R00147 44323

C0-DXA-277

CHICAGO PUBLIC LIBRARY
HAROLD WASHINGTON LIBRARY CENTER

R0014744323

REF
LB
2899   Haar, Jerry
.B8
H32   The politics of
         higher education
         in Brazil

DATE DUE

REFERENCE

FORM 125 M

Cop1   SOCIAL SCIENCES AND HISTORY DIVISION

The Chicago Public Library

Received   JAN 12 1978

The Politics of Higher Education in Brazil

Jerry Haar

Published in cooperation with the
Institute of Higher Education,
Teachers College, Columbia
University, New York, N.Y.

The Praeger Special Studies program—
utilizing the most modern and efficient book
production techniques and a selective
worldwide distribution network—makes
available to the academic, government, and
business communities significant, timely
research in U.S. and international economic, social, and political development.

The Politics of Higher Education in Brazil

PRAEGER SPECIAL STUDIES IN INTERNATIONAL POLITICS AND GOVERNMENT

Praeger Publishers   New York   Washington   London

Library of Congress Cataloging in Publication Data

Haar, Jerry, 1947-
  The politics of higher education in Brazil.

  (Praeger special studies in international politics
and government)
  Bibliography: p. 203
  1. School management and organization—Brazil.
2. Education and state—Brazil. I. Title.
LB2899.B8H32   379'.151'0981   75-23967
ISBN 0-275-55630-1

PRAEGER PUBLISHERS
111 Fourth Avenue, New York, N.Y. 10003, U.S.A.

Published in the United States of America in 1977
by Praeger Publishers, Inc.

All rights reserved

© 1977 by Praeger Publishers, Inc.

Printed in the United States of America

For Sabina

PREFACE

The idea for this book emerged from a course on comparative politics and education in the fall of 1971 at Teachers College, Columbia University. The politics of educational access so aroused my intellectual curiosity that I began a thorough search for material on the topic. It seemed that all roads led not to Rome, but Brazil.

To begin with, Brazil was the most glaring example of a nation where the social demand for access to higher education was tremendous and intense, yet its government traditionally had been unwilling or unable to meet that demand. Also, there were recent indications that the modernizing authoritarian regime that came to power in 1964 had begun to take significant steps to deal with the problems of educational access. Finally, I was awarded a Fulbright-Hays grant for dissertation research, enabling me to utilize primary sources and empirically assess the current situation regarding access to higher education in Brazil, both educationally and politically.

Many individuals and institutions both in Brazil and the United States contributed to the realization of this study. Unfortunately, it is not possible to cite all those who willingly offered their time and insights into Brazilian higher education and the process of public policy making.

I would, however, like to acknowledge the contribution of those persons and organizations without whose help and cooperation this study would not have been possible.

During my stay in Rio de Janeiro and travels throughout Brazil, I received invaluable assistance and vital information from the Fulbright Commission; the Getúlio Vargas Foundation; the CESGRANRIO Foundation; Cecilia Malizia Alves, Wilma Larangeira, Jader de Medeiros Britto, Teresinha Rêgo, and Fidelina dos Santos of the Brazilian Center of Educational Research, Rio de Janeiro; Sergio Lorenzato of the State University of Campinas; Denise das Chagas Leite and Frank Taylor of the Inter-American Development Bank in Rio de Janeiro; Professor Maria Judith Costa Lins; Professor Carlos Corrêa Mascaro; and Deputy Carlos Flexa Ribeiro.

In the United States, thoughtful comments and sound advice were offered from Professors Walter E. Sindlinger, Harland G. Bloland, Kempton Webb, and Douglas Chalmers of Columbia University, and Professor Arnold Spinner of New York University. The Institute of Higher Education at Teachers College kindly assisted in the publication of this work.

I am especially grateful to Fay Haussman, a New York-based research associate of the Institut d'Etudes sur l'Education (Brussels, Belgium) and a specialist on social development in Brazil. She generously shared with me her voluminous, well-organized files on Brazilian education. This saved me about one year of research. Ms. Haussman's vast knowledge and brilliant insight into Brazilian education also aided immeasurably to the realization of this study.

I alone assume all responsibility for any shortcomings or errors in this work.

Barbara Eckel merits acknowledgment for typing the manuscript. I wish to express special thanks to my wife and parents for their great encouragement and moral support.

I would like to offer six caveats. First, because of the paucity of academically published materials on, and the rapidly changing environment of, educational access, it was necessary to rely heavily upon newspapers and magazines. Second, when the study was conducted (1972-73), the monetary exchange rate of the cruzeiro to the U.S. dollar was approximately CR$6 = US$1, the financial statistics in the book reflect that rate (currently it is more than ten cruzeiros to the dollar). Third, in 1975 as a result of metropolitan government, a new State of Rio de Janeiro was created, comprising the former states of Rio de Janeiro (capital: Niterói) and Guanabara (capital: Rio de Janeiro). Fourth, the term "professor" is used in the context of Brazilian culture: professor and teacher are synonomous and apply to both formal and nonformal education, university and nonuniversity instruction. Fifth, The Politics of Higher Education in Brazil focuses, for the most part, on policy making rather than politics in the broader sense, and it deals with one arena—access to higher education—rather than the entire postsecondary educational system. Sixth, although the concluding chapter offers some brief comments on the 1974 and 1975 developments in access policy in Brazil, the main concern and thrust of the study cover the formative years of 1964 through 1973.

Finally, I wish to express my gratitude to the Brazilian people for their kindness and hospitality and offer my good wishes in their quest for order, progress, and justice in their system of education, as well as in other areas of national life.

CONTENTS

	Page
PREFACE	vii
LIST OF TABLES AND CHART	xiii

Chapter

1 INTRODUCTION: EDUCATIONAL ACCESS AND PUBLIC POLICY — 1

    College Entrance Examinations and the Access Issue — 1
    Focus of the Book — 2
    Notes — 4

2 EDUCATIONAL POLITICS AND THE POLICY-MAKING PROCESS — 6

    Reviews of the Politics of Education — 6
    Policy Making Defined — 8
    Notes — 11

3 INCREMENTALISM AND POLICY FORMATION — 15

    Precepts of the Strategy — 16
    Methodology — 19
    Notes — 21

4 PLANNING AND POLICY MAKING UNDER THE MILITARY GOVERNMENTS — 23

    The Political Environment of Planning and Policy Making — 23
    The ESG and the Role of the Military — 25
    The Military-Technocrat Policy-Making Alignment — 27
    Structural and Functional Considerations — 28
    The Outputs of Planning and Policy Making — 31
    Planning on the Micro-Level: Higher Education — 37
    Notes — 43

Chapter		Page
5	HISTORICAL ROOTS OF BRAZILIAN HIGHER EDUCATION	46
	Higher Education During the Colonial and Empire Periods	46
	The Republican Period	53
	Notes	58
6	THE SYSTEM OF HIGHER EDUCATION	60
	Organization, Administration, and Finance	60
	Students	63
	Cursinhos	65
	Reform Policies	67
	Economic Aspects of Higher Education	69
	Social Demand for Higher Education	69
	Supply of Higher Education	71
	Labor Market Conditions	74
	The Process and Problems of Access to Higher Education	78
	Process: The Exame Vestibular	78
	Problems of Admission	80
	Notes	83
7	THE SEQUENCE OF POLICY DEVELOPMENT	86
	Stage One: Planning the First Experiment and Reaction to Planning Initiatives	86
	Planning the First Experiment	87
	Reaction to Planning Initiatives	101
	Stage Two: Modifications for the Second Experiment and Reaction to the First Experiment	104
	Modifications for the Second Experiment	105
	Reaction to the First Experiment	113
	Press	115
	Secondary Schoolteachers	117
	Cursinhos	118
	University Professors and Rectors	120
	Isolated Colleges	122
	Students	124
	Government	125
	Stage Three: Preparations for the Third Experiment and Reaction to the Second Experiment	128

Chapter		Page
	Preparations for the Third Experiment	128
	Reaction to the Second Experiment	135
	Secondary Schoolteachers	136
	Cursinhos	136
	University Professors and Rectors	137
	Isolated Colleges	137
	Press	138
	Students	140
	Government	140
	Notes	144
8	THEORETICAL ANALYSIS	150
	The Eight Stages of Disjointed Incrementalism	150
	Margin-Dependent Choice	150
	Restricted Variety of Policy Alternatives	153
	Restricted Variety of Policy Consequences	155
	Adjustment of Objectives to Policies	158
	Reconstructive Treatment of Data	163
	Serial Analysis and Evaluation	165
	Remedial Orientation of Analysis and Evaluation	167
	Social Fragmentation of Analysis and Evaluation	171
	CESGRANRIO: Some Behavioral Observations	173
	Notes	179
9	CONCLUSION	181
	Theoretical Findings	181
	Educational Findings	183
	Epilogue	187
	1974	188
	1975	190
	Notes	192

Appendix

A	GLOSSARY OF EDUCATIONAL TERMS	193
B	STATUTE OF THE CESGRANRIO FOUNDATION	196
C	ORGANIZATIONAL CHART OF THE CESGRANRIO FOUNDATION	199
D	CESGRANRIO: PARTICIPATING HIGHER EDUCATION INSTITUTIONS	200

	Page
BIBLIOGRAPHY	203
ABOUT THE AUTHOR	223

LIST OF TABLES AND CHART

Table		Page
4.1	Earnings and Participation in Total Income by Income Level	33
4.2	Income Distribution According to Sector and Level of Education	35
4.3	The Influence of Education, Age, and Sector on the Distribution of Income, 1970 Percentages	36
4.4	Federal Resources Allocated to Education	39
4.5	Federal Budget in the Education Program by Subprogram, 1971, 1972, and 1973	40
4.6	Increase in Federal Budget from 1972 to 1973 by Program Budgets	41
6.1	Federal Government Expenditures in Higher Education, 1965-73	62
6.2	Growth of Candidates for College Admission and Number Passing the Entrance Examinations, 1960-73	70
6.3	Candidates for the Vestibular per Place, by Field of Study, for Some Federal Universities, 1965-72	72
6.4	Total Enrollment and Growth of Higher Education in Brazil, 1964-73	74
6.5	Increases and Relative Distribution of Undergraduate College Enrollment by Course of Study, 1958, 1965, 1971	75
7.1	Proposed Format of Test Requirements by Subject Matter Areas and Course of Study: Greater Rio de Janeiro College Entrance Examinations, 1972	97
7.2	CESGRANRIO Statistical Report: General Summary, 1972	106

Table		Page
7.3	CESGRANRIO Program Plan for the 1973 Entrance Examinations	108
7.4	CESGRANRIO Comparative Statistical Report: General Summary	111
7.5	CESGRANRIO Comparative Statistical Report: COMBIMED	112
7.6	CESGRANRIO Comparative Statistical Report: COMCITEC	113
7.7	CESGRANRIO Comparative Statistical Report: COMSART	114
8.1	Income and Expenditures for Entrance Examinations of Selected Private Higher Education Institutions in Greater Rio de Janeiro, 1972	162
8.2	Technical and Financial Assistance from the Department of University Affairs, Ministry of Education and Culture, to Nonfederal Member Institutions of CESGRANRIO, 1971-73	164

Chart		
4.1	Distribution of Income in Brazil, 1970	34

The Politics of Higher Education in Brazil

CHAPTER 1

INTRODUCTION: EDUCATIONAL ACCESS AND PUBLIC POLICY

Strikes by public schoolteachers in Italy. Military intervention in university governance in Chile. The mobilization of parents in opposition to court-ordered busing of schoolchildren in Boston and Louisville.

The incidents, participant groups, and places may be different; there is a common element, however, that binds the three examples listed above: they are all issues of public policy.

Concerning education and public policy, one of the most striking features of the postwar period has been the tremendous and rapidly increasing worldwide demand for education.[1] This phenomenon is an outgrowth of the modernization process that has enveloped traditional societies as well as the quest for adjustment to modern and postmodern societies among the developed nations of the West. Specifically, the rising social demand for education, with its inherently political implications, can be attributed to three factors: the mounting educational aspirations of parents and their children; the belief held by governments that education is a key to national development; and the population explosion.[2]

COLLEGE ENTRANCE EXAMINATIONS AND THE ACCESS ISSUE

It is an undeniable fact that the social demand for schooling and governmental recognition of education as a catalyst of national development have jointly elevated access to education as one important public policy issue in a great many nations. With regard to higher education (the area of most concern here), a number of countries have traditionally relied upon college entrance examinations as the key mechanism for access. Consequently, initiatives to review and reform the system of access to higher education have centered on these exams. In systems heavily dependent upon the mechanism of entrance exams as a determinant of access to higher education, focusing on the mechanism sheds light upon the interrelationship between social demand, educational access, entrance exams, and public policy actions.

In recent years, college entrance examinations have become an important part of the access issue in nations whose educational systems depend exclusively, or almost exclusively, upon them: the <u>baccalaurèat</u> exam in France, the <u>Abitur</u> in West Germany, the <u>aptitud acadêmica</u> in Chile, the <u>General Certificate of Education</u> examination in England, and the <u>exame vestibular</u> in Brazil.

All of the systems mentioned above have been publicly criticized by large segments of the citizenry who believe that the entrance examinations are excessively demanding, too rigid in their composition, discriminatory toward lower socioeconomic groups, and designed to perpetuate elitism. At the same time, a small yet influential coterie of academicians and bureaucrats have sought to maintain the status quo with respect to entrance examinations: the preservation of "academic standards" and "high social cost/low social benefits" (more accurately, the national treasury cannot afford it and the labor market cannot absorb the surplus of graduates) has dominated their argument.

Upon observation, one can rightly conclude that college entrance examination policy is an important and timely political issue in many countries.

FOCUS OF THE BOOK

While access to higher education via entrance examinations in France, West Germany, and the United States has received attention from scholarly researchers, there has been no attempt to do the same for Brazil.[3] Perhaps no other country has been so engulfed in access to higher education as a political issue; certainly, few nations have depended so heavily upon tests for university admission.

This book will examine the formation of public policy regarding access to higher education in Brazil from 1964 to 1975, and it will reveal why, how, and when policy change developed, and the individuals and groups involved. In addition to presenting the current situation regarding access to higher education, some prognostication will be made as to future directions of access in Brazil.

Among the questions addressed are the following: What conditions prompted the federal government to consider changes in policy relating to access to higher education? What were the roles and power

INTRODUCTION

configurations among individuals, interest groups, and various sectors of society in reforming educational policy? What alternatives were proposed, and how were choices made? What was the nature of conflict in policy formation and how, if at all, was it resolved? Does the new access policy satisfy both social demand and national development needs? What are the survival chances of the new policy?

The above questions, however, collectively lead to a larger, more fundamental question: Can a nation with a traditionalist educational system depart from past policy practices and initiate reforms commensurate with the exigencies of a modernizing society? Given the deep strains of tradition which run through Luso-Brazilian culture plus the historically retarded development of Brazil's higher educational system, one would be inclined to answer this question in the negative. On the other hand, upon examination of the far-reaching changes in Brazil's socioeconomic and political structure since the end of World War II—most notably that nation's incredible economic growth—one may observe the currents of pragmatism and modernization running strongly against traditionalism. Consequently, one could answer the question in the affirmative.

Dichotomies such as those just mentioned place limitations on the selection of viable frameworks for policy analysis with regard to issues in Brazilian national development. In undertaking any study involving policy formation, planning, and administration in Brazil, one must be constantly cognizant of the perennial struggle between traditionalist and modernizing forces. For there are, as Jacques Lambert points out, two Brazils existing today—one archaic, one modern.[4]

A nation of uneven development, with great disparities in income distribution and a high concentration of political power, Brazil is also a giant. It is the fifth largest country in the world, occupying 3,286,470 square miles and exceeded in territorial extent only by the Soviet Union, Canada, China, and the United States.[5] In addition, Brazil's population exceeds 99 million (1973 estimate) and grows at a rate of approximately 3.5 percent annually.[6] The economic growth rate was a phenomenal 10 percent in 1974; however, analysts project a slower rate of growth in the future.*

Furthermore, Brazil is a land of great variation in topography, climate ecological characteristics, and ethnic composition.

In short, these four major variables (traditionalism versus modernity, disparity, gigantism, and diversity) influence and shape public policy.

---

*Data compiled from the Fundação Getúlio Vargas, Rio de Janeiro, 1975.

A number of theoretical frameworks were carefully considered for purposes of analysis. Braybrooke and Lindblom's theory of "disjointed incrementalism" was finally chosen for analysis.[7] Disjointed incrementalism holds that "what is feasible politically is policy only incrementally, or marginally, different from existing policies" and it proceeds in a piecemeal, remedial, or satisficing manner.[8]

An examination of educational politics in Brazil, focusing on the formulation and implementation of public policy, can reveal not only how one nation deals with the problem of access to higher education, but the explanatory force of disjointed incrementalism as a theory of policy formation.

NOTES

1. George Z. F. Bereday and Joseph A. Lauwerys, eds., The World Year Book of Education, 1965: The Education Explosion (New York: Harcourt, Brace and World, 1965), p. 1.

2. Philip H. Coombs, The World Educational Crisis (New York: Oxford University Press, 1968), p. 18.

3. For a discussion of French government policy on the baccalauréat exam and access to higher education see Carol Browning, "The Democratization of Higher Education in France During the DeGaulle Administration of the Fifth French Republic" (Ph.D. diss., Columbia University, 1971). The politics of the Abitur is treated by John H. Van de Graaff in "West Germany's Abitur Quota and School Reform," Comparative Education Review 11 (February 1967): 75-76. A sociological analysis of access to higher education in the United States, in historical perspective, is provided by Michael S. Schudson, "Organizing the 'Meritocracy': A History of the College Entrance Examination Board," Harvard Educational Review 42 (February 1972): 34-69. Nádia Franco da Cunha's Vestibular na Guanabara (Rio de Janeiro: Ministério da Educação e Cultura, 1968), provides a compilation of sociological facts and figures on the 1964 Brazilian college entrance examinations in one state; however, the treatment is concerned with pedagogical, rather than policy, analysis.

4. Jacques Lambert, Os Dois Brasís (Rio de Janeiro: Centro Brasileiro de Pesquisas Educacionais, 1959).

5. Ministério do Planejamento e Coordenação Geral, Sinopse Estatística do Brasil, 1971 (Rio de Janeiro: Fundação IBGE, 1971).

6. William Harris and Judith S. Levey, eds., The New Columbia Encyclopedia (New York: Columbia University Press, 1975), p. 359; Kempton E. Webb, "The Geography of Brazil's Modernization and Implications for the Years 1980 and 2000 A.D.," in The Shaping

of Modern Brazil, ed. Eric N. Baklanoff (Baton Rouge: Louisiana State University Press, 1969), p. 145.

7. David Braybrooke and Charles E. Lindblom, A Strategy of Decision (New York: Free Press, 1968).

8. Charles E. Lindblom, The Policy-Making Process (Englewood Cliffs, N.J.: Prentice-Hall, 1968), pp. 26-27.

CHAPTER

2

EDUCATIONAL POLITICS AND THE POLICY-MAKING PROCESS

> Despite certain notable exceptions, and the recent and current work that is beginning to fill the void, political scientists in general have paid very little attention to the over-all character of the education-polity nexus, and very few empirical studies have been made which focus explicitly upon specific ways in which educational systems affect the functioning of political systems.[1]

More than a decade has passed since James S. Coleman made this observation. In that time, there has been a marked increase in interest in the politics of education. Both political scientists and educators have shown growing concern about the political dimension of education[2] as well as the educational dimension of politics.[3] Education, with its multiplicity of functions, has become an increasingly important and influential variable in the processes of social, economic, and political development, both in modern and modernizing societies. For the many political scientists who are concerned about the holistic imperative[4]—the interrelatedness and interdependence of systems—the interface of politics and education is a legitimate and vital area of inquiry.

REVIEWS OF THE POLITICS OF EDUCATION

Rather than review here the literature of the politics of education, the reader is referred to several excellent and comprehensive reviews published elsewhere.

In their critique and synthesis of selected literature in the politics of American education, Laurence Iannacone and Peter J. Cistone focus on arenas and issues in educational politics, urban education, government and education (on local, state, and federal levels), and conceptual and methodological approaches to the study of educational politics. Three themes recur throughout their monograph: the dynamic relationship between educational politics and societal change; political culture as a powerful determinant of the style and structure of educational politics; and the dominance of professional and employee interests in the governance of education.[5]

Paul E. Peterson's review of the politics of American education is divided into two parts: one dealing with the autonomy of school politics, the other discussing the politics of school finance.[6] Peterson finds school autonomy and school finance the dominating topics in the study of educational politics; and, with regard to the former, he questions whether school politics are really more autonomous than politics in other policy areas. He concludes by suggesting that research on school autonomy and school finance consider the impact of external political variables on the school system and school politics.

It is regrettable that neither of the aforementioned reviews touches upon the politics of American higher education; nor do they discuss the politics of education in comparative perspective. Fortunately, these topics are covered in a fairly extensive, well-organized bibliography by Grant Harman.[7] The bibliographical guide treats the politics of education in comparative perspective and briefly discusses such political phenomena as interest groups, elites, and political socialization.

Several other bibliographies and reviews that merit attention are Frederick S. Lane's selected bibliography on the politics of higher education;[8] Philip Altbach and David Kelly's bibliography of higher education in developing nations;[9] John Meyer and Richard Rubinson's review of research on education and political development;[10] and Michael Kirst and Edith Mosher's early analysis and synthesis of the literature on the politics of American education.[11]

It is Kirst and Mosher who offer a very useful scheme for classifying studies in educational politics. According to them, research on the politics of education may be categorized as follows:

citizen perceptions, opinions, attitudes, and voting practices with regard to educational issues;
habitual strategies, information sources, and perceived self-interest of relevant policy makers;
roles in the policy-making process;
premises and context for authoritative decision making;

groups as interacting pluralities of individuals who share common political interests and goals;

structure and impact of governmental institutions and processes;

influence of elites or community power structures on educational policies and programs.[12]

One particularly useful approach to the study of educational politics focuses on policy making. The process of policy making is broad, intricate and complex. In fact, it could be argued that policy formation encompasses, in varying degrees, all categories of Kirst and Mosher's classification scheme.

Since this is the approach the author has chosen by which to analyze the politics of higher education in Brazil, it is necessary to define policy making, what it is and what its components are.

POLICY MAKING DEFINED

The social, economic, political, and ideological changes which engulfed the world during and after World War II presented awesome and monumental challenges to national governments. They were faced with many problems which urgently needed to be solved--and for which solutions often lacked a precedent.

From close observation of the course of events, the pattern of conflict, and the trends which were emerging, social scientists began to realize that the policy process was a legitimate and important object of study. In the seminal work on the subject, economists, sociologists, psychologists, anthropologists, and political scientists focused upon developments in the scope and method of policy science with relation to their respective disciplines.[13] Over the past few years, among the most innovative and influential contributions to the study of public policy have been the works of Yehezkel Dror.[14] He has integrated the theoretical approaches of policy analysis, behavioral science, and systems analysis in examining public policy making. Through the use of an interdisciplinary scientific orientation, Dror's endeavors are notable in the effort to make policy science a true science of policy.

However, Charles E. Lindblom, commenting on the state of policy science to date, observes that:

> The idea of making "the policy-making process" itself a major focus for specialized inquiry is still so new that no one seems to want to answer the question of what is supposed to be included in the process and what excluded from it. The usefulness of the concept is even implicitly

called into question by many political scientists who
now come close to defining politics as a whole as a
policy-making process.[15]

The definitions to which Lindblom refers are those by Meyerson and Banfield who maintain that "politics is the activity . . . by which an issue is agitated or settled";[16] and Van Dyke's assertion that "politics consists of struggle among actors pursuing conflicting desires on public issues."[17]

The next logical questions which arise are the following: What is "policy"?, and what does "policy formation" consist of? In answer to the first question, Raymond A. Bauer suggests:

> If the [decisions and actions] are trivial and repetitive and demand little cogitation, they may be called routine actions. If they are somewhat more complex, have wider ramifications, and demand more thought, we may refer to them as tactical decisions. For those which have the widest ramifications and the longest time perspective, and which generally require the most information and contemplation, we tend to reserve the term policy.[18]

Of course, the pattern and flow of bureaucratic decisions and actions create a behavioral situation in which the perception of what is "policy" will vary. In other words, looking at levels of authority in organizations, a tactical decision from above may be construed as "policy"; and while the subordinate may feel that he, in turn, is making tactical decisions, within the wider parameters of bureaucracy he is merely engaging in routine actions.

Bauer acknowledges this dilemma, however, and maintains that, regardless of one's perspective, true "policy" is a "parameter-shaping" act—one that is given serious consideration, is "most difficult to arrive at, and at the same time most difficult and most important to study."[19]

With regard to "policy formation," this activity consists of three processes: decision making; management; and policy revision.[20] One generally assumes that the implementation, management, and readjustment of policy to internal and external changes are major features of "policy formation"; this is correct. Many individuals, however, erroneously consider "decision making" synonymous with "policy formation," rather than a feature of it. In fact, "decision making" is specifically a cognitive activity:

> This model assumes a single decision-making unit
> with a single set of utility preferences; knowledge of
> a reasonably full range of action alternatives and of
> their consequences; this intention of selecting that
> course of action of maximum utility; and, the oppor-
> tunity, disposition, and capacity to make the appro-
> priate calculations. In the process of policy formation
> every one of these assumptions is violated. However,
> both the connotations of the term decision-making and
> the ordinary discussion of decision-making on policy
> issues preserve the illusion of these assumptions.[21]

It is worth noting several aspects of "policy formation" which will provide some indication of the complexity and challenges involved in this activity and, at the same time, reveal the inappropriateness of considering "decision making" as either the exclusive or dominant feature of "policy formation."

To begin with, it is essential to recognize the most fundamental pillar of "policy formation," namely that there is no best solution to a policy problem. Yet one may ask, "Cannot agricultural economists and econometricians produce models and calculations to predict the optimal conditions and point at which wheat cultivation in a given state will produce the best financial return to the farmer?" Statistically, yes; but statistical decision theory, mathematics, and operations research provide only part of the picture in a complex universe in which human influences and actions play major parts. Therefore, statistical decisions to aid the wheat farmer would, indeed, prove unreliable if they did not provide for a contingency input to account for a multi-billion-dollar grain sale to the Soviet Union, a product of American foreign policy formation in the area of detente.[22]

If a best solution in "policy formation" cannot be found from reliance upon numbers, what about "morality" and human behavior? Here, too, there are limitations. Morality often intervenes in the policy process, not as a guiding light, but as a "mechanism for making one's values evident."[23] True, conflicting values and interests are important and must be dealt with by policy makers—but within the vital context of the allocation of scarce resources. The policy maker cannot depend solely upon moral considerations as determinants of policy. He simply does not function in an environment where a set of moral values, or even agreement on the importance of moral considerations in policy formation, is uniform.

In the complex arena of public-policy formation, both quantitative and qualitative criteria are subjugated to a greater consideration: politics. Moreover, the nature of politics and its role in the policy process dictate the ways in which quantitative and qualitative criteria enter into the decision-making process.

Public policies are determined by small groups of individuals or by negotiation involving interested parties. As a result, policy formation proceeds along several lines. First, the interests and values of policy makers, their colleagues, and their constituencies will vary. Second, there will be differential benefits from the same policy to individuals within an organization who pursue identical values. Third, different preferences and inequity (that is, in the distribution of benefits) to some person or unit within the system mean that there can be no "optimal" policy, only a "good" policy at best—one in which the system as a whole gains to some extent. Fourth, because other events intervene and policy makers maintain different priorities, the amount of time, attention, and energy they give to a particular problem differs considerably. Fifth, and finally, the lines along which the policy process proceeds limit one from distinguishing a designated beginning and termination point of a given issue.[24]

Because of the characteristics of the policy-making process described above, two things are immediately apparent: bargaining is an exceedingly important feature of the policy process, for without a "minimum winning coalition"[25] policy formulation is practically impossible; and the nature of the policy-making process (and, one could argue, politics itself) requires a far greater dependency upon descriptive or behavioral theory (how individuals actually proceed in formulating policy) rather than upon normative theory (how individuals should proceed).

Returning to the realm of educational politics, this study examines the process of public policy making in Brazil as it relates to higher education and the issue of access. There are a number of approaches one may take in analyzing public policy, focusing upon either the individual in the policy-making process or the policy-making process as an activity within a political system—or both.[26] The analytical framework chosen to examine policy formation on access to higher education is presented in the following chapter. Its theoretical properties give particular attention to priority allocation from its conception at the individual level through its function in, and dependence upon, the policy-making process.

NOTES

1. James S. Coleman, ed., Education and Political Development (Princeton: Princeton University Press, 1965), p. 8.
2. This includes analyses of inputs, processes, and outputs of political systems as they affect the educational system. For examples

of politics and education in the United States see: Stephen K. Bailey and Edith K. Mosher, ESEA: The Office of Education Administers a Law (Syracuse: Syracuse University Press, 1968); Jerome T. Murphy, "Title I of ESEA: The Politics of Implementing Federal Education Reform," Harvard Educational Review 41 (February 1971): 35-63; Frederick M. Wirt and Michael W. Kirst, The Political Web of American Schools (Boston: Little, Brown, 1972); Alan Rosenthal, Pedagogues and Power: Teacher Groups in School Politics (Syracuse: Syracuse University Press, 1969); and Mike M. Milstein and Robert E. Jennings, Educational Policy-Making and the State Legislature: The New York Experience (New York: Praeger, 1973). Some foreign examples are: Maurice Kogan, The Government of Education (London: Macmillan, 1971); James M. Clark, Teachers and Politics in France (Syracuse: Syracuse University Press, 1967); David B. Abernethy, The Political Dilemma of Popular Education: An African Case (Stanford: Stanford University Press, 1969); Philip G. Altbach, ed., Turmoil and Transition: Higher Education and Student Politics in India (New York: Basic Books, 1969); Albert A. Blum, ed., Teacher Unions and Associations: A Comparative Study (Urbana: University of Illinois Press, 1969); Arthur Liebman, Kenneth Walker, and Myron Glazer, Latin American University Students: A Six Nation Study (Cambridge: Harvard University Press, 1972); and Herbert C. Rudman, The School and the State in the U.S.S.R. (New York: Macmillan, 1967).

3. This encompasses analyses of inputs, processes, and outputs of educational systems as they affect the political system. Several United States illustrations are: David Easton and Jack Dennis, Children in the Political System: Origins of Political Legitimacy (New York: McGraw-Hill, 1969); Robert D. Hess and Judith V. Torney, The Development of Political Attitudes in Children (Chicago: Aldine, 1967); K.P. Langston and M. Kent Jennings, "Political Socialization and the High School Civics Curriculum in the U.S.," American Political Science Review 62 (September 1968): 852-67; M. Kent Jennings and R.G. Niemi, "The Transmission of Political Values from Parent to Child," American Political Science Review 62 (March 1968): 169-84; Richard M. Merelman, Political Socialization and Education Climates: A Study of Two School Districts (New York: Holt, Rinehart and Winston, 1971); and Harmon Ziegler, The Political Life of American Teachers (Englewood Cliffs, N.J.: Prentice-Hall, 1967). The educational dimension of politics outside the United States is explored in such notable works as: Paul R. Abramson and Ronald Inglehart, "The Decentralization of Systematic Support in Four Western Systems," Comparative Political Studies 2 (January 1970): 419-42; Samuel H. Barnes, "Participation, Education and Political Competence: Evidence from a Sample of Italian Socialists," American

Political Science Review 60 (June 1966): 348-53; Stephen K. Douglas, Political Socialization and Student Activism in Indonesia (Urbana: University of Illinois Press, 1970); Peter John Georgeoff, The Social Education of Bulgarian Youth (Minneapolis: University of Minnesota Press, 1968); Richard R. Fagen, Transformation of the Political Culture of Cuba (Stanford: Stanford University Press, 1969); Andreas Kazamias, Education and the Quest for Modernity in Turkey (London: George Allen and Unwin, 1966); and A.B. Hodgetts, What Culture? What Heritage?: A Study of Civic Education in Canada (Toronto: Ontario Institute for Studies in Education, 1968).

4. Coleman, Education and Political Development, p. 13 f.
5. Laurence Iannacone and Peter J. Cistone, The Politics of Education (Eugene, Oregon: ERIC Clearinghouse on Educational Management, 1974).
6. Paul E. Peterson, "The Politics of American Education," in Review of Research in Education 2, Fred N. Kerlinger and John B. Carroll, eds. (Itasca, Ill.: F.E. Peacock, 1974), pp. 348-89.
7. G.S. Harman, The Politics of Education: A Bibliographic Guide (St. Lucia, Queensland, Australia: University of Queensland Press, 1974).
8. Frederick S. Lane, The Politics of Higher Education: A Selected Bibliography, mimeographed (New York: Bernard M. Baruch College, City University of New York, June 1974). An up-dated supplement to this bibliography is planned.
9. Philip G. Altbach and David H. Kelly, Higher Education in Developing Nations: A Selected Bibliography, 1969-1974 (New York: Praeger, 1974).
10. John W. Meyer and Richard Rubinson, "Education and Political Development," in Review of Research in Education 3, Fred Kerlinger, ed. (Itasca, Ill.: F.E. Peacock, 1975), pp. 134-162. Also see a special issue on the politics of education in Comparative Education Review 19 (February 1975).
11. Michael W. Kirst and Edith K. Mosher, "Politics of Education," Review of Educational Research 39 (December 1969): 623-40.
12. Ibid.
13. Harold Lasswell and Daniel Lerner, eds., The Policy Sciences (Stanford: Stanford University Press, 1951).
14. Yehezkel Dror, Public Policymaking Reexamined (Scranton, Pa.: Chandler, 1968); idem, Design for Policy Sciences (New York: American Elsevier, 1971); idem, Ventures in Policy Sciences: Concepts and Applications (New York: American Elsevier, 1971).
15. Lindblom, The Policy-Making Process, p. 3.
16. Martin Myerson and Edward C. Banfield, Politics, Planning and the Public Interest (Glencoe, Ill.: Free Press, 1955), p. 304.

17. V. Van Dyke, "The Optimum Scope of Political Science," in A Design for Political Science: Scope, Objectives, and Methods, ed. J.C. Charlesworth (Philadelphia: American Association of Political and Social Science, 1966), p. 2.

18. Raymond A. Bauer, "The Study of Policy Formation: An Introduction," in The Study of Policy Formation, ed. Raymond A. Bauer and Kenneth J. Gergen (New York: Free Press, 1968), pp. 1-2.

19. Ibid., p. 2.

20. Joseph Bower, "Capital Budgeting Is a Management Problem," mimeographed (Cambridge, Mass.: Harvard Graduate School of Business Administration, 1966); See also Raymond A. Bauer, "Social Psychology and the Study of Policy Formation," American Psychologist 21, no. 10 (1966): 933-42.

21. Raymond A. Bauer, "The Study of Policy Formation: An Introduction," p. 11; also, Martin Patchen, "Decision Theory in the Study of National Action: Problems and a Proposal," Journal of Conflict Resolution 9 (June 1965): 164-76.

22. Two economists, discussing mathematical models and modern economic theories, conclude that although quantitative techniques of decision making are very useful in solving a number of problems, they are useless in functioning as a neutral, final arbiter of interest conflict centering upon major policy issues. See Richard Zeckhauser and Elmer Schaefer, "Public Policy and Normative Economic Theory," in The Study of Policy Formation, eds. Raymond A. Bauer and Kenneth J. Gergen (New York: Free Press, 1968), pp. 28-101.

23. Ibid., p. 10.

24. Bauer, "The Study of Policy Formation: An Introduction," pp. 11-17.

25. Theodore Riker, The Theory of Political Coalitions (New Haven: Yale University Press, 1962).

26. Enid Curtis Bok Schoettle, "The State of the Art of Policy Studies," in The Study of Policy Formation, eds. Raymond A. Bauer and Kenneth J. Gergen (New York: Free Press, 1968).

CHAPTER 3

INCREMENTALISM AND POLICY FORMATION

In A Strategy of Decision, philosopher David Braybrooke and political scientist Charles E. Lindblom focus upon policy evaluation as a social process and analyze the operating procedures of individual policy makers in a political system.[1] From their respective disciplines, Braybrooke and Lindblom examine the phenomenon of incrementalism and its importance within the policy process.*

From their scholarly endeavors there emerges a theory to explain the processes of evaluation and decision with regard to alternative public policies. This theory accounts for the costliness of analysis in terms of resources such as time, attention, energy, and money, and considers the impossibility, at times, of carrying analysis to conclusion. Furthermore, it explains how

---

*It is most appropriate for the author to mention why he selected disjointed incrementalism as a theoretical framework for analyzing policy on access to higher education in Brazil. Having been a student of Brazilian affairs for six years prior to undertaking this study, the author was not unfamiliar with the political, economic, and social dimensions of Brazilian society. A major presumption which the author had—and which was confirmed after arrival in Brazil—was that apocalyptic change has not been a feature of Brazilian development. Consequently, although many theoretical frameworks could have been used in the study, the strategy of disjointed incrementalism (the antithesis of apocalyptic change) was given special consideration by the author. Only after careful and considerable deliberation and actual field research did the author finally select Braybrooke and Lindblom's strategy as the best theoretical approach to utilize.

considered evaluations of policy can be reached when
the rationales suggested by conventional theories of
choice cannot be provided.[2]

Braybrooke and Lindblom refer to their approach as the "strategy of disjointed incrementalism."

PRECEPTS OF THE STRATEGY

The first of eight intercorrelated attributes of the strategy which the authors present is margin-dependent choice. Braybrooke and Lindblom distinguish the characteristics of incremental or margin-dependent choice as follows:

> only those policies are considered whose known or expected consequent social states differ drom each other incrementally . . . only those policies are considered whose known or expected consequences differ incrementally from the status quo . . . examination of policies proceeds through comparative analysis of no more than the marginal or incremental differences in the consequent social states . . . choice among policies is made by ranking in order of preference the increments by which social states differ.[3]

It can be seen that margin-dependent choice differs considerably from a rational-deductive system of problem solving. Moreover, the highest priority given the status quo means policy analysts need not concern themselves with controversial and time-consuming philosophical and moral discussions about all possible social states (for example, constitutional democracy versus one-party dictatorship).

Value conflicts which do arise, however, center upon "trading ratios at the margin between pairs of values" and are resolved by determining "how much of one value is worth sacrificing, at the margin reached in a given situation, to achieve an increment of another."[4]

The second attribute of the strategy is its restricted variety of policy alternatives. It would follow that if policies which differ only incrementally from the status quo are the only ones that policy makers will decide upon, alternative choices will subsequently consist of a restricted variety. For a society which practices incremental politics will naturally seek incremental alternatives.

As for nonincremental alternatives, policy analysts lack an organized way to systematically deal with such alternatives; they cannot be "rationally explored."

A third characteristic of the strategy of disjointed incrementalism is its restricted variety of policy consequences. Policy analysts will surely neglect the unimportant consequences of policies; and although their attention will be devoted exclusively to important policy consequences, this does not mean they will assess all important consequences. Of the policies they consider important, they often choose not to tackle: "the uninteresting (to them), the remote, the imponderable, the intangible, and the poorly understood, no matter how important."[5]

The fourth feature of the strategy is its adjustment of objectives to policies. This implies a reciprocal relationship between means and ends or policies and values. In other words, although policies are sought to achieve specified objectives, it is also true that objectives are sought to support specified policies. Objectives are contingent upon means and, subsequently, will shift with the degree of "possibility" (that is, costliness). Costliness depends upon the relative importance of means available to pursue certain objectives; and objectives are examined in terms of their appropriateness to a defined alternative or a small group of fixed alternatives.

Two additional aspects of ends-means relationships are as follows: objectives at times become meaningful only after the means have been selected; and certain objectives become irrelevant once one means has been decided upon.[6]

Fifth, the strategy of disjointed incrementalism entails a reconstructive treatment of data. As the authors point out:

> evaluation . . . is not rigidly bound to treat problems in their original forms . . . it transforms problems in the course of exploring data. Old possibilities are discarded, and new urgencies appear. Fact systems are restructured as new ones are discovered. Policy proposals are redesigned as new views of the facts are adopted.[7]

In this sequence, shifts in values emerge; the reverse, however, can also take place, commencing with shifts in values, thus establishing another reciprocal relationship.

Values, in the strategy of disjointed incrementalism, are expressed as themes rather than as rules which prescribe or prohibit. Changing views with regard to facts are molded by changes in evaluative themes. To illustrate, Braybrooke and Lindblom suggest that facts regarding specific federal agencies will be restructured when concern moves away from efficiency in performance towards their link to the maintenance of party organizations. They go on to say that the multiplicity and fluidity of values invite exploratory responses—imaginative, innovative, and speculative.[8]

A sixth component of the strategy is serial analysis and evaluation. As this implies, analysis and evaluation proceed in a series of steps which are adapted to incremental changes. Federal legislation in the United States regarding social security, public education, and revenue sharing are examples.

The authors state that:

> it is a characteristic of political processes in most governments that any single office, organization or agency pursues a never-ending series of attacks on more or less permanent, though perhaps slowly changing, problems that lie within its field of interest or authority. [9]

Consequently, analysts (if they are experienced and realistic) accept the fact that alleviation rather than solution is the best they can expect in confronting most problems.

At times, "frames of reference shift" in serial analysis and evaluation; this does not, however, necessarily mean abandonment of the problem. For example, in American higher education the shift from federal aid to institutions to federal aid to students should not be interpreted as a governmental retreat from support of higher education: institutions are still receiving federal support; only now the student is the "donor".

Seventh, besides being incremental, exploratory, serial, and meansdependent, the strategy is characterized by a remedial orientation of analysis and evaluation. These characteristics both aid and influence the analyst to "identify situations or ills from which to move away rather than goals toward which to move."[10] For example, universal higher education is considered to be an important national goal in the opinion of a number of educators. Although they cannot agree upon the kind of education and structure for such a system nor how to bring it about, they can, however, direct themselves to ameliorative methods such as: compensatory and remedial education programs offered within the universities; massive provisions for financial assistance and work/study programs; campaigns to recruit students who ordinarily would not consider postsecondary education; modifications in curricula to include nontraditional study; extension education; and adoption of flexible course scheduling to include evenings and weekends.

The eighth and final aspect of the strategy is social fragmentation of analysis and evaluation. As this suggests, analysis and evaluation occur at a great number of points in society and in centers by analysts who take many different approaches and maintain less than perfect communication with each other. For example, the education of handicapped children is a topic of study in the American Foundation for the Blind, the National Institutes of Health, the U.S. Office of Education, and the Center for Research and Demonstration in the Education of the Handicapped at Teachers College, Columbia University, to name but a few types of complex organizations which deal with this problem.

The disjointed process by which analysis and evaluation of problems and policy take place at various points, lacking both articulation and coordination, is certainly an obstacle to a complete and conclusive treatment of any issue. Nevertheless, as Braybrooke and Lindblom point out:

> Disjointedness has its advantages—the virtue of its defects—chief among them the advantage of preserving a rich variety of impressions and insights that are liable to be "coordinated" out of sight by hasty and inappropriate demands for a common plan of attack. There are circumstances to which no one plan is especially suited.[11]

The strategy of disjointed incrementalism, as outlined in this chapter, provides a comprehensive framework for explaining the policymaking process in a political system. In the studies done by Wildavsky;[12] Davis, Dempster, and Wildavsky;[13] Hyneman;[14] and Rostow and Millikan,[15] disjointed incrementalism clearly demonstrates its usefulness in the analysis of various policy-making phenomena.

Although the strategy is "widely practiced" and can usefully be codified as Braybrooke and Lindblom assert, the authors are quick to recognize that "it is only one of many possible sets of adaptations."

The extent to which this particular set of adaptations explains the public policy-making process concerning access to higher education in Brazil will be examined in the following chapters.

METHODOLOGY

The assembly of a substantial data base is vital to the analysis of public policy formation. Unfortunately, data on the process of public policy formation are sparse and unsystematic. This may be attributed to the fact that there have been the following factors: difficulties in identifying policymakers and participants in the process; a lack of theories in which pertinent issues and variables are involved; and problems stemming from the fact that public policy formation is generally historically bound.[16]

With respect to techniques of assessments, the author chose to employ Gergen's methodological approach of assessing "leverage points" in the process of policy formation.[17] According to Gergen, the identification of a core group of persons is vital to the success of any approach dealing with policy analysis:

> The subunits of greatest importance are individual persons rather than organizations or institutions, and that a thorough understanding of public policy will ultimately depend on knowledge of individual participants.[18]

Gergen utilizes the notion of leverage points, rather than "power" and "influence," because the first, he believes, is more appropriate for analysis of both an entire society and a single community. He proposes a three-dimensional model for identifying leverage points and asserts that any individual in a society can be compared along these lines.[19] The first dimension is issue relevance—the extent to which public policy on a particular issue affects an individual and modifies his normal behavior. The second dimension is subphase resources. They provide the participant with leverage at various stages of policy formation: initiation; staffing and planning; communication and publicity; institutional sanction; intra-elite organizing; financing; and sanction and control. The third dimension is personal efficacy; this denotes a "personality constellation" or "set of social capacities" which are linked to an individual's effective leverage.

Gergen's model possesses some dynamic properties that are worth mentioning. To begin with, issue evaluation is a dynamic characteristic of the model in which a policy maker's basic attitude towards an issue—the degree to which he is for or against an outcome—determines the extent of leverage he will employ. Another dynamic property deals with potential and actual leverage. A strong leverage position does not, in itself, mean the individual will actually operationalize it on every issue; this will depend upon the extent to which his position is polarized, thereby prompting him to exert actual leverage. Related to actual and potential leverage is leverage configuration. This is synonymous with the concept of coalitions in which persons possessing disparate degrees of leverage unite to collectively affect an issue outcome. Lastly, the process of policy formation through time brings an additional dynamic characteristic to the model. Leverage configuration is highly fluid; therefore, the formation of public policy is continuously being altered and modified.

A two-stage procedure which Gergen proposes for assessing leverage[20] was adopted and adapted by the researcher to the exigencies of the strategy of disjointed incrementalism and the nature of the specific issue being analyzed. The technique assesses the main dimensions of the model and accounts for its dynamic characteristics as well.

It is necessary to point out, however, that the formation of public policy is a "continuing process . . . almost impossible to freeze . . . at any one point and gain an adequate conceptualization."[21] Consequently, research on public policy formation practically requires a "strategy of interlocking research phases."[22] In other words, selected techniques of assessment may be utilized during different stages of data gathering. For example, after the actual leverage and leverage configuration are determined, role analysis could be initiated followed by a standardized interview. This was precisely the procedure followed by the author. The method offers the researcher flexibility, enabling him to make the methodological techniques of assessment fit the theoretical framework rather than vice versa.

Clearly, certain techniques are more appropriate, valid, and reliable at certain stages of policy formation (an inherently fluid process) than others. For the investigator engaged primarily in qualitative rather than quantitative research on public policy formation, an eclectic use of methodology is not only convenient—it is essential.

Having presented the theoretical framework and methodology that were utilized in analyzing public policy making in Brazil, it is now necessary to discuss the planning and policy-making environments of access to higher education.

NOTES

1. David Braybrooke and Charles E. Lindblom, A Strategy of Decision (New York: Free Press, 1968).
2. Ibid., p. vi. A number of their premises parallel assertions made by Karl Popper in his The Open Society and Its Enemies, vol. 1 (London: George Routledge and Sons, 1945), 139-44. There he states that one can simplify the problem of evaluation by focusing upon social maladictions instead of ideal constructs or utopias; that because man's competence is limited, only minor units of the social structure may be changed at any one time; and continuous readjustment alleviates the necessity of being correct in any single decision.
3. Braybrooke and Lindblom, A Strategy of Decision, pp. 85-86.
4. Ibid., pp. 87-88.
5. Ibid., p. 90.
6. Ibid., pp. 97-98. See John Dewey, Logic (New York: Henry Holt, 1938) in which he discusses the interdependence of means and ends and proposes evaluating ends in the light of means.
7. Braybrooke and Lindblom, A Strategy of Decision, p. 98.

8. Ibid., p. 99.
9. Ibid., p. 100.
10. Ibid., p. 102.
11. Ibid., p. 106. See R.G. Lipsey and Kelvin Lancaster, "The General Theory of Second Best," Review of Economic Studies 24 (1956-57): 11-32.
12. Aaron Wildavsky, The Politics of the Budgetary Process (Boston: Little, Brown, 1964).
13. Otto A. Davis, M.A.H. Dempster, and Aaron Wildavsky, "A Theory of the Budgetary Process," American Political Science Review 60 (September 1966): 529-47.
14. Charles S. Hyneman, Bureaucracy in a Democracy (New York: Harper, 1950).
15. W.W. Rostow and Max F. Millikan, A Proposal: Key to an Effective Foreign Policy (New York: Harper, 1957).
16. Kenneth J. Gergen, "Methodology in the Study of Policy Formation," in The Study of Policy Formation, eds. Raymond A. Bauer and Kenneth J. Gergen (New York: Free Press, 1968), pp. 206-07.
17. Kenneth J. Gergen, "Assessing the Leverage Points in the Process of Policy Formation," in The Study of Policy Formation, eds. Raymond A. Bauer and Kenneth J. Gergen (New York: Free Press, 1968), pp. 181-203.
18. Ibid., p. 182.
19. Ibid., pp. 183-90.
20. Ibid., pp. 198-200. Gergen's proposed technique combines the advantages found in the reputational, positional, social participation, opinion—leadership, and demographic approaches for the identification of leaders and policymakers.
21. Gergen, "Methodology in the Study of Policy Formation," p. 232.
22. Ibid.

CHAPTER

4

**PLANNING AND
POLICY MAKING UNDER
THE MILITARY GOVERNMENTS**

Access to higher education does not proceed in a vacuum. It is a fluid phenomenon which affects, and is affected by, both the subsystem of which it is a part (education), as well as other systems—political, economic, social, and cultural. These interrelationships are important, particularly when one seeks to analyze a process as broad and far-reaching as policy formation. Therefore, before embarking upon a presentation and discussion of policy making on access to higher education, one must first understand government planning and policy making on the macro-level of Brazilian society, as well as the micro-level of higher education.

THE POLITICAL ENVIRONMENT OF PLANNING AND POLICY MAKING

Economic and social chaos, corruption, and the perceived threat of communism prompted the military to act on March 31, 1964, by overthrowing the constitutionally-elected, leftist government of President João Goulart. The "March Revolution" was carried out not by extremists but by moderate groups (predominantly middle-class). Although its climactic phase was accomplished by military action, the leadership behind the scenes was supplied by civilians.[1]

In his thorough analysis of the emergence of a "modernizing authoritarian regime," Ronald Schneider asserts that Brazil has gone through eight distinct stages since 1964:

>1. Creation of an "Institutional Act" in early April 1964 which set aside parts of the Constitution and served as a legal basis for purging those politically associated with the old order.

2. General Humberto Castelo Branco's inauguration as President in mid-April and the fruition of an eighteen-month period of military-civilian coexistence, in which the administration sought to move from a pseudo-democratic system toward the reestablishment of a completely reformed [open and democratic] political system.

3. A power struggle within the military in October 1965 in which the hard-liners, opposing Castelo Branco, won significant gains—most importantly, the assurance that their candidate, General Arthur da Costa e Silva, would be the next President.

4. The abolition of political parties, as they then existed, and the creation of a bipartite system consisting of the government-sponsored ARENA (National Renovating Alliance) and the MDB (Brazilian Democratic Movement), a catch-all political organization for opposition elements.

5. Costa e Silva's inauguration in March 1967 and the growing disillusionment of many who saw him renege on his commitment to "humanize" the revolution by pursuing liberal social and political policies.

6. The resort to violence and terrorism in 1968 by anti-government elements, as arbitrary use of the vast powers stipulated in the 1967 Constitution was applied by the government to stifle even legal forms of opposition.

7. Increasing conflict between the government and opposition groups, particularly students and the progressive wing of the Catholic Church; and the subsequent development of a power struggle among rival right-wing elements, culminating in Institutional Act No. 5 (December 1968)—a hard-line measure in which federal, state, and municipal legislatures were recessed, and habeas corpus was suspended indefinitely.

8. The ascension to the presidency of General Emilio Garrastazú Médici in November 1969, a close friend of Costa e Silva and former Chief of the SNI (National Intelligence Service).[2]

In the five years since Schneider made these observations, there have been several important political developments which may be considered additions to the eight stages outlined above. Stage Nine would be the election of General Ernesto Geisel, brother of Médici's army minister, as president on January 15, 1974, and the attempt at distenção (relaxation of tensions). Stage Ten would be the upset of the government party, ARENA, in the November 1974 federal and state legislative elections. The opposition party, MDB, increased its number of federal deputies from 87 to 162 while ARENA's representation declined from 223 to 202. MDB gained 17 federal senate seats (from 3 to 20), while ARENA's representation declined from 63 to 46. The election results for state deputies were even more startling: MDB won majorities in the States of São Paulo, Rio Grande do Sul, Rio de Janeiro, Acre, and Amazonas.

In sum, from April 1, 1964 to December 13, 1968 (the date of the Fifth Institutional Act), an evolutionary process was operating by which the level of involvement of the Brazilian military rulers had broadened while the base of their support had narrowed. It was apparent that "the military government of tutelary democracy had, in fact, become an open military dictatorship, while the military as an institution had become deeply divided and split."[3]

The result, then, was the evolution of an authoritarian political system that displays the following characteristics: centralization of authority, depoliticization, repression, political apathy among the populace, and—to some extent—ideological indoctrination (namely, national security and nationalism).[4]

THE ESG AND THE ROLE OF THE MILITARY

The military—firmly and completely in control—operated in a power vacuum, sharing part of that power only with the technocratic elite upon which it depended. For only a highly centralized technocracy could provide the institutional framework and functions needed for economic planning.

According to Brazilian political scientist, Cândido Mendes de Almeida, the military rulers could thoroughly and safely dominate the system because of the following: the national bourgeoisie, capable of taking upon itself a major role, had been politically eroded; the weak bargaining position of wage earners resulted in low political autonomy; the most dynamic middle-class sectors had been absorbed by the government apparatus; also, state economic infrastructure enterprises had expanded significantly; and the traditional landowning sectors, rebuked by deposed President Goulart when he was in office, were dependent upon the military for their survival.[5]

The key element in the policy-making apparatus—particularly dominant during the government of President Castelo Branco—has been the Escola Superior de Guerra (Superior War College). In 1949, a presidential decree formally established the Escola Superior de Guerra (ESG). However, it was designed to be significantly different from the American National War College; the charter decreed its purpose as preparing university graduates who are civilians, as well as graduates of the military schools, for management and advisory positions in the areas of policy formulation, development, planning, and administration of national security policies (for example, military, intelligence, economic, political, social).[6] The ESG's academic program, its mixed civilian-military student body, and its faculty (military, university professors, government technocrats) resembles what can best be described as a combination military post-graduate college/university graduate school of public administration.

The ideology of the ESG focuses upon the interrelationship between national security and national development. Among its policies are the following: strong government, including greater centralization; authority in policy making; planning and rationality in decision making; anti-Communism; a pro-United States posture; limiting the number of political parties; eliminating demagoguery by union bosses and populist politicians; and support of private and foreign participation in development, while maintaining a strong state role in the economy.[7]

The military rulers, however, were divided into factions. The "liberal internationalists" (also known as the Sorbonne group), representing the ESG ideology, and typified by President Castelo Branco, were opposed by "authoritarian nationalists," known as hard-liners (linha dura). The latter comprised junior officers whose position was more militant and authoritarian, less able to distinguish between subversion and national reform, less pro-United States, less pro-private enterprise, and more nationalist.

Nevertheless, basic policies of the military governments have not changed; and the tremendous influence of the ESG's educational program, as well as the school's active alumni association, have not waned appreciably. Stepan cogently affirms this when he states:

> The central idea formulated at the ESG was that development and security issues are inseparable. Even when differences over specific policies developed between the Castelo Branco government and the Costa e Silva government . . . almost all military officers agreed that since labor, fiscal, educational, and other problems were intrinsic to the security of the nation, it was legitimate and necessary for military men to concern themselves with these areas.[8]

THE MILITARY-TECHNOCRAT POLICY-MAKING ALIGNMENT

The Brazilian military governments have relied upon "technocrats" for program planning, policy formulation, decision making, and administration. Technocrats are individuals, both civilian and military, whose administrative abilities and expertise are distinguished by their technical managerial skills. These public administrators rely heavily upon economics, quantitative methods, and systems analysis to carry out the management of government. Many have received postgraduate training in economics and public administration from major U.S. universities.

The government, using constitutional amendments, institutional acts, and executive decrees to bypass the legislative and judicial branches, assumed complete control and drew upon technocrats to diagnose complex economic problems and suggest alternative solutions. It was, however, the presidency, not the technocratic elite, which filled the vacuum left by other power centers.

To illustrate this important point (that the technocrats were important shareholders but not partners in political power), Carlos Castello Branco, one of Brazil's most respected political columnists, offers a prime example. He relates that Roberto Campos, upon assuming the post of planning minister in 1964, offered the president several alternative policies for combating inflation. The president did not agree to the alternative that was the distinct preference of his monetarist planning minister, but instead chose a gradualist approach based upon his evaluation of a number of factors, neither exclusively nor predominantly technical.[9]

A thorough, scholarly analysis of the role of technocrats in the Brazilian military governments has been done by Barry Ames.[10] The elite informants he questioned stated that they expected técnicos (technocrats) to make decisions on technical criteria, but did not expect perfectly rational and omniscient policy makers.[11] Ames concludes that decision-making behavior varies with each group and setting and also ascertains that:

> While the regime has relied more than its predecessors on técnico decision makers, this did not substantially affect policy outcomes. . . . Técnicos seemed able to achieve their objectives only when the elite had an intense interest in the policy problem and when no clientele groups of the regime opposed the técnicos.
> The desire to institute rational decision making may have been a rhetorical synonym for the desire to

institute decision making that would produce certain kinds of outputs.[12]

The political interventions and constraints placed on the technocrats have not left them, on the whole, disenchanted; nor have they hampered the technocrats' ability to perform. With great zeal, technocrats have forged ahead to create new ministries, such as the Ministry of Planning and General Coordination (similar in ways to the U.S. Office of Management and the Budget); remove authority to initiate new programs from other ministries (for example, Ministry of Education and Culture); and strive to better the bureaucratic performance in government agencies by fostering full-time work scheduling. The technocrats' responsibility for the remarkable economic progress made and the coherent economic policy making implanted during the last ten years has brought about tacit acceptance of the authoritarian political system by most middle-class Brazilians.

Consequently, the result is a working alliance, as Thomas Skidmore observes, between the military and the technocrats:

> Each has his own reasons for wanting an authoritarian regime. Each needs the other. The hardline military need the technocrats to make the economy work. The high growth rates in turn give pragmatic legitimacy to the authoritarian system—"it works." The technocrats and managers need the military in order to stay in power, or at least in order to have the power and authority to carry out their policies.
>
> The partners in the alliance have found no single rationale for their authoritarianism. The technocrats and middle sectors do not share the political paranoia of the hard-liners and the latter do not really understand the economic strategies of the former.[13]

STRUCTURAL AND FUNCTIONAL CONSIDERATIONS

The technocrats did not need many new administrative structures when the authoritarian regime came to power in 1964. They inherited the institutional machinery created by President Vargas during the Estado Nôvo (1937-45) and expanded after the Second World War. Centralized economic planning by the national government and the omnipotent presence of the administrative state have been, continually, essential elements of government since 1945.

As Skidmore keenly observes, "the presidency has been the most important single institution in this structure."[14] The president has possessed legal and extra-legal authority, and the extensive power of appointment combined with the tremendous growth of the public sector have given the president vast power for influencing public policy.

Another extremely important unit in the administrative network has been state corporations and regulating agencies. The government has controlled the key manufacturing and transportation industries, utilities, energy, and major commodities, among others.

The military government also inherited a system of compulsory representative organizations, most importantly labor unions. The Labor Ministry has closely controlled the syndicates and thoroughly dominated their activities.[15]

Finally, the compulsory, state-controlled social security system has been an important feature of the administrative state. Practically the entire urban sector—the most politically conscious—and the rural sector have been integrated into a comprehensive welfare system. The social-security system puts a damper on urban discontent; for although the services (for example, medical care, recreational facilities) are below standard, "the real benefits are nonetheless significant in a society of low wage levels and high underemployment and disguised unemployment."[16]

In order to grasp the structural and functional features of policy planning in Brazil, it is necessary to delve deeper. For that purpose, it is useful to draw upon the comprehensive work, both empirical and theoretical, of Robert Daland.

The central point of Daland's dissection of Brazilian public administration is that there exists a "political paradox of planning" by which rules, controls, and other devices are utilized in planning implementation to limit individual freedom in the short-run in order to produce its expansion in the long-run.[17] Relevant to our discussion here are Robert Daland's analysis of the problem, attempted solution, and obstacles.

The main problem, as he sees it, concerns constraints: technical, political, and administrative. The first of these, technical, pertains to planning capability and availability of data. He asserts, however, that postwar Brazil has progressively overcome these problems. Brazilian governments, regardless of ideological posture, have worked closely with the United States in the training of Brazilian economists and public administrators. Consequently, today they rely only occasionally on U.S. technical assistance in economic planning. Also, there has been continuity in planning during the past three decades, the major difference concerning strategy (structuralist versus monetarist) rather than analysis. Data available for research design and analysis, have also improved considerably. Economists of the Brazilian Economic Institute of the Getúlio Vargas Foundation, and the Institute of Economic and Social Planning of the Ministry of Planning are skillfully able to produce and analyze data and engage in such activities as monitoring inflation and generating sophisticated micro-economic sector plans.[18]

The second constraint, political, has been eliminated since the revolutionary governments have provided political stability and have had carte blanche in producing plans, planning institutions, and implementation.

It is the third constraint, administrative, that has proven to be continually problematic for Brazilian governments. Plans have often been useless and dysfunctional because of low performance capabilities and poor central direction within the government bureaucracy. There are various explanations for the inefficiency of the bureaucracy—the use of bureaucracy to defuse opposition by carrying over employees of the former regime, to have it function as a patronage system for the incumbent regime, and its use as a substitute social security system to maintain regime stability. Poor central direction can be explained by the fact that the president and cabinet ministers often cannot effectively control the bureaucracy due to inertia within the agencies, an enormous de facto span of control, and inability to vitalize programs because of the multitude of ceremonial, political, and routine tasks which are not delegated.[19]

The military governments have attempted to solve the administrative problems of planning. Their efforts have been channeled into major development plans and programs. In addition to comprehensiveness, the strategy called for utilizing newly created decision centers. Each government agency was supervised by 1 of 16 ministries. The ministries, in turn, were obligated to follow a uniform pattern of central organization at the ministerial level. One notable feature of this was the creation of the position of secretary-general in each ministry for the purpose of directing programming and serving as a liaison with the Ministry of Planning.[20]

Nevertheless, obstacles still exist; but these are confined largely to administrative constraints (for example, the bureaucracy's low level of performance capacity). The strategy of creating a parallel bureaucracy for policy making, funding, and providing incentives has been advantageous to the military regime in certain instances. By and large, however, it has been disadvantageous. Robert Daland cites a number of the disadvantages, such as:

> the duplication of bureaucratic entities (increasing the complexity of the bureaucracy and the need for further top-level coordinative structures, thus compounding the already severe bottleneck at the top) . . . the use of interagency centers—called work

groups, executive groups, councils, commissions, etc.—means that the formal hierarchy is not a command hierarchy, despite the fact that many perceive it to be so. As a result, the real centers of decision are disguised, in part intentionally and in part accidentally, so that considerable administrative slippage occurs as people behave as if each minister controls the agencies under his formal jurisdiction. Frequently he does not, and a buffer is produced so that legitimate elements within the bureaucracy are expending effort fruitlessly and in the wrong arena.[21]

In a sense, the major weakness of the parallel strategy seems to be the extension of the norms long associated with the Brazilian bureaucracy to the new elements of the parallel bureaucracy.[22]

THE OUTPUTS OF PLANNING AND POLICY MAKING

The major thrusts of the military government's activities have been economic planning and policy making. Undisputedly, they have been successful in attaining their goals of controlling inflation and fostering high economic growth rates. Although the Castelo Branco government was concerned almost exclusively with the former, and the Costa e Silva and Médici administrations with the latter—in the aggregate their economic development plans and actions are quite similar.[23]

Shortly after the military came to power in 1964, the top priority was an anti-inflation program. Planning Minister Roberto Campos and Finance Minister Octávio Gouvêa de Bulhões sought to stabilize the economy by cutting both the growth rate of the money supply as well as public spending and also froze the federal minimum wage. The immediate results were disheartening: an industrial recession in São Paulo and a marked drop in the employment rate.[24]

The government consequently sought to increase employment and energize industrial production by decreasing taxes on consumer items. But the large coffee surplus, traditionally subsidized by the federal government, necessitated a considerable increase in the stock of money—an inflationary measure.

The ministers of planning and finance reapplied monetary constraints at the end of 1965. Although the negative effect of such measures reappeared, the government was successful in reducing the rate of inflation (from 91.9 percent in 1964 to 34.5 percent in

1974).* In addition, another government accomplishment was the notable reduction in the federal deficit from 3.2 percent of the Gross Domestic Profit to 1.1 percent of the GDP at the time Costa e Silva assumed the presidency.25 (By 1971 the figure was 0.2 percent of the GDP.)

True, the stabilization goals of Campos took twice as long to be reached and, too, the Castelo Branco government had failed to initiate a resumption of growth. However, as Skidmore argues, "relative success in controlling price increases was itself a prerequisite for renewed expansion."26 In addition, Campos and his team had reduced the government deficit, promoted improved government management, instituted tax reform thus increasing revenues, brought about increased efficiency in the private sector, and strengthened the nation's balance of payments position.

Under the governments of Costa e Silva and Médici, their Finance Minister Antônio Delfim Neto had to modify the anti-inflation strategy to deal with "cost-push" inflation. The money supply was increased and the minimum wage kept in line with cost of living increases. Demand was restored, fostering an impressive growth rate in the Gross Domestic Product: 10 percent a year since 1968. Only Japan experienced a higher rate of growth.27 In order to maintain equilibrium, a residual inflation rate of approximately 20 percent has been tolerated. In addition, the "crawling peg" system of mini-devaluations has tremendously boosted exports; and both increased exports and net capital inflows have produced large surpluses in the balance of payments.28

Nevertheless, the military governments have yet to deal satisfactorily with such issues as land reform, urbanization, population growth, and regional disparities. Moreover, they have not launched an all-out effort to solve one of the most serious problems gripping the Brazilian people: the decline in real wages of low income groups and the maldistribution of income.

The real minimum wage has fallen steadily since 1964.29 Lower income groups have borne the brunt of stabilization policies. Their purchasing power has declined, and the only thing that has kept families from going under financially has been the increasing number of housewives and children entering the labor force. And even so, per capita food consumption has declined—not to mention a decline in nutrition.30

The earnings of various classes and their participation in the total income are shown in Table 4.1. As one can readily see, the

---

*Statistics compiled from the Fundação Getúlio Vargas, Rio de Janeiro.

TABLE 4.1

Earnings and Participation in Total Income
by Income Level

Classes of Monthly Income (in 1970 cruzeiros)	Number of Persons 1960	Number of Persons 1970	Percentage of the Total Income Groups 1960	Percentage of the Total Income Groups 1970
Below 98	4,899,932	7,452,929	25.2	28.6
Between 99 and 154	3,318,008	5,707,926	17.1	21.9
Between 155 and 210	2,534,189	4,682,106	13.0	17.9
Between 211 and 280	2,955,074	1,580,858	15.2	6.1
Between 281 and 466	3,247,010	3,166,785	16.7	12.1
Between 467 and 934	1,776,356	2,167,000	9.1	8.3
Between 935 and 2,333	569,267	1,038,199	2.9	3.9
2,334 and above	104,585	283,940	0.5	1.1
Average monthly income	206	282	—	—

Source: "A renda dos brasileiros," Veja, 7 June 1972. Based upon data from Albert Fishow, "Brazilian Size Distribution of Income," American Economic Review 62 (May 1972): 391-402; and Carlos Geraldo Langoni, Distribuição da Renda e Desenvolvimento Econômico do Brasil (Rio de Janeiro: Editora Expressão e Cultura, 1973).

gap between rich and poor had widened considerably since the 1960 Census. The distribution of income in Brazil is shown in Chart 4.1.

Most relevant to the researcher's study, however, is the importance in Carlos Langoni's findings of education as a key variable in income distribution. Table 4.2 shows the distribution of income by geographic sector and level of instruction. Basically, the changes from 1960 to 1970 point to the following: a decrease in the economically active rural sector and a parallel increase in the urban sector; a drop of 24 percent among illiterate wage earners; an increase in monthly earnings of all groups except illiterates; a drastic increase in the proportion of the economically active population that possesses a level of instruction above primary school; and the higher the level of instruction, the greater the income. Additional data are furnished in Table 4.3 that reveals, among other things, that the 40 percent of the population with the lowest income is more likely to be illiterate, under 20 percent, and employed in the agricultural sector.

CHART 4.1

Distribution of Income in Brazil, 1970

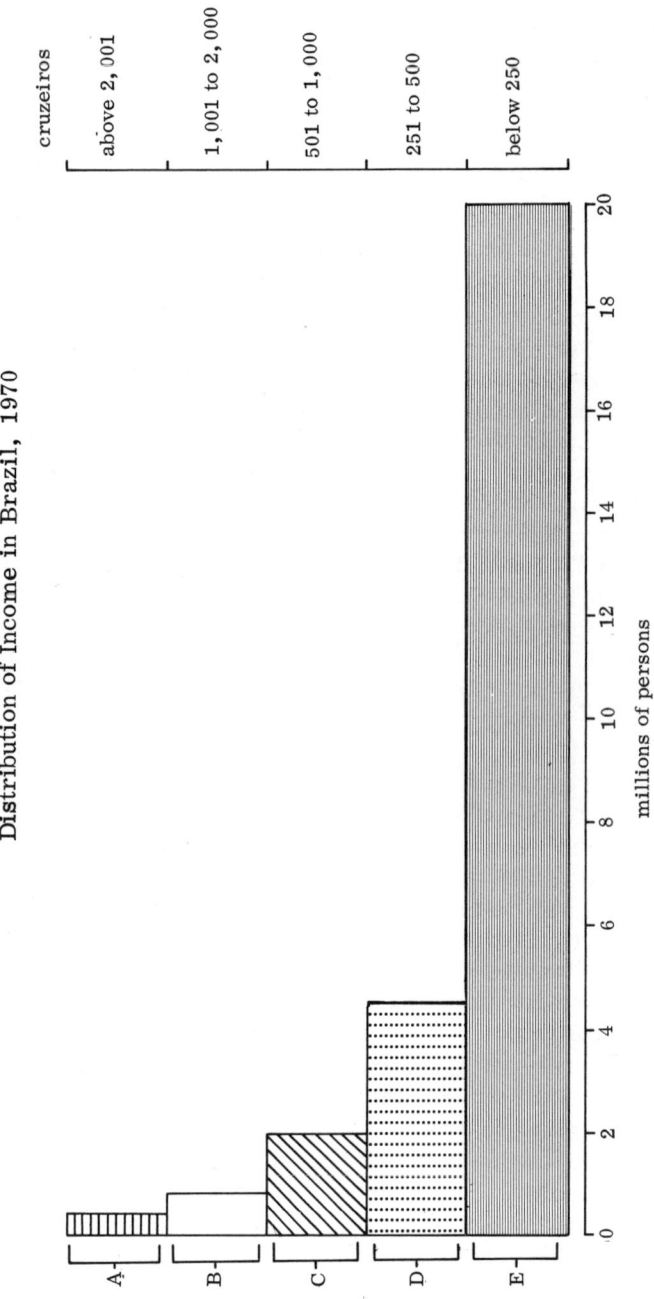

	cruzeiros
A	above 2,001
B	1,001 to 2,000
C	501 to 1,000
D	251 to 500
E	below 250

millions of persons

Note: Of the 27,872,070 possessing income, the distribution, from the wealthiest to the poorest, is as follows: A level, 328,538; B level, 752,953; C level, 1,965,790; D level, 4,623,288; E level, 20,201,501.

Source: Census data (1970), Instituto Brasileiro de Geografia e Estatística (IBGE).

TABLE 4.2

Income Distribution According to Sector
and Level of Education

	Percent of the Economically Active Population*			Monthly Income in 1970 Cruzeiros		
	1960	1970	Percentage Variation	1960	1970	Percentage Variation
Sector						
Rural	46.56	40.05	-13.98	129	138	+7
Urban	53.44	59.95	+12.18	273	378	+38
Level of education						
Illiterate	39.05	29.75	-23.81	111	112	—
Primary	51.71	54.47	+5.34	211	240	+14
Junior high	5.16	8.03	+55.62	440	482	+9
Senior high	2.67	5.24	+96.25	536	688	+28
University	1.40	2.51	+79.28	1,123	1,706	+52

*Economically active population: in 1960, 19,404,421; in 1970, 26,079,743.

Source: Carlos Geraldo Langoni, Distribuição da Renda e Desenvolvimento Econômico do Brasil, p. 86.

Langoni concludes that Brazilian economic development is a mechanism which naturally differentiates people, principally by education. Because education is the major determinant of income distribution, Langoni asserts that the overall situation would be much worse if the possibilities for access to education were diminishing while the concentration of wealth was increasing. However, he acknowledges the expansion of educational opportunity—a 55 percent increase on the junior high school level; 96 percent, high school; and 79 percent, higher education. Finally, Langoni ascertains that when educational supply (that is, opportunity) can be adjusted to educational demand, there will be a reduction in the inequalities—the nation will be better equipped and income will be better distributed. *

---

*What Langoni means when he uses the phrase "the nation will be better equipped" and talks about the need for "qualified manpower" is technically-trained or skilled manpower.

TABLE 4.3

The Influence of Education, Age, and Sector on the
Distribution of Income, 1970 Percentages

	40 Percent of Economically Active Population with Lowest Income Levels	20 Percent of Economically Active Population with Highest Income Levels
Participation in the total income	10.00	62.24
Education		
Illiterates	50.00	3.60
With higher education	0.01	9.10
Age		
Minors 20 years of age	25.00	1.20
Sector		
Agricultural	64.50	9.30
Industrial	7.40	27.20
Service	28.10	63.50

Source: "A renda dos brasileiros," Veja, 7 June 1972. Based on Carlos Langoni, Distribuição da Renda e Desenvolvimento Econômico do Brasil.

In sum, government planning and policy making are made by a military-civilian elite in a technocrat-dominated system of military government. There is no dispute over basic goals. Fundamental issues are decided in secret by the military high command; and since 1965, those who believe that an open political system is incompatible with dynamic economic growth in the short run have exercised a dominant role. The major concern of the government since 1964 has been in the area of economic policy making; and although plagued by an inefficient bureaucracy, the military governments have made remarkable gains.

Even in the economic field, however, there remain problems to surmount—most seriously, income redistribution. As Kempton Webb cogently states:

> The so-called "Brazilian miracle" of economic growth
> since 1964 is an undeniable achievement but it is equally

undeniable that the resulting improvements to the country have been highly selective.[31]

In other areas, concerning social policy, there is also much to be done. Reform has been slow and piecemeal. Again, Webb captures the fluid process in operation:

> There are more innovations; more new elements and procedures on the landscape. These innovations can be viewed as successive waves passing over the national territory and those propagation waves of innovation tend to carry upon their crests the more buoyant (adaptive, capable, and modernized) elements of the society while the more backward or traditional elements tend to be swamped and left behind.[32]

One such innovation concerning access to higher education will be closely examined. Before doing so, however, it is necessary to see how the nature and elements of government planning and policy making for the system as a whole operate on the micro-level: in this case, higher education.

PLANNING ON THE MICRO-LEVEL: HIGHER EDUCATION

The major government bodies responsible for planning and policy-making in higher education are the Ministry of Education and Culture (MEC) and the Federal Education Council (CFE). The MEC (formerly the Ministry of Health and Education) was created in 1930 and by 1970 had grown into a massive, unmanageable bureaucracy in which coordination and communication were very poor and productivity was low. (No less than 73 directors and chiefs were directly responsible to the minister.) This was changed, however, in July 1970 by an administrative reform decree which created eight departments and instituted an innovative budgetary system. Since then, planning, programming, and budgeting have brought positive changes to Brazilian education.

These functions are carried out by a secretary-general. The general secretariat is the central organ of planning, coordination, control, and financial inspection, and the secretary-general is the minister's chief operations and financial manager.

The Department of University Affairs (DAU) replaced the Directorate of Higher Education. Its responsibilities, authority, and autonomy increased; and, consequently, so did its importance.

The Federal Education Council, of which the director of DAU is a member, is a normative body consisting of twenty-four members nominated by the president and is responsible for authorizing and accrediting all undergraduate and graduate programs. General policy guidelines, program duration and course content are all activities of the Council.[33] The CFE also works closely with the Council on the Improvement of Higher Education Personnel (CAPES), an autonomous federal agency which offers scholarships for study in Brazil and abroad to upgrade university teaching staffs.

Broadly speaking, the Ministry of Planning also exercises some responsibility for education since it is in charge of budget development for all ministries. In addition, the Ministry of Planning's Institute of Economic and Social Planning (IPEA) engages in studies related to the economics and finance of education and manpower planning.

Turning to the performance of the federal government in the area of education, the Human Resources Office of USAID, in its sector analysis of education in Brazil, reports that:

> The present federal government has made education a priority area, and its recent actions substantiate this. Federal and state expenditures are rising in real terms; at the federal and state levels planning units have identified key problems in the education sector, meaningful goals have been set, and implementation programs have been initiated which are designed to ameliorate those problems; MEC and the state secretariats of education have undergone, and continue to undergo, administrative reform; and laws and decrees have been promulgated which have had, and will continue to have, profound effects on improving the education system and relating it more closely to the social and economic development needs of Brazil. The system can be characterized as one that is in a state of rapid change.[34]

An excellent indicator by which to assess the priority level of education—and particularly higher education—under the military governments is budget allocation. As one can note in Table 4.4, the federal budget for education rose from CR$196,900,000 in 1964 to CR$2,869,000,600 in 1973—an increase of 1,357 percent. Furthermore, broken down by subprogram (Table 4.5), the data illustrate the highest educational priority given to higher education, which has consistently claimed over 50 percent of federal education funds.

Returning to Table 4.4, however, one can see that resources in education as a percentage of the total federal budget have actually declined from a high in 1968 of 10.69 percent to a low of 6.55 in 1973.

TABLE 4.4

Federal Resources Allocated to Education
(in millions of 1973 cruzeiros)

	Federal Budget in Education	Total Federal Budget	Resources in Education as a Percent of Total Budget
1964	196.9	3,010.7	6.80
1965	387.9	5,098.9	6.97
1966	483.0	7,062.6	7.28
1967	630.0	9,272.0	8.50
1968	874.6	11,547.0	10.69
1969	1,163.5	14,709.0	10.04
1970	1,511.0	19,124.0	9.70
1971	1,838.0	23,100.0	10.05
1972	2,098.4	32,176.8	8.50
1973	2,869.6	43,833.5	6.55

Source: USAID, "Education Fact Sheet No. 13: Budgets, Costs, Expenditures," Human Resources Office, Rio de Janeiro; Government of Brazil, Federal Budget, 1973.

True education outlays as a percent of the total federal budget have declined; however, this has not affected the position of education relative to other areas. In Table 4.6, the federal budgets by program for 1972 and 1973 are presented. Excluding the first three categories under the program heading (these are administrative and bureaucratic rather than programmatically oriented), one can see that, among the 15 programs or spheres of governmental activity, education ranked fourth in both 1972 and 1973. Brazil spent more only in transportation, defense and security, and social assistance. Although educational expenditures as a proportion of the total budget have declined, the percentage increase in the education budget from 1972 to 1973 was above the mean for all programs.

Further clarification of the trend of government expenditures in education and insight into the actual educational policy-making process in this area is provided by Barry Ames.[35] According to him, the high levels of educational spending (1968-69) were due to the fact that "other ministries were not prepared to begin new projects and because education was politically popular."[36] The MEC, however, was very wasteful in the use of funds; consequently, the technocrats

TABLE 4.5

Federal Budget in the Education Program by Subprogram, 1971, 1972, and 1973
(in thousands of 1973 cruzeiros)

Subprogram	1971 Expenditures	1971 Percent	1972 Expenditures	1972 Percent	1973 Expenditures	1973 Percent
Administration	143,867.6	8.3	116,293.9	5.5	106,416,700	3.7
Studies and Research	15,714.2	1.0	16,178.7	0.8	17,730,600	0.6
Staff Training and Upgrading	40,295.6	2.3	90,871.9	4.3	102,572,200	3.6
Divulgence of Technical Information	1,262.0	0.1	3,723.8	0.2	3,800,100	0.1
Fundamental Education	285,708.5	16.5	336,070.7	16.0	412,860,700	14.4
Secondary Education	164,965.6	9.5	227,440.7	10.8	382,055,300	13.3
Higher Education	946,036.3	54.7	1,167,836.5	55.7	1,659,223,000	57.8
Adult Education*	4,722.7	0.3	354.6	0.02	—	—
Student Assistance	77,773.6	4.5	93,166.6	4.5	133,739,200	4.7
Cultural Affairs	32,017.7	1.9	41,702.4	2.0	34,712,500	1.2
Sports and Physical Education	6,432.7	0.4	1,703.0	0.1	1,800,000	0.1
Complementary Education	10,263.4	0.5	3,049.1	0.1	14,659,800	0.5
Total	1,729,061.9	100.0	2,098,391.9	100.0	2,869,570,100	100.0

*A great many government-sponsored adult education programs, such as MOBRAL (Adult Literary Program), operate as semi-autonomous foundations with separate budgets not tied to the MEC. In addition, other ministries (for example, Labor, Industry and Commerce) run adult education programs; and nongovernmental groups such as the Church, business, and community groups conduct adult education programs.

Source: USAID, "Education Fact Sheet No. 25; Budgets, Costs, Expenditures," Human Resources Office, Rio de Janeiro.

TABLE 4.6

Increase in Federal Budget from 1972 to 1973
by Program Budgets
(in cruzeiros)

Program	1972	1973	Percent Increase
Administration	3,347,232,200	4,944,928,000	47.7
Grants to state and local governments	4,990,937,600	6,540,500,400	31.0
General expenditures	4,911,284,900	7,715,189,800	57.1
Agriculture/livestock	556,037,200	674,693,100	21.3
Social assistance	3,831,712,100	4,681,590,000	22.2
Science and technology	355,719,800	473,605,300	41.1
Colonization and agrarian reform	56,229,300	54,706,000	-2.7
Commerce	8,271,300	8,509,900	2.9
Communications	386,136,000	660,761,900	71.1
Defense and security	4,343,915,800	5,381,464,400	23.9
Education	2,098,391,900	2,869,570,100	36.8
Energy	864,279,900	1,123,980,000	30.0
Housing and urban planning	170,420,300	188,052,700	10.3
Industry	188,638,600	489,646,400	159.6
Foreign policy	225,000,000	360,320,000	60.1
Natural resources	278,716,300	300,667,200	15.8
Health and sanitation	817,579,600	1,146,622,800	40.2
Transportation	4,716,297,200	6,218,691,100	31.9
Total	32,176,800,000	43,833,500,000	36.2

Source: USAID, "Education Fact Sheet No. 23: Budgets, Costs, Expenditures," Human Resources Office, Rio de Janeiro, February 1973.

were able to assert their influence and gain some control over education allocations and management at the expense of professional educators. The Ministry of Planning, already playing an increasing role in government policy making, assumed control of fiscal operations in the area of education. In fact, the Ministry of Planning gained control over every department in ministries dealing with spending. As previously mentioned, the 1970 Administrative Reform created the office of secretary-general in each ministry—the liaison position between the Planning Ministry and each ministry. The IPEA within the Planning Ministry was responsible for cost-benefit and other economic analyses of MEC projects that called for additional funds.

The IPEA technocrats had expertise in manpower economics, systems analysis, and the allocation of educational resources. For them, secondary education was deemed the highest educational priority.[37] National development, they asserted, demanded a great many more people with high school-level technical skills. High levels of spending for higher education was considered by the technocrats to produce underemployment and unemployment among professionals.

Antagonism between the technocrats and the professional educators both within and outside the MEC bureaucracy accelerated:

> The IPEA staff criticized MEC as incapable of carrying out anything, full of political appointees and incompetents, and dedicated to self-aggrandizement at the expense of programs. MEC bureaucrats thought tecnicos were interested in quantity rather than quality and were unwilling to listen to people who had spent their lives in the field.[38]

The technocrats, however, were unsuccessful in gaining the power and influence required to shape public policy. As Ames points out:

> [A] natural ally of tecnicos seeking expansion of secondary education would be parents' and teachers' organizations. However, the activity of such organizations was generally inhibited by the repression of groups articulating lower-class interests. Teachers organizations had to spend most of their time trying to get paid. No groups could be found whose primary purpose lay in expanding educational opportunities for poor rural children.
> The structure of the budgetary process encouraged demand articulation by representatives of the universities, whose beneficiaries are mainly upper-middle and upper-class groups.[39]

Finally, the minister of planning, João Paulo dos Reis Velloso, was not a major advocate of the position held by the young technocrats in IPEA; this naturally deprived the technocrats of political clout on the inter-ministerial and presidential levels. In addition—and most importantly—Minister of Education Jarbas Passarinho and his chief advisors were committed to a policy which considered higher education of central importance. This is not to say that secondary education was deemed inconsequential and thus, ignored; on the contrary, in 1971 the minister's plan for far-reaching reform of primary and secondary education became law. Minister Passarinho, however, would not zealously embrace the strategy proposed by the IPEA technocrats, a strategy that was not attuned to many intervening political variables with which the minister of education had to deal.

This chapter has presented the nature, structure, and spheres of government planning and policy making.

It has been shown that government planning and policy making proceed within an authoritarian political environment. Power is centralized and rests with the military. Immune from serious challenge or vociferous criticism, they are assisted in policy making, planning, and administration by a civilian technocratic elite. The only constraints placed on the military are administrative ones due to the low-performance capabilities of the Brazilian bureaucracy.

One of the principal concerns of the federal government has been economic growth and development. While its accomplishments have been remarkable in this sphere of activity, the government has yet to ameliorate such severe problems as maldistribution of income.

The sections following present the historical roots of higher education and an overview of the system of postsecondary schooling.

NOTES

1. Among the abundant literature on the events leading to the 1964 Revolution, several notable contributions are: Alberto Dines, ed., Os Idos de Março e a Queda em Abril (Rio de Janeiro: José Alvaro Editor, 1964); Thomas Skidmore, Politics in Brazil, 1930-1964: An Experiment in Democracy (New York: Oxford University Press, 1967); Fernando Pedreira, Março 31: Civis e Militares no Processo de Crise Brasileira (Rio de Janeiro: José Alvaro Editor, 1964): Oliveiros S. Ferreira, As Forças Armadas e o Desafio da Revolucão (Rio de Janeiro: Edição GRD, 1964; Alfred C. Stepan, "Patterns of Civil-Military Relations in the Brazilian Political System" (Ph.D. diss., Columbia University, 1969).

2. Ronald M. Schneider, The Political System of Brazil: Emergence of a Modernizing Authoritarian Regime, 1964-1970 (New York: Columbia University Press, 1971), pp. 109-10.

3. Alfred Stepan, The Military in Politics: Changing Patterns in Brazil (Princeton: Princeton University Press, 1971), p. 216.

4. H. Jon Rosenbaum and William G. Tyler, eds., Contemporary Brazil: Issues in Economic and Political Development (New York: Praeger, 1972), pp. 5-13. An important analytical work on the Congress' loss of its traditional functions and incapacity to find new spheres of activity is: Sérgio Henrique Abranches et al., As Funcoes do Legislativo (Brasília: Department of Social Sciences, University of Brasília, 1972).

5. Cândido Mendes de Almeida, "Sistema político e modêlos de poder no Brasil," Dados, no. 1 (second semester, 1966), pp. 7-15.

6. Stepan, The Military in Politics, p. 76. To illustrate the importance of the Escola Superior de Guerra (ESG) in shaping the civilian postwar political elite, Stepan cites data revealing that of the 1,276 graduates in the period 1950-67, 626 (49 percent) were civilians.

7. Ibid., pp. 178-83. See also Joseph Novitski, "Brazil's Policies Shaped at War College," New York Times, 2 August 1972.

8. Stepan, The Military in Politics, p. 186.

9. Carlos Castello Branco, "O emprêgo da técnica," Jornal do Brasil, 19 September 1972.

10. Barry Charles Ames, "Bureaucratic Policy Making in a Militarized Regime: Brazil After 1964" (Ph.D. diss., Stanford University, 1972).

11. Barry Ames, "Rhetoric and Reality in a Militarized Regime," Sage Professional Paper in Comparative Politics, vol. 4, no. 01-042 (Beverly Hills: Sage, 1973), p. 9. This monograph is based on Ames' dissertation in which public policy making is empirically assessed in three areas: urban housing, salary policy, and the allocation of federal resources in education.

12. Ames, "Bureaucratic Policy Making in a Militarized Regime."

13. Thomas E. Skidmore, "Politics and Economic Policy Making," in Authoritarian Brazil: Origins, Policies, and Future, ed. Alfred Stepan (New Haven: Yale University Press, 1973), p. 19.

14. Ibid., p. 32.

15. The corporatist representation system is the subject of a detailed and comprehensive examination by Philippe C. Schmitter, Interest Conflict and Political Change in Brazil (Palo Alto: Stanford University Press, 1971).

16. Skidmore, "Politics and Economic Policy Making," p. 35.

17. Robert T. Daland, "The Paradox of Planning," in Contemporary Brazil, eds. Rosenbaum and Tyler, p. 30. See also his Brazilian Planning: Development Politics and Administration (Chapel Hill: University of North Carolina Press, 1967); and "Development Administration in the Brazilian Political System," Western Political Quarterly 21 (June 1968): 325-39.

18. Daland, "The Paradox of Planning," p. 31.
19. Ibid., pp. 32-33.
20. Ibid., pp. 37-38.
21. Ibid., p. 42.
22. Ibid., p. 44.
23. See Ministério do Planejamento e Coordenação Econômica, Programa de Ação Econômica do Governo, 1964-66 (Rio de Janeiro: Documentos IPEA, 1964); Ministério do Planejamento e Coordenação Geral, Programa Estratégico de Desenvolvimento, 1968-1970 (Rio de Janeiro: IBGE, 1967); Brazil, I Plano Nacional de Desenvolvimento (PND), 1972/74 (Rio de Janeiro: IBGE, 1971).
24. Skidmore, "Politics and Economic Policy Making," pp. 6-7.
25. Albert Fishlow, "Some Reflections on Post-1964 Brazilian Economic Policy," in Authoritarian Brazil, ed. Alfred Stepan, p. 72.
26. Skidmore, "Politics and Economic Policy Making," p. 12.
27. Fishlow, "Some Reflections on Post-1964 Brazilian Economic Policy," p. 72.
28. Skidmore, "Politics and Economic Policy Making," pp. 12-14.
29. Conjuntura Econômica, January 1975.
30. Jornal do Brasil, "Pesquisa revela queda no poder aquisitivo dos trabalhadores," 29 October 1972.
31. Kempton E. Webb, The Changing Face of Northeast Brazil (New York: Columbia University Press, 1974), p. 181.
32. Ibid., pp. 181-182.
33. Agnes E. Toward, "Some Aspects of the Federal Education Council in the Brazilian Education System" (Ph.D. diss., University of Texas, 1966).
34. U.S. Agency for International Development, Brazil: Education Sector Analysis (Rio de Janeiro: Human Resources Office, USAID, 1972), p. 1.
35. Ames, "Rhetoric and Reality in a Militarized Regime."
36. Ibid.
37. Carlos Geraldo Langoni, "A rentabilidade social dos investimentos em educaçao no Brasil," in Ensaios Econômicos, 1972, pp. 343-78; Cláudio de Moura Castro, Eficiência e Custos das Escolas de Nível Médio: Um Estudo-Pilôto na Guanabara, Relatório de Pesquisa No. 3 (Rio de Janeiro: IPEA/INPES, Ministério do Planejamento e Coordenação Geral, 1971).
38. Ames, "Rhetoric and Reality in a Militarized Regime," p. 40.
39. Ibid., pp. 40-41.

CHAPTER
5
HISTORICAL ROOTS OF BRAZILIAN HIGHER EDUCATION

In a very real sense, the problem of educational expansion in Brazil—and, therefore, the question of access to higher schooling—can be linked to the clash between the cultural legacy of a colonial and imperial past and the economic realities of a modern nation aspiring to become a world power. Therefore, it is only fitting that attention be given to those developments in Brazil's cultural history that relate to the issue of access to higher education, thereby providing a background for the understanding of Brazilian federal educational policy on access to higher education since 1964.

HIGHER EDUCATION DURING THE COLONIAL AND EMPIRE PERIODS

The historical roots of Brazilian education can be traced to the first colonization by the Portuguese in 1549. Among those accompanying colonial Governor General Tomé de Souza, under orders of King Dom João III, were six Jesuit priests. The Jesuits were concerned, initially, with providing religious instruction and literacy training to the Indian children. Soon after, however, they extended their efforts to schools for the preparation of clergymen and education for those colonists of considerable means. The classical nature of Jesuit education appealed to the upper class of colonial society and abetted the social integration of that elite group from the North to the South.[1]

The Jesuit colégios (translated as "colleges" but actually high schools) were practically the only institutions of cultural and intellectual development in colonial Brazil. Portuguese colonial policies viewed Brazil in terms of short-range exploitation of raw materials rather than long-term investment; as such, the mother country took a position on cultural development that was at the least indifferent and at the most antagonistic. Robert Havighurst and J. Roberto Moreira point out:

> In a society which developed at the mercy of economic cycles, the product of an almost blind search for means of survival and maintenance, without orientation or planning, it was difficult to achieve a cultural consciousness that would bring about the development of satisfactory educational institutions. Had it not been for the catechistic activities of the Jesuits, probably the first educational institutions would have appeared only at the time of independence from Portugal.[2]

Of the token higher education offered during the Colonial period (1500-1808), the most notable college was at Bahia. In 1575 the first bachelor degrees were conferred, in 1576 the licenciate, and in 1578 the master of arts. The recipient of the last degree was, in the words of Fernando de Azevedo, "that colonial equivalent of the college graduate today.[3] Graduates of the college who wished to continue their education would stay in Bahia or go to Rio de Janeiro for theological studies in preparation for the priesthood, or they would go to either the University of Coimbra in Portugal for study in law or the University of Montpellier in France for study in science and medicine.[4]

In 1759 the colonial educational system—as poor as it was—suffered a serious setback that would last for 50 years. Caught up in the "Age of Enlightenment" that was spreading over the European continent, the Marquês de Pombal, prime minister of Portugal, issued an order expelling the Jesuits from the kingdom and its colonies. Many monarchs and their advisers in Catholic countries criticized the Society of Jesus for pursuing educational methods and content that were authoritarian, dogmatic, inflexible, and antiquated. Enlightened European rulers sought the reform of instruction through the introduction of sciences, mathematics, secular philosophy, and modern languages.

While historians have either vigorously condemned the actions of Pombal or enthusiastically supported his decision regarding the Jesuits, it could well be argued that Pombal's policy of expulsion was not as significant and far-reaching as many would believe. To begin with, the Portuguese prime minister's decree affected only the Brazilian landed aristocracy since they, and not the general public, were the ones for whom the colleges were exclusively maintained. Furthermore, while Pombal's educational reform plans for both Portugal and the colonies seemed to broaden educational opportunity, in actuality he achieved no more than the Jesuits. The "regal courses" of study he introduced were frequented by the very same social class that had previously attended the Jesuit colleges.[5]

The establishment of higher education, exclusively professional in character, came about 1808. That date marks the flight of Dom João VI and the Royal Family from Portugal upon news of an imminent invasion of that country by the forces of Napoleon. The immediate purpose of King João's educational endeavors was to attend to the needs of the Portuguese Court; for an immediate return to the mother country was not anticipated. During the reign of Dom João VI in Brazil, the following cultural accomplishments were realized: courses in anatomy, surgery, obstetrics, medicine, and economics in 1808; founding of the Naval Academy in that same year; creation of the Botanical Nursery, Military Academy, and Public Library in 1810; courses in agriculture and founding of the Chemical Laboratory in 1812; additional studies in agriculture in 1814; the Royal Academy of Design, Painting, Sculpture, and Architecture in 1816; courses in chemistry in 1817; courses in mechanical drawing and creation of the National Museum in 1818.[6]

The educational policies and programs of Dom João VI can be described as highly utilitarian in nature—a complete break with the scholasticism of the literary period (that is, before the expulsion of the Jesuits). Dom João clearly sought the creation of special schools with competent teaching staffs whose graduates would serve the public and promote the economic advancement of Brazil. It cannot be determined to what extent João VI's actions were inspired by the anti-university, pro-professionalization ideology of the French Revolution.[7] It will suffice to say that his educational policies set a precedent and laid the basis for the future pattern of the development of higher education in Brazil.

The continuation of King Dom João VI's efforts regarding higher education for the professions, as well as the initial development of primary and secondary school systems, came about during the Empire, 1822-1889. One year after the king returned to Portugal, Brazilian patriots under the leadership of José Bonifácio de Andrada e Silva persuaded the prince regent, Dom Pedro, not to return home. On September 22, 1822, Brazil claimed independence as an empire under Dom Pedro I. The liberal elite which came to power was greatly influenced by the ideas of the French Revolution; and in the realm of education, the imperial government created numerous laws and proposed many plans and programs.

Probably the most important educational law promulgated during the Empire was the Additional Act of 1834. This law decentralized the organization and administration of primary and secondary education, assigning the responsibility to the states; and only higher education and schools in the "neutral township" of Rio de Janeiro were to be administered by the federal government.[8] The impact of the Additional Act on the shape of institutional development (as well as socioeconomic development) during the following 227 years cannot be underestimated. The retrogressive and divisive nature of the 1834 law is amply described by the Brazilian social historian Fernando de Azevedo:

> The decentralization of the fundamental education begun by the Additional Act and maintained throughout the period of the Republic as far as primary education is concerned, attacking one of the essential points of the structure of education, did not permit for a whole century the building on a solid, wide basis of common education, of a superstructure of higher education, either general or professional, nor did it permit the reduction of the intellectual distance between the lower social strata and the elite of the country. Public education was condemned not to have an organization, its links being broken and its central, directive force paralyzed, that center from which an educational policy should be spread to the school institutions of various grades and which should have coordinated in its system the civilizing forces and institutions scattered throughout the national territory. Neither were the provinces under whose supervision there remained only primary and secondary education, able to complete their systems and raise them to the level of higher education, nor was the Imperial government able to raise upon a solid basis of elementary and middle education a national system of education. The very Constitution, reformed in 1834, consequently established the breakdown of education and the duality of systems; the federal and provincial, both of them necessarily mutilated and incomplete; one without the necessary base, the other without the natural crown of a higher professional or disinterested education.[9]

If there was no vertical connection between primary and secondary education, there was a lack of horizontal linkages among higher educational institutions. The growth of faculdades isoladas (isolated or single-purpose colleges) in the professional fields occurred in a haphazard fashion and without an effort towards affiliation or merger. A law school and an economics school could be located near one another in the same town, with each being oblivious to the other. There was no serious effort to build what could be called a university.

Other than the Additional Act of 1834, the other development that profoundly affected the evolution of education in Brazil was the professionalization of higher education.

To begin with, the leadership structure in colonial society initially rested with the landed aristocracy, Portuguese nobility in transition, and the clergy (the Jesuits in particular). There soon emerged, however, a new social category: "intellectuals." Products of Jesuit primary and secondary education, these young men went to Portugal for higher educational studies at the University of Coimbra, afterward returning to Brazil. Their degrees provided them with the means of easy access to the noble class; but their education—largely literary and exclusively Latin—could not make these "intellectuals" anything but men of letters.[10]

Although this literary intellectual formation fell apart with Pombal's expulsion of the Jesuits in 1759, it was resurrected under the Empire, tied to liberal culture and the preparation of lawyers, physicians, engineers, and military officers:

> A culture which had been tributary to religion became thus tributary to the liberal professions, without being stripped of its old humanistic and ecclesiastical content.[11]

Thus, there was established the indelible influence of professionalization in higher schooling. While Dom João VI seriously attempted to establish schools and institutions of agriculture, economics, and veterinary medicine, and restructure the military and naval academies, his efforts were fruitless. The upper classes, throughout the periods of the Empire and the Republic, exerted their influence through the liberal professions, particularly law and medicine. The graduates of the law schools, most of whom did not practice their profession, were highest on the social ladder and exercised the greatest political power. The law schools were training grounds for the elite, the most important stepping stones for young men outside the upper class, and embryos of political life in which the nature of juridical study more closely embodied the spiritual, moral, and cultural values of the land.

The role of the liberal professions cannot be underestimated in examining the evolution and reform of education in Brazil. It will be shown in subsequent chapters that this historical legacy was influential in developments in contemporary higher education.

Returning to the discussion of the historical development of higher education in Brazil, one finds little progress during the Empire period. The law of August 11, 1827 created two courses in law: one at the Convent of São Francisco in São Paulo and the other at the Monastery of Sao Bento in Olinda. Havighurst and Moreira remark:

> These schools were of the utmost importance in training the political elite and in shaping the juridical mentality of the Empire.[12]

By way of the reorganization in 1874 of the Central School, which became the Polytechnical School, courses were offered in engineering and the physical and natural sciences; and in 1875 the School of Mines of Ouro Prêto was founded. With these exceptions, however, the major educational activities during this period dealt with secondary education, the most notable accomplishment being the national government's founding in 1837 of the Colégio Pedro II in Rio de Janeiro—the official model for secondary educational development throughout the nation.

With respect to higher education, the Empire period demonstrates a proclivity for debate rather than a call for action. In the debates of the Constituent Assembly of 1823, a number of proposals were set forth regarding the creation of a university; and even Article 250 of the Constitution of 1823 contains a measure to set up universities in appropriate locales.[13] Nevertheless, this did little except abet the creation of isolated colleges. In 1843 and again in 1870 federal proposals were put forth for the creation of a university, but these efforts did not materialize. Even in the last "Speech from the Throne," just before the abdication of the Emperor (May 3, 1889), Pedro II called for the creation of two universities, one in the North and one in the South, and faculties of sciences and letters in the provinces.

Why was it not possible for a university system—or at least one university—to take hold in Colonial or Imperial Brazil? From the early years of the Empire, there developed a pattern of isolated colleges exclusively for the benefit of the upper classes and geared to professional training. The strong influence of French culture and Napoleon's reorganization of the universities into bodies that emphasized professional higher education were very important. Another major influence was the positivist thought of Auguste Comte which emerged in Brazil during the last years of the Empire. Positivists in public office opposed the creation of a university on grounds that it would limit spiritual liberty, atrophy scientific development, and give even greater intensity to the already "deplorable pedantic pretensions" of the bourgeoisie.[14]

It is Fernando de Azevedo, however, whose truculent observation of Brazil in the Colonial and Empire periods captures the essence of his nation's retarded higher educational development and points out the historical legacies which have affected the development of Brazilian educational institutions up until the present:

> All our culture . . . is marked in its most typical aspects by this purely literary and professional type of training under the influence of which, without the ballast of solid scientific and professional studies, a tendency toward brilliant generalizations was developed rather than one of fruitful specialization, a taste for rhetoric and bookish erudition, a superficiality barely concealed by verbal pomp, a one-sidedness of vision and a dilettantism which leads the individual to examine superficially all questions of doctrine without studying any of them deeply. The fact is that during the whole nineteenth century, at the root of this culture and at its source, there lay a system of education of the intellectual elite made up of a literary and rhetorical secondary education and a higher education that was exclusively professional and in which there were lacking those institutions destined to systematic, philosophical studies and scientific research, in which the critical and experimental spirit and a taste for observation and facts might be developed. This tendency to put quantity above quality, erudition above culture, the value of eloquence above the position of ideas, the "more or less" instead of exactitude, if it did not have its origins in it, certainly was strengthened by the traditional type of teaching, utilitarian and informative, in which it was not so much a question of appreciation as of sheer accumulation, and in which the spirit of exactitude, profundity, penetration, critical and aesthetic maturity was (as it still is today) sacrificed to the acquisition of an encyclopedic learning.[15]

In short, education, in general, did not occupy a position of high priority in either Colonial or Imperial Brazil. The colony of Brazil was for Portugal nothing more than a source of wealth to be exploited immediately—without consideration for long-term colonization and development. Since there were no plans to develop an infrastructure of any kind in this sparsely-populated and feudalistic society, there was no need for a developed educational system. The aristocracy did take advantage of, and encourage among their own, what little higher education was available: the classical, European model disseminated by Jesuit teachers. Higher education was, then, nothing more than a literary, humanistic ornament for the nobility. Despite the efforts of the Marquês de Pombal to centralize and reform education in the colony, the transfer of the Portuguese Court to Brazil in 1808, and the shift of the country's economic center from the Northeast to Rio de Janeiro in the South—the educational situation remained more or less the same.

During the Empire period there was much debate and genuine efforts to create a free, public educational system as well as higher educational institutions. Traditional values, however, and a juridical mentality collectively prevented the realization of these goals. Compared with the Colonial period there definitely was some progress: increased primary and secondary education, governmental action establishing professional higher studies, and the sporadic and scattered appearance of isolated colleges.

Nevertheless, primary education consisted mostly of literary training and involved no more than 15 percent of the population;[16] secondary education became exclusively "preparatory," rather than "formative" in concept—functioning primarily to prepare students for higher study;[17] and higher education, while offering a professional, utilitarian education, was still influenced by classical instruction and catered to the same upper-class groups. When the Republic was proclaimed in 1889, Brazil was still very much a "backward and underdeveloped country."[18]

THE REPUBLICAN PERIOD

In 1889, the Emperor was deposed by liberal military officers under the influence of civilian republican leaders. The government which came to power during this period of nationalism was by no means "popular," but rather composed of a "politically liberal elite" which would maintain control of the political process for the next thirty years.[19]

The Constitution of 1891 created a dual system of education, divided between the states and the federal government. The states would develop their own system of primary, secondary, and higher education; and the central government would supervise a system of secondary and higher education.[20] Minister of Education Benjamin Constant, a positivist like most of his colleagues, did formulate a reform of primary and secondary education and reorganized a number of public isolated colleges, with, however, only a modicum of success.

Higher education expanded during the Republican period with 8 schools of medicine, 8 of engineering, and 17 of law being erected between 1890 and 1930. The fact, however, that only nine research institutes were founded up until 1940 clearly shows the dominant trend of professional education.[21] On September 7, 1920, President Epitácio Pessoa decreed the creation of Brazil's first university, the University of Rio de Janeiro. However, this "university" was merely an aggregation of three professional training schools—law, medicine, and engineering—and did not create structural, functional, or pedagogical changes. The creation of the University of Minas Gerais, seven years later, amounted to the same thing.

Thirty years after the Proclamation of the Republic, Brazil rapidly began to enter the stages of economic growth which were to serve as a prelude to the economic developments of the post-war period. Coffee still remained the main agricultural product, but industrialization, urban migration, increasing disparities in income, inflation, and an elitist federal government characterized Brazilian society. Moreover, the country did not have at its disposal an educational system to meet the needs of the nation's economic development.

Social and political stagnation, combined with the economic crisis of 1929, brought about the Revolution of 1930 in which Getúlio Vargas came to power. It was during the early part of the Vargas era that public education surfaced to serve as a major issue in national affairs. The Associação Brasileira de Educação (ABE) was founded to function as a forum for contemporary educational ideas. And one group in particular, the Escola Nova (New School), was especially influential in advocating the adoption of John Dewey's educational thought to the Brazilian experience.

In Francisco Campos, President Vargas chose a capable and dedicated proponent of the Escola Nova to head up the newly created Ministry of Education and Health. Campos was primarily concerned with secondary education, and his 1931 Law alters the character of secondary education by creating two cycles of schooling: a five-year "functionalist" one and a two-year "complementary" one. The idea was to add a formative concept to the institutionalized "preparatory" concept of secondary education. That is, besides preparation for higher education, the student should be educated in developing the right habits, attitudes, and behavior to function as a useful and responsible member of society.[22] Minister Campos centralized educational authority to the point where the Constitution of 1934, in which the government assumed complete responsibility for national education, was a natural extension of the Minister's administrative policies.

In the area of higher education, Francisco Campos' most notable reform was Decree 19,851 of April 11, 1931. Known as the "Statute of Brazilian Universities," the decree set forth the concept of a university system as the pattern to follow for higher educational development. According to the decree, a university could be organized with three faculties: law, medicine, and engineering; or the substitution of a faculty of education, sciences, and letters for any one of the three.[23] Under the provision of the "Statute of Brazilian Universities," the first true Brazilian university was the University of São Paulo founded in 1934. Its Faculty of Philosophy, Sciences and Letters became the backbone of the institution, and scientific research also came into full fruition. In 1935, the University of the Federal District was created; although the University was abolished in 1939, its School of Philosophy and Letters and the School of Science were incorporated into the University of Brazil (formerly the University of Rio de Janeiro).

These developments, along with the founding of the Catholic University of Rio de Janeiro in 1940, were landmarks in the growth of the university idea in Brazil—a type of growth which can be described as extremely slow and marked with obstacles, as scientific research and learning for learning's sake fought to coexist with utilitarianism.[24]

The Republican period was interrupted in 1937 when President Vargas staged a coup d'etat, dissolved Congress and set up a dictatorship. This period, from 1937 to 1945, is called the Estado Nôvo (New State). Vargas had skillfully manipulated the extremists of left and right to the point where the military and the middle class developed an attitude of "profound pessimism about the viability of open politics."[25] Disenchanted with liberalism as the political course for Brazil to follow, politically socialized Brazilians beckoned the authoritarianism of the Estado Nôvo.

In the area of education, the policy of compromise, adjustment, and balance were shunned as the dictatorship sought a short-term solution to the problem of education.[26] The Deweyist "progressive education" of the Escola Nova became distorted as the State insisted all education must serve its objectives.[27] The Vargas government glossed over the real substantive, pedagogical challenges of the nation in favor of expedient and nationalizing policies.

Educational expansion did occur, of course, on all levels; and the emphasis given vocational-technical education and universal primary education in the Constitution of 1937 were, indeed, revolutionary for Brazil.

Moreover, Minister of Education Gustavo Capanema undertook a reorganization of the Ministry of Education by which a pedagogical research institute was created and administrative services were more efficiently coordinated with the objectives of educational planning. Capanema also formulated the "Organic Law of Secondary Education" in 1942—a document which, although calling attention to the need for better articulation among the various types of secondary education (commercial, industrial, normal, and college-preparatory), was a "retrogression in the history of secondary education" and highly authoritarian as it "institutionalized, from without, and 'imposed' from the top, a rigid federal system of education which all schools, public as well as private were subordinated to."[28]

Education during the Estado Nôvo was characterized by a stress on quantity over quality, uniformity and rigid curricula and teaching methods, acute bureaucratization, neglect of teacher training, stopgap measures, and encouragement of private education on the secondary level (with federal regulation, however) to alleviate the financial burden placed on the national treasury.

Mediocrity also characterized higher education, since most of the expansion at the time was among professional, isolated colleges, often of dubious academic quality. The quantitative expansion of higher education during the Vargas period was, according to one educational historian, an unsuccessful effort to bring the masses to the "fountain of culture" and elevate their level of knowledge; consequently, newly created universities tended to be "cities of stone, without an enlivening spirit, without a creative spirit."[29]

After World War II, Vargas was deposed and the Republic restored in 1946. Elections were held and Eurico Dutra, Vargas' war minister, became president. Economically, Brazil was in a very good position. The nation prospered through the sale of raw materials and agricultural products to the Allies during the war, and was thus able to industrialize considerably, increase the rate of employment, and expand public services and communications. As living standards improved greatly in large, urban areas, rural inhabitants flocked to the cities to find employment.

However, the nation was not without its problems. Inflation plagued the economy, and the economic development of the country was uneven: the gap between rich and poor widened further.

For the next 18 years, Brazilian socioeconomic development would proceed with great momentum: rapid industrialization and urbanization, centralized planning, galloping inflation, tremendous population growth, increases in real income, high levels of production, disparities in regional development, expansion of a diversified middle class, political and ideological struggle, and educational reform.[30] In short, Brazil would be irrevocably immersed in the process of modernization.

The postwar governments were faced with an educational system woefully inadequate for Brazil's development. Minister of Education Clemente Mariani appointed a commission in 1947 to come up with a national plan for education as authorized in the Constitution of 1946. The intention of Mariani was to give Brazil, for once, a comprehensive educational law for public education, long-term in plan, and geared to the concepts of modernization, democratization, and decentralization. The bill was submitted to Congress in 1948 and for the next 13 years was the focus of intense debate: liberals versus conservatives, proponents of centralization pitted against defenders of decentralization, private school interests versus advocates of public schooling. The bill died, surfaced, died again, and finally arose in 1957 when it was vigorously debated by public school and private school advocates. According to one scholar of Brazilian education, the "prejudicial effect of conflicting interests and compromise solutions flawed the basic unity and spirit of the Law."[31] The bill was passed in 1961 as the "Law of Directives and Bases of National Education"—an ambiguous and contradictory national education law. Soon after approval of the legislation, the new law was implemented only partially and with varying degrees of success, however.[32]

In essence, the 1961 Law decentralized the Brazilian educational system, creating a dual system: federal and state. A Federal Education Council would oversee the transfer of responsibility for education to various sources. In reality, the 1961 Law decentralized administration on the local level, but still maintained supervision of state and private schools to assure compliance with the law. As one keen observer notes, "the Law of Directives and Bases did not establish a new educational system . . . it modified the already functioning educational system of Brazil."[33]

Although the 1961 Law focused primarily on primary and secondary education, there were provisions for higher education; however, nothing was promulgated to radically alter the structure and function of postsecondary education. The Law retained federal administrative responsibility for higher education through the newly created Conselho Federal de Educação (Federal Education Council). However, the relationship between the Ministry of Education and higher education centered on individual faculties and universities. The constitutions and bylaws of universities and independent faculties would be subject to governmental approval, and the Federal Education Council would establish the minimum curriculum for programs in which diplomas could be used for licensing. University autonomy would be recognized; it could, however, be suspended if the institution did not comply with the law.

While the 1961 Law was being debated in Congress, higher education was expanding at a pace previously unseen; independent, isolated colleges as well as universities (the newer institutional phenomenon) sprang forth. Postwar modernization necessitated a system of higher learning to meet the manpower requirements of economic growth, and the Brazilian middle class—a product of this socioeconomic transformation—demanded increased access to higher schooling, as a means of insuring both social and material benefits for their children.

To illustrate the kind of growth Brazilian universities underwent in the postwar period, it is noted that in 1946 alone Minister of Education Ernesto de Souza Campos inaugurated the Universities of Paraná, Bahia, and Recife. At the same time, the Catholic Universities of Pôrto Alegre, São Paulo, and Rio de Janeiro restructured their organizational frameworks.[34] From 5 universities in 1940, Brazil had created 32 by 1961: 22 public institutions financed by the federal government; 3 state universities; 6 Roman Catholic; and 1 private, nonchurch administered institution. Furthermore, over 400 isolated colleges were founded. Enrollments increased from 21,000 in 1939 to 38,000 in 1949, to 102,000 in 1961. Private institutions claimed 44 percent of the student enrollment; federally-supported, 38 percent; state institutions, 17 percent; and 1 percent in municipal institutions.[35]

Be that as it may, one must realize that the powerful and overwhelming forces of modernization often cannot extirpate the legacies of history and tradition. In the case of Brazil, there are four currents which have run through the course of higher educational development: the absence of a firm federal commitment to education; an alternating pattern of centralization-decentralization which has characterized federal involvement; exclusive emphasis on training for the professions; and the absence of a university tradition.

As subsequent chapters will reveal, these legacies of history and tradition would become enmeshed in the controversy over access to higher education.

NOTES

1. Fernando de Azevedo, Brazilian Culture (New York: Macmillan, 1950), pp. 165-67.
2. Robert J. Havighurst and J. Roberto Moreira, Society and Education in Brazil (Pittsburgh: University of Pittsburgh Press, 1965), pp. 54-55.
3. Maria do Carmo Tavares de Miranda, Educação no Brasil (Recife: Imprensa Universitária, 1966), p. 25; Azevedo, Brazilian Culture, p. 168.
4. Harold Benjamin, Higher Education in the American Republics (New York: McGraw-Hill, 1965), p. 32.
5. Havighurst and Moreira, Society and Education in Brazil, pp. 57-58.
6. Miranda, Educação no Brasil, pp. 41-43.
7. Azevedo, Brazilian Culture, p. 372.
8. Brazil, Additional Act of August 6, 1834, Clause No. 2, Article 10.

9. Azevedo, Brazilian Culture, pp. 376-77.
10. Azevedo, Brazilian Culture, pp. 165-66.
11. Ibid., p. 170.
12. Havighurst and Moreira, Society and Education in Brazil, p. 72.
13. Brazil, Project of the Constitution, 1 September 1823, Article 250.
14. Miranda, Educação no Brasil, pp. 57-58.
15. Azevedo, Brazilian Culture, p. 388.
16. Havighurst and Moreira, Society and Education in Brazil, p. 71.
17. Benno Sander, "Educational Law and Practice in a Developing Country: An Empirical Study of the Impact Made by Brazilian Law No. 4024 on Secondary Education in the State of Rio Grande do Sul" (Ph.D. diss., Catholic University of America, 1970), pp. 42-43.
18. Havighurst and Moreira, Society and Education in Brazil, p. 76.
19. Ibid., p. 77.
20. Brazil, Constitution of 1891, Article 35.
21. Azevedo, Brazilian Culture, p. 431.
22. Adalberto Corrêa Sena, Legislação Brasileira do Ensino Secundário (Rio de Janeiro: Livraria Central, 1929), p. 10.
23. Benjamin, Higher Education in the American Republics, p. 33.
24. Azevedo, Brazilian Culture, pp. 475-76.
25. Thomas E. Skidmore, Politics in Brazil, 1930-1964: An Experiment in Democracy (New York: Oxford University Press, 1967), p. 22.
26. Azevedo, Brazilian Culture, p. 457.
27. Humberto Grande, A Pedagogia no Estado Nôvo (Rio de Janeiro: Gráfica Guarany Ltda., 1941), p. 8.
28. Sander, "Educational Law and Practice in a Developing Country," pp. 48-49.
29. Miranda, Educação no Brasil, p. 77.
30. Sander, "Educational Law and Practice in a Developing Country," pp. 30-32.
31. Agnes Toward, "Some Aspects of the Federal Education Council in the Brazilian Education System" (Ph.D. diss., University of Texas, 1966), p. 63.
32. William A. Harrell, Educational Reform in Brazil: The Law of 1961 (Washington, D.C.: U.S. Office of Education, 1968), p. 48.
33. Ibid., p. vi.
34. Miranda, Educação no Brasil, pp. 79-80.
35. Havighurst and Moreira, Society and Education in Brazil, p. 197.

CHAPTER

6

THE SYSTEM OF HIGHER EDUCATION

In presenting the system of higher education in Brazil, it is important to note its organization, administration, and finance; economic and manpower considerations; and the process and problems of access to higher education.

ORGANIZATION, ADMINISTRATION, AND FINANCE

The organization of higher education in Brazil consists of universities or university "foundations" and isolated, independent colleges. The former must comprise five or more institutes, colleges, or schools (the three terms are interchangeable) and be recognized by the Federal Education Council. Isolated colleges, on the other hand, are single-purpose colleges—mostly private—which are unaffiliated with a larger institution such as a university or consortium of colleges. In 1973 there were 69 universities (federal, state, municipal, and private), enrolling 45.37 percent of the students in higher education, and 712 isolated colleges, both public and private, enrolling the remaining 54.63 percent of the students.[1]

Although the federal government maintains a dominant role in the governance of higher education, universities nevertheless do maintain normative and governing structures. The most important of these, and the principal lobby for higher education, is the Council of Rectors, a private, voluntary association of presidents of universities. It meets during the year to discuss, debate, and sponsor conferences on a variety of issues and subjects pertaining to the reform and improvement of higher education.

Within the university, a University Council (senate) makes policy for the institution; it is composed of the directors and full professors of the various schools plus representatives of associate and assistant professors and students. Formerly a professor catedrático (loosely translated as a professor holding an endowed chair) controlled each discipline within the school. This has been replaced by a system of professorial rank—assistant, associate, and full professor—in which tenure may be granted, but the power and autonomy is far less than that of the cátedra (chair). In addition, in accordance with the 1968 Reform Law, a system of "departmentalization" is being implemented.

The undergraduate program of instruction varies from three to six years in duration; and, in contrast to the United States, comprises a number of courses of study which American universities offer exclusively on the graduate level. For example, medicine is a six-year program; law and engineering are five-year programs; and journalism, library science, and physical education are three years in length.[2] Graduate education has expanded in recent years, and universities now offer M.A. and Ph.D. degrees.

Also, in recent years the academic program has moved from the curriculum as the basic unit of evaluation to the credit system in which the basic unit is the subject. Books and course texts are expensive, and libraries are small and decentralized; consequently, students constantly complain about these weaknesses and do not make much use of library facilities.[3]

With respect to the teaching body, the number of college teachers increased from 30,872 in 1964 to 63,754 in 1971. However, because of the tremendous growth of the higher education student body in that period, the students-per-teacher ratio increased from 4.7 to 8.9.[4] An accurate accounting of the stock of college teachers cannot be determined because most professors (84 percent) teach part-time and most give classes in more than one institution.[5] A continuous campaign to hire more full-time teachers can partly explain the increase in the students-per-teacher ratio, as part-time professors are being replaced.

Concerning faculty salaries for full-time professors in federal universities, the monthly salary, calculated in 1971, was as follows: assistant professors, US$709; associate professors, US$811; and full professors, US$913.[6] As for faculty affairs (for example, hiring, firing, scheduling), these are handled exclusively by the institution. Although apparently only 25 percent of college teachers have graduate degrees, efforts have been made during the past 15 years to remedy this. A study by the Fundação Getúlio Vargas reported that 1,200 Brazilians returned from abroad during 1960-1970 with an M.A. or Ph.D. More than two-thirds returned to teach exclusively; and from 1970-1974 the number is probably quite high.[7]

Almost all financing of federal higher education comes from the national government; and in the case of state colleges and universities, state governments. Federal funds, however, are also allotted in small amounts to state and private institutions, usually for financial aid to poor students. As to the financing of nonpublic institutions:

> Private schools have varied sources of financing: from students in the form of tuition, from foundations or religious organizations; and from the federal government mostly in the form of scholarships for needy students. Data on the detailed sources of financing for various types of institutions are not readily available.[8]

The public colleges and universities, in contrast from the private, charge only minimal tuition (actually fees). The federal government is interested in introducing a system of graduated tuition for those who can afford to pay, but this has not yet materialized.

As Table 6.1 reveals, there has been a steady increase in federal funds allocated to higher education. It must be noted that the growth in the percentage of federal expenditures for higher education has been uneven partially because of funding variations of primary and secondary education, as well as the rapid growth of enrollments and expenditures among the private institutions since 1969.

TABLE 6.1

Federal Government Expenditures in Higher Education, 1965-73

Year	Federal Government Expenditures (in 1973 CR$1,000)	Percent Growth Over Previous Year	Growth in Constant Prices*
1965	188,488	00	100
1966	219,399	16	84
1967	332,649	52	100
1968	450,166	35	109
1969	669,003	49	134
1970	810,364	21	135
1971	946,036	17	132
1972	1,167,837	23	137
1973	1,659,223	28	n.a.

*1965 = 100.

Source: USAID, Brazil: Education Sector Analysis and data compiled from the Human Resources Office, Rio de Janeiro, Brazil.

THE SYSTEM OF HIGHER EDUCATION

STUDENTS

It is unfortunate that comprehensive socioeconomic data on Brazilian university students currently do not exist. A partial, regional analysis of students done in 1968 is very much out of date.[9] A modest effort, however, was made in 1972 to scientifically collect and analyze data on candidates for admission to higher education.[10] Although important limitations of the study are the facts that the information deals only with a population concentrated in Greater Rio de Janeiro and excludes candidates who are not competing in the unified college entrance examinations, the findings, nevertheless, are worth citing. The data are pertinent because they focus on the unified college entrance examination system that was developed in Rio de Janeiro and implemented in 1972.

The exam competition was divided into three distinct areas, each area given a Portuguese acronym: science and technology (COMCITEC); biomedical sciences (COMBIMED); and human and social sciences, arts, and letters (COMSART).

The greatest proportion of students approved in the three areas was between 17 and 19 years of age. Female students outnumbered males in absolute numbers in COMBIMED and COMSART: and in all three areas, females achieved a higher proportion of approved candidates. With respect to family income, high family income is correlated with the higher rates of passing on the exams. Also in absolute numbers and percentages, the majority of students did not work, and their families assumed all financial responsibility. Candidates whose fathers had a higher education and whose occupation was in the liberal professions (for instance, law, medicine, engineering) showed the highest percentages of approvals on the entrance examinations. It is important to note the miniscule representation in the exam competition of candidates from the lowest socioeconomic class.

Concerning secondary school related data, both in absolute numbers and percentages the approved students had never failed a course, had been daytime pupils, and had frequented a cursinho (preparatory course for the college entrance exam). The number of times which a candidate took the entrance exams had nothing to do with his chances of passing.

With respect to the students' career orientation, the survey reveals that reading materials were the major source of influence in candidates' career choices; however, this had little influence on the percentage of students approved in the exam competition. Most students denied that there was less competition for freshman places in the career area they selected; and even for those who answered in the affirmative, this fact was not especially influential in their career choice.

As for employment prospects, most students felt it would not be easy to find work in their career areas. Those who believed otherwise and considered this the decisive factor in choosing a career showed the smallest percentage of those passing the exams. A majority of students, however, believed that their career area offered good economic possibilities, yet asserted that this was not very important in their career choice. Those who acknowledged that economic considerations were of prime importance in choosing a career showed the smallest passing rate on the examinations.

Concerning social prestige, a majority of the approved students believed that their career provided social prestige and was very important to the nation's development.

Finally, the overwhelming majority of students who passed the exams asserted that the career they chose was the one most suited to their aptitudes and interests. Those for whom this fact served as the major basis for their career choice showed the highest passing rate in all areas except science and technology (COMCITEC). In the COMCITEC area, however, the absolute number of students was extremely small; hence, the number of approved students in this category inflates the percentage rate.

It must be stressed that this portrait of the Brazilian university student should not be used to infer that students throughout Brazil manifest the same pattern of socioeconomic characteristics. However, since the data findings are derived from a recent survey in Greater Rio de Janeiro, the geographical focus of the study, they are particularly relevant.

It is necessary to mention something about student politics under the military regime. Like their Hispanic American peers, Brazilian university students have an activist tradition. The principal concern of these students has always been university reform. From 1937 to 1964 the leading collective voice of the students was the National Union of Students (UNE), an activist organization which was funded, in part, by the federal government. Leftist and nationalist in its orientation, the UNE became increasingly radicalized during the regime of President João Goulart. When the military came to power, extremist elements in the UNE had come to dominate the organization.[11]

In November 1964, the government declared the UNE illegal. This directive, known as the Suplicy Law (after Minister of Education Flávio Suplicy de Lacerda), did not, however, abolish structures for student representation in the universities or on the state level. The government replaced the UNE with a National Directorate of Students (DNE), but the new organization did not have the legitimacy which the UNE still retained despite its legal extinction.[12]

Over the next few years, student protest demonstrations and government repression increased and intensified. From 1967 to 1968 the situation worsened considerably. Students launched a campaign aimed at the recent agreements between the Ministry of Education and Culture (MEC) and the U.S. Agency for International Development (USAID). Under the MEC-USAID Accord, a team of American university professors were sent to advise the Brazilian government on higher educational reform.[13] Student activists saw this as imperialist infiltration in Brazilian education.

In March 1968, a high school student participating in a demonstration in Rio de Janeiro was killed by police. A wave of protests followed, and demonstrations, confrontations, violence, and arrests resulted.

Shortly thereafter, President Costa e Silva appointed a commission, headed by General Carlos Meira Mattos, to study the student movement and its manifestations. Reporting to the President in May, the Meira Mattos Commission concluded that "excessive repression will give rise to excessive reaction"; the government must liberalize its relations with student movements, respecting student demands, attending to those which are justified, and recognizing the existence of deficiencies in the system; and authorities must realize that it is incorrect to qualify the whole student movement as subversive.[14] Meira Mattos, himself, urged the government to open up more places in the universities.

Students, professors, and other members of the academic community virtually lost their right to dissent when the government issued Decree-Law No. 477 of February 26, 1969. The decree defined disciplinary infractions practiced by workers in public and private teaching institutions; outlawed strikes, work stoppages, and any activities of a subversive nature; and specified a three-year suspension of students and a five-year prohibition of employment for professors and administrators convicted of violating the decree.[15]

It must be stressed, however, that the student movement has comprised a minority of the total university population. Nevertheless, it has made an important mark on the Brazilian educational panorama and has gained the attention of the government.

CURSINHOS

Although not a formal part of the system of secondary or higher education, the cursos pré-vestibulares, also known as cursinhos (little courses), serve an extremely important function and, in so doing, consequently affect the formal educational system on both levels. Therefore, it is worth mentioning something about these institutions: what they are and how they function.

The cursinhos were created and continue to exist because: candidates for higher education outnumber university places; selection for higher education is based solely on performance on entrance exams; secondary education generally is of poor quality and does not adequately prepare students to confront the exams; and consequently, students do not give much credence to, nor show much interest in, secondary education.

The overwhelming number of cursinhos are privately-owned and operated; a few are run by private and public colleges and student councils. Proponents of the cursinhos assert that education, rather than training, is the exclusive function of these important institutions. Opponents counter that cursinhos are commercialized, fact-cramming, training courses.[16]

The teaching staff consists of salaried teachers, cooperatives of teachers, and instructors who receive remuneration per class taught. The staff is largely part-time and has a great many young teachers. The teachers are mostly public and private schoolteachers, university professors, and college students. The pay is often much better than that offered in formal educational institutions, and the instructors must know not only content but—equally as important— how to teach. Although hired by cursinho directors, the teachers are evaluated several times by the students; those who are found "unsatisfactory" are fired.

Tuition at the cursinhos varies, depending upon such factors as the prestige of the cursinho, the competition for the area (for example, medicine), and the section of the city where the courses are given. The competition among the cursinhos is fierce, each one trying to undercut the other; and in some cases, coalitions—formal or informal—are formed to drive certain competitors out of business.

Students who attend cursinhos fall into three categories: individual students who are preparing for the exams for the first time; individual students who failed the entrance exams previously and are repeating the cursinho; and students who attend private high schools which have <u>convênios</u> (agreements) with the cursinhos. This last category deserves attention.

In 1963 many private high schools sent their students to a cursinho for part of the time. Consequently, the federal government prohibited this action in 1964. In turn, private high schools, led by Colégio Brasileiro de Almeida, responded by bringing the cursinho to the high school! Under this arrangement, the cursinho would substitute the senior year of formal high school education.[17] Eventually, in 1966, the Federal Education Council permitted certain private high schools, which so requested, to send their seniors to cursinhos, providing the distance from the high school to the cursinho was not great.

The financial arrangements of the agreements between the high schools and the cursinhos provide for the student to pay the high school tuition only. Nothing is paid directly to the cursinho. The high school, in turn, shares this inomce with the cursinho. To illustrate, Curso Bahiense has agreements with a number of high schools with the provision that the high school keeps 30 percent of its tuition income and the cursinho receives 70 percent.[18]

The cursinhos will be mentioned further in the sections dealing with the sequence and analysis of policy development on access to higher education.

REFORM POLICIES

The efforts of the Brazilian government to reform higher education have aimed at modernizing the entire system and, in many ways, adopting features of the American and, to some extent, British systems.

The cornerstone of the government's reform policies is the 1968 University Reform Law:

> The main item of the general overhaul is the breakingup of the faculties [semi-autonomous colleges within the university], the establishment of departments for specific branches of learning, a greater flexibility in the curricula, the extension of the "credit system" and the appropriation of sufficient resources from public funds in order to guarantee, together with just and sufficient wages, the full-time dedication of professors to do their job.[19]

In 1969 the government operationalized the provisions of the Law relating to teaching schedules and salaries. In federal universities wages were increased and a system of instructors, assistant, associate, and full professors was adopted. The MEC also set up COMCRETIDE, a special commission to financially assist universities in contracting professors for new work schedules. At the same time, the government has moved to more closely regulate professors, courses of study, and the creation of new institutions.

The government has also encouraged the use of instructional technology in the universities and provided large amounts of funds for physical facilities—institutional construction and expansion. Improved management procedures have also been encouraged.

Less success has greeted the 1968 Law's provisions for a basic cycle of general education in the university, because of the lack of full-time professors, the small number of facilities with auditoriums, and the lack of counselors.

Following the student protest movement in 1968, as mentioned, the federal government sought to involve students and professors in national development by integrating Brazilian universities with regional development plans. The most notable innovation in this area has been Projeto Rondon—a domestic Peace Corps program created in 1967. Initiated through the Ministry of Interior, it recruited university students to spend their vacation periods working on service projects in depressed areas of the nation. By 1972 more than 30,000 students had participated in the program, and its success gave rise to other community service efforts.[20]

Also set up were rural university centers for training and community action (CRUTAC). Concentrated largely in the North and Northeast, these extension centers were created to offer students an internship and to provide the rural poor with social and educational services. Today there are 22 CRUTACs in federal universities throughout Brazil.

The federal government has also sought to stimulate the development of postgraduate education. The emphasis has been on the preparation of university teachers and the development of graduate programs leading to the M.A. and Ph.D. degrees. The graduate programs are offered mainly at institutions in the well-developed Southeast of the nation (Guanabara-São Paulo). Enrollments have grown 156 percent between 1965 and 1970; and in recent years, graduate study in the traditional field of law has declined sharply while agriculture, engineering, science, business, and education have sharply increased.

An excellent indicator and source of government reform policies is the Sector Plan for Education and Culture,[21] published in English by the Ministry of Education and Culture. It is part of the I Plano Nacional de Desenvolvimento (PND) 1972/74 (First National Development Plan). The Sector Plan establishes the great importance and interdependence of education in national development and presents 33 priority projects which were to be initiated in the 1972-74 period. Thirteen of these projects deal with higher education.

The focus of this study, however, is on reform policies which concern another dimension of higher education—the issue of access. For the federal government, this has been one of the highest—if not the highest—educational priority in recent years.

ECONOMIC ASPECTS OF HIGHER EDUCATION

Since economic factors are of prime importance to the Brazilian government—in every area of its activity—and because federal policy makers do maintain an influence on private as well as public higher education, a discussion of economic aspects is most relevant. Essentially, economic aspects of higher education center upon the social demand for higher education, on the one hand, and the labor market for college-trained manpower, on the other. As economist Samuel Levy points out in an extremely important study on the subject:

> At the macro-economic level, the planning of higher education consists essentially in attempting to influence the interaction between the forces of supply and demand in two distinct, and only remotely related markets, which is at the root of the problems of higher-education planning.[22]

Social Demand for Higher Education

A startling revelation produced by the tabulation of the 1970 Census data shows that during university attendance very little earnings need be foregone; in fact, during university attendance earning capacity increases even beyond high school.[23]

There is, however, need for qualification. Socioeconomic background shapes the demand for certain careers. The few poor students who attend private universities are restricted, in a sense, from choosing engineering, architecture, and medicine because tuition for these programs of study are considerably higher than for courses in law, economics, and philosophy and letters. In addition, the former professions require full-time university attendance (meaning additional foregone income); this further dissuades poor students from pursuing study in such fields even at the tuition-free public universities.

The annual rate of increase of secondary school graduates has been steady over the years, averaging 13.7 percent per annum. The effective demand, however, for higher education has greatly expanded (see Table 6.2). In analyzing the data, it should be pointed out, one must understand "applicants" to include multiple applications. Nevertheless, even considering the factor of multiple applications, the growth rates are impressive—particularly in light of the fact that since 1971 the practice of multiple applications has diminished tremendously.

TABLE 6.2

Growth of Candidates for College Admission
and Number Passing the Entrance
Examinations, 1960-73

Year	Applicants	Annual Increase of Applicants (in percent)	Number Passing	Proportion Passing (in percent)
1960	64,637	—	23,753	36.7
1961	70,147	8.52	24,705	35.2
1962	70,942	1.13	29,896	42.1
1963	86,716	22.24	37,205	42.9
1964	97,481	12.41	47,219	48.4
1965	110,834	13.70	48,141	43.4
1966	123,379	11.33	51,223	41.5
1967	183,150	48.42	70,915	38.4
1968	214,996	17.39	82,781	38.5
1969	276,904	28.80	109,281	39.5
1970	328,931	18.80	135,600	41.2
1971	400,958	21.90	191,585	47.8
1972	476,154	18.75	268,815	56.46
1973	508,615	6.82	318,028	62.53

Source: SEEC (Service for Educational and Cultural Statistics, MEC); DAU (Department of University Affairs, MEC); Estatísticas da Educação Nacional, 1960-1970, vol. 1, MEC, 1972.

It is important to note that a considerable part of the demand for higher education is repressed demand—those who have postponed entry to higher education and others who have failed to gain admission in earlier attempts.[24] The roots of this situation are structural. First, many students seek admission to higher education because secondary education has been largely college-preparatory and does not train students for jobs following high school graduation. Second, if the high school graduate does enter the labor market he must compete, unfavorably, with college students who work part-time, receive higher wages, and have better prospects of higher earnings in the future. Third, higher education is an attractive form of investment because of the low private costs: tuition is free in public institutions and many private colleges do not charge excessively high fees. (Again, these generalizations do not apply to the poor student.) Furthermore, foregone earnings may be very low, since many university programs do not require full-time attendance. Fourth—and most importantly—higher education is the number one route for upward social mobility, "a filter, controlling the access to the ranks of the middle classes, permitting just that inflow which is necessary to replenish and supplement the professional cadres."[25]

With low private costs of higher education and a system of free tuition in public colleges, the middle class thus reaps "windfall profits," in a sense. It would seem the candidate need concern himself only with passing the difficult college entrance examinations. It is essential, however, to note that selection for higher education is largely economic in character. Even discounting foregone earnings at earlier levels, the costs of education are often great because of the shortage of public school education. To illustrate, in 1970, 38.4 percent of junior high school enrollments, 41.1 percent of senior high school enrollments, and all enrollments in the cursinhos were in the tuition-charging private sector.[26]

The demand for places in higher education has been most pronounced in the biomedical and technological areas. Table 6.3 reveals candidate/place ratios in 1970 of 6.27 in the former and 5.09 in the latter field. Recent demand pressure has subsided in these fields. Other fields have remained stable in terms of demand; although arts and letters (since 1969) and social and economic sciences (since 1970) have seen increased demand. The former is most likely because of expanded curricula offerings and the candidacy of poorer and less able students, and the latter because of the sheer popularity of the course offerings.

Supply of Higher Education

It is vital to understand that in a developing country with a population of over 99 million and gross socioeconomic disparities, the tasks of planning and statistical projection are very often formidable. In fact, the tremendous social demand for higher education has taken planners by surprise. From the earliest to the latest calculations of higher education enrollment projections—using both the "manpower requirements" and social demand approaches—estimates have all lagged one or two years.* Actually, public higher education,

---

*The planning study I Plano de Desenvolvimento, 1973/74 (Rio de Janeiro: IBGE, 1971) projected a target of 820,000 enrollments in higher education in 1974. Figures reveal that 837,000 was reached in 1973.

TABLE 6.3

Candidates for the Vestibular per Place, by Field of Study, for Some Federal Universities, 1965–72

Year	Exact Sciences Number of Universities	Exact Sciences Candidates Per Place	Biomedical Sciences Number of Universities	Biomedical Sciences Candidates Per Place	Technology Number of Universities	Technology Candidates Per Place	Human Sciences Number of Universities	Human Sciences Candidates Per Place	Letters and Arts Number of Universities	Letters and Arts Candidates Per Place	Socioeconomic Sciences Number of Universities	Socioeconomic Sciences Candidates Per Place
1965	8	2.65	13	2.60	11	3.70	13	1.97	12	1.27	12	2.28
1966	9	2.25	13	4.02	10	3.20	13	2.08	12	1.90	12	2.47
1967	10	2.47	13	4.00	10	3.27	13	1.40	11	1.57	13	2.40
1968	9	1.98	13	3.67	10	3.64	13	1.51	12	1.92	11	2.90
1969	11	2.28	14	4.58	12	4.32	13	2.50	13	1.82	13	3.47
1970	12	2.45	14	6.27	13	5.09	14	2.50	12	1.87	11	3.51
1971	10	2.27	12	5.74	10	4.58	12	2.45	10	3.24	8	3.03
1972	6	2.38	9	3.88	6	3.43	9	1.97	5	2.03	4	3.11

Source: A survey of 17 Federal Universities; Samuel Levy, *The Demand for Higher Education and the Labour Market for Professionals in Brazil*, contract no. AID-12-692 (Rio de Janeiro: Human Resources Office, USAID, 1972).

THE SYSTEM OF HIGHER EDUCATION 73

even with its increase in capacity-utilization to meet social demand, has not expanded nearly as rapidly as the private institutions. By 1970 private higher education enrollments had significantly outnumbered enrollments in the public sector.[27] In addition to the obvious, heavy public investment costs needed to accommodate student demand, policy makers were no doubt aware that the private cost of higher education was low and the private rate of return substantially higher than the social rate.

Operating precariously, and in many cases not formally recognized, private isolated colleges do serve an important function:

> Despite their disorderly growth, the generally low quality-level of the instruction they offer, and the fact that many of them are motivated exclusively by profit considerations, it should be emphasized that the new private establishments have performed an important social function: that of relieving some of the pressure of demand from public universities, and absorbing those who could not gain admission elsewhere.[28]

Total enrollments in higher education in Brazil are illustrated in Table 6.4. The absolute number of matriculations as well as the growth rate are impressive. Since 1964 undergraduate student enrollment has risen from 142,386 to 836,469 in 1973. This represents a percentage increase of 487.5 percent and an average annual rate of increase of 21.9 percent. Over a 15-year period, from 1958 to 1973, enrollments in higher education grew by 890.1 percent.

As to enrollments in major courses of study, Table 6.5 reveals the distribution of undergraduate enrollments by courses of study from 1958 to 1971. In addition to the tremendous growth in the aggregate (564.5 percent) and large increase in the absolute number of enrollments for all courses of study, the percentage contribution to total enrollments by all courses of study, except for philosophy, letters and science, and physical education, has declined. For example, the combined enrollments in law, medicine, and engineering accounted for 50.4 percent of total enrollments in 1958, yet only 26.3 percent in 1971. On the other hand, philosophy, letters, and science, combined with basic cycle enrollments, accounted for 53.3 percent of the total enrollments in 1971. Two major trends are discernible: business administration and economics have supplanted law as "the fashionable course in a society where technocrats play such important roles"[29] (the former courses grew by 664.8 percent over a 15-year period as compared with 244.8 percent for the latter course); and particularly large enrollment increases have occurred in fields where

TABLE 6.4

Total Enrollment and Growth of Higher Education
in Brazil, 1964-73

Year	Total Enrollment	Percent Growth from 1964	Percent Annual Increase
1964	142,386	—	—
1965	155,781	9.4	9.4
1966	180,109	26.5	15.6
1967	218,099	53.2	21.1
1968	278,295	95.4	27.6
1969	342,886	140.8	23.2
1970	425,478	198.8	24.1
1971	561,397	294.3	31.9
1972	688,052	383.2	22.6
1973	836,469	487.5	21.6

Source: Estatísticas Nacional da Educação, 1971, vol. 1, MEC, 1972; Ministério da Educação e Cultura, Encontro de Dirigentes (Brasília: MEC, 1974).

institutional costs are low (for example, philosophy, science, and letters; basic cycle; physical education).

Labor Market Conditions

Information on the geographical distribution and average annual income of secondary school and college graduates amply reveals some of the glaring disparities in the Brazilian economy. Levy produces data which show that:

> The center-south region, with 60.6 percent of the population, and an income per capita which is 21.5 percent higher than the national average, is where 76.5 percent of university students, 79.9 percent of [college graduates] and 80.0 percent of those with completed secondary-education . . . are located. Moreover, 53.0 percent of university graduates, 46.9 percent of university students and 47.2 percent of [high school] graduates are concentrated in São Paulo and Guanabara, with a combined population

TABLE 6.5

Increases and Relative Distribution of Undergraduate College Enrollment by Course of Study, 1958, 1965, 1971

Courses	1958 Enrollments	1958 Percent	1965 Enrollments	1965 Percent	1971 Enrollments	1971 Percent	Percent Growth, 1958-71
Basic cycle	—	—	—	—	142,937	25.5	—
Philosophy, letters, science	17,372	20.6	36,314	23.3	156,187	27.8	799.0
Law	22,302	26.4	33,608	21.6	76,906	13.7	244.8
Engineering	9,672	11.5	21,986	14.1	39,433	7.0	307.7
Business and economics	6,812	8.1	19,751	12.7	52,098	9.3	664.8
Medicine	10,535	12.5	15,574	10.0	30,990	5.6	194.2
Dentistry	5,145	6.1	6,044	3.9	8,571	1.5	66.6
Agriculture	1,627	2.0	4,397	2.8	6,482	1.2	298.4
Social work	1,265	1.5	3,086	2.0	6,352	1.1	402.1
Architecture	1,720	2.1	2,601	1.7	4,591	0.8	166.9
Pharmacy	1,583	1.9	2,350	1.5	4,185	0.8	164.4
Art	*	*	2,056	1.3	4,889	0.9	137.8
Veterinary medicine	763	0.9	1,740	1.1	2,743	0.5	259.5
Communications	*	*	1,322	0.8	4,305	0.8	225.6
Nursing	*	*	1,056	0.7	2,882	0.5	172.9
Physical education	*	*	980	0.6	8,615	1.5	779.1
Others	5,685	6.8	2,916	1.9	9,231	1.7	62.4
Total	84,481	100.0	155,781	100.0	561,397	100.0	564.5

*Included in the "others" category of 1958 enrollments and percentage.

Source: USAID, Brazil: Education Sector Analysis, 1972; SEEC, Ministry of Education and Culture.

of 23.7 percent of the total. This illustrates well the degree of concentration of the modern and dynamic sector in the Brazilian economy.[30]

The professions of law, agronomy, dentistry, economics, engineering, and medicine were selected by Levy for analysis, as they account for 34.0 percent of all those who had completed higher education in Brazil, according to the 1970 census estimates. In his study:

> the average annual earnings for each of the six professions is presented as a proportion of the average annual earnings for all those with a completed university course, for the country as a whole. Thus, lawyers, who exercise their profession, earn, on the average, 12.6 percent more than all university graduates. Economists, engineers and physicians, respectively, earn 9.8, 45.1 and 28.5 percent more than the average for all university graduates. On the other hand, agronomists' and dentists' annual earnings are respectively, 20.0 and 24.3 percent lower than this average.[31]

Of the six professions, only dentistry and agronomy offer recent college graduates labor conditions which are less favorable than those of all university graduates. However, when one accounts for the private costs of higher education that are higher in medicine, engineering, dentistry, and agronomy than for other courses of study—the private rates of return are not significantly higher for medicine and engineering graduates and are actually considerably lower for dental and agronomy graduates in comparison both with other professions and—more crucially—all university graduates as a whole!

Labor market conditions are still favorable for college graduates as a whole, and especially favorable for those in the professions; however, earnings of dental and agriculture professionals are less than those of the average university graduate. It is vital to realize that university students are not sensitive to market factors in selecting a career. To illustrate, from 1960 to 1969 the number of students graduating from dental school increased very little; during the same time, agriculture school graduates grew by almost 370 percent. Economics and engineering graduates increased by 702.4 percent and 452.8 percent, respectively, while annual graduations in medicine and law were considerably smaller—116.8 and 93.1 percent, respectively.[32]

In his summary analysis, Levy states:

> The great increase in the demand for higher-education can be understood only in broad socioeconomic terms— as a manifestation of a relatively well defined social group which expects very high social and economic benefits on its investment. . . .
> Many of the problems which characterize the professional labour markets in Brazil, do not result from a <u>general</u> overproduction of university graduates, but rather from the overly-rigid nature of the higher-education system, inadequate professional orientation to students and early specialization. There is little evidence to suggest that unemployment among university graduates is a serious problem. Instead, what often happens is that university graduates are absorbed in jobs previously occupied by secondary school graduates. The demand for at least a part of the annual output of university graduates is closely interdependent with the supply of them, both curves shifting simultaneously.
> The increase in the supply of university graduates probably has had a depressing effect on the relative earnings of secondary-school graduates, especially due to the fact that much of secondary education is still nonprofessionalizing in character. The earnings of university graduates, however, seem to be administered prices, subject to social and institutional conventions, and not so sensitive to the action of market forces. This results in a very wide disparity between the earnings of university graduates and those of [high school] graduates—again indicating the substantial private benefits to be reaped from a university degree.[33]

Among his policy recommendations, Levy asserts that massive public expenditures for higher education are unjustified, and that money should be invested instead in primary and secondary education. He does recognize that increasing social demand for higher education must be accommodated somehow and suggests that this be done in priority areas where shortages are acute.

THE PROCESS AND PROBLEMS OF ACCESS TO HIGHER EDUCATION

Before examining public policy making on access to higher education, it is necessary to explain briefly the process and problems of access which existed at the time the federal government decided to focus its attention on the issue.

Process: The Exame Vestibular

Admission to higher education in Brazil was determined exclusively by the candidate's performance on the exame vestibular (college entrance examination). Few educational systems in the world rely so heavily upon one criterion for university admission or on an external examination as the sole basis for access to higher schooling.

The exame vestibular was brought about by Minister of Education Rivadávia Correa in 1911. The purpose of the examination's creation was to exercise greater federal control over secondary education by means of a State examination. Along with federal accreditation of secondary schools, the exame vestibular was a mechanism for carrying out the policy of the new Republican government to centralize all of secondary education, particularly "non-official" (private) institutions.[34] In 1915, Carlos Maximiliano broadened the function of the examination with the purpose of having it serve as a unit of common measurement among higher education institutions in assessing the abilities of candidates for admission.

The reforms of Minister Francisco Campos, embodied in the 1931 Education Law, contained a proposal to select candidates for higher education by means of a curso complementar (complementary course). This proposal, however, was never enacted.[35] Another reform-minded Minister of Education, Gustavo Campanema, indirectly dealt with the examinations. Law no. 20 of October 2, 1947, gave the Minister of Education authority to prescribe the procedures for holding the examinations in all "official" (that is, under federal jurisdiction) higher education establishments. It is important to note that in this law the examinations are not referred to as concurso de habilitação (ability examination) but concurso vestibular (entrance examination).[36] Ten years later, the Ministry of Education and Culture set down the subjects required for the college entrance examinations; this was embodied in Portaria (Regulation) no. 453 of December 21, 1956, and Portaria no. 14 of January 1957.[37]

The monumental Law of Directives and Bases of National Education (no. 4,024 of December 20, 1961), also known as LDB, established the exame vestibular as compulsory for access to the university and reaffirmed the autonomous right of higher education institutions to organize competitive examinations for college entrance (article 69a). Furthermore, the LDB allowed secondary schools to use the last year of colégio (high school) as a pre-university course of study in preparation for the exame vestibular (article 46, paragraph 2). Universities could also, if they so chose, offer the last year of high school by creating a colégio universitário (article 79, paragraph 3).

Students, upon completing high school, had two options: immediately take the college entrance exams; or spend an additional year preparing for the examinations. Invariably, those who decided on the second alternative would enroll in one of the cursinhos, where the sole purpose was to undergo an intensive program to pass the exams. Most of these students had attended high schools that did not have agreements established with the cursinhos. (It is significant to note the absence of a guidance component in the process of admissions to higher education.)

The next step the student followed was registration for the exam competition at the college or colleges he wished to attend. After furnishing the necessary documents, the student paid the inscription fee for the tests. The amount varied with the institution and program—no limit was set on the fee a college could charge.

All during this process, the candidate came in contact with school clerks, never professors. Even the notice of the examination schedule, place, and so on, was provided impersonally—posted or published in the newspapers. There was no personal notification or communication by mail; in essence, there was no contact between the candidate and the school.

When the candidate confronted the college entrance examinations, he could expect to find both written and oral tests; and for certain courses of study, practical tests were also required. As already mentioned, the Ministry of Education in 1957 established the minimum subjects required in the exams for admission to each major course of study in higher education. Institutions of higher education could legally introduce additional subjects on the entrance examinations. Even aptitude, ability, and vocational tests could be given.

Because of the great size of the potential admissions group (recent high school graduates, those who graduated earlier but decided to postpone taking the exams, and those who had failed the tests previously and were trying again)—logistical considerations for test taking were of prime concern. Consequently, thousands of candidates were herded into sports stadiums and other huge, centralized locations. Administrative convenience was deemed far more important than the physical comfort of the candidates.

Following the grading of the tests, the results were published in the newspapers, along with the names of those who passed. These fortunate candidates then enrolled in higher education (the competition was valid only for the school year for which it was held). As for the others:

> the great majority take it [the exam] as an experience, and try again the next year, or abandon their hopes. . . . Among those who keep on trying, some make the attempt two, three, four, five, six, and even seven times. Each new attempt means the passing of a year, except in the case of a second call; this occurs only in certain schools where the number of passing candidates has not reached the number of places offered.[38]

The examinations, it should be noted, were eliminatório (eliminatory). The entrance examination used an arbitrary, predetermined score as a cutoff point for passing. As a consequence, however, the number of candidates achieving a passing score was often greater than the number of available freshman places (called vagas). Students who had passed the exam competition but were denied admission were considered excedentes, and there was often tremendous pressure to allow them to enter college. As Teixeira pointed out:

> This results in the custom of making the examinations more difficult in proportion as the number of candidates is greater than the fixed number of openings, thus guaranteeing that the number passing will be equal to, or smaller than, the number of available places.[39]

In the large cities, particularly Rio de Janeiro and São Paulo, the examinations were often very difficult, and the failure rate was quite high. Not surprisingly, the proportion of students going to cursinhos to prepare for the tests was exceedingly high.

This was the process by which candidates were selected to higher education. It was a process which was by no means satisfactory, as we shall now see.

Problems of Admission

The process of selection for higher education created a number of major problems of admission[40]—problems which concerned students, educational institutions, manpower economics and politics (many of these have already been discussed or alluded to). The problems were as follows.

THE SYSTEM OF HIGHER EDUCATION

First, secondary education, being exclusively preparatory rather than formative, led the vast majority of its graduates to seek university admission. This situation, in addition to inflating the number of candidates for admission, was responsible in part for Brazil's critical shortage of middle-level manpower.

Second, colleges and universities followed a policy of numerus clausus. Each institution made available only a limited number of places, under the pretext of maintaining high academic standards. Candidates' opportunities for higher education were limited further by the fact that government policy restricted public colleges and universities from expanding significantly; the only expansion was in private isolated colleges, a great many of which were of dubious quality.

Third, the exams were inherently designed to limit the size of the actual admissions group of each college and university in five ways:

a. The tests depended quite heavily on fact memorization; and they were exceedingly difficult in content, often exceeding the level of what could reasonably be expected of a high school graduate. The written and oral tests included trivial and trick questions as well as items requiring great detail. Overall the exams were highly selective. In addition, the tests were constructed and graded exclusively by college professors: there was no collaboration with secondary education specialists.

b. Generally, the core of test subjects, material content, the type of tests, and the system of grading and selecting candidates differed among institutions and fields of study.

c. The candidates took the examinations for admission to one major course of study only; they were not allowed more than one career choice.

d. The exams prejudiced the candidates both mentally and physically. The tests served as the only means of access to higher education; this, combined with the fact that the nature of the tests and the selection of candidates were designed to eliminate the majority of students, created widespread and severe anxiety and fear. Compounding the situation, the test-taking conditions brought physical difficulties to the candidates. The huge stadiums in which most candidates took the exams were extremely hot, poorly ventilated, excessively bright or dim in various locations, and installed with wood and concrete benches which were hot, hard, and rough.

e. The college entrance exam competition was eliminatory based on an arbitrary passing score. This produced a gross injustice by creating excedentes, candidates who passed the exams but were denied admission due to lack of freshman places. These candidates and their families, infuriated by the situation, reacted strongly to this unfair practice: they resorted to legal means to force admission.

Fourth, the system of access to higher education, with its total reliance upon entrance exams, compounded by the academic weakness of secondary education, gave rise to cursinhos and the heavy dependence by candidates for admission on these private preparatory courses. Consequently, secondary education became downgraded and depreciated even more.

Fifth, the lack of articulation between secondary and higher education was further perpetuated by the process of selection for higher education for the following reasons:

a. The college entrance exams were the only criterion for admission to higher education; secondary school work and letters of recommendation meant absolutely nothing.

b. The tests were constructed and graded exclusively by college professors.

c. The content of the tests was geared to higher—not secondary—education's concept of what a candidate should know.

d. The cursinhos undermined the legitimacy of secondary education, further hampering cooperation between middle level and higher level education.

Sixth, the system of access to higher education fostered economic discrimination against poor candidates. The cursinhos, which definitely improved a candidate's chances for admission, were expensive to attend; the monthly charges were often equal to or greater than three-fourths of the monthly minimum wage of workers. Also, the inscription fee for registering for the exams was approximately one-half the monthly minimum wage. Furthermore, because various colleges and universities held their entrance exam competition on different dates and at different times—those who could afford multiple inscription fees could improve their chances for admission by taking entrance examinations at more than one college.

Seventh, the federal government could not obtain an accurate accounting of the demand for higher education. Multiple inscriptions for exams inflated the true number of candidates for admission; also, there was the inability to identify repeater candidates for admission, further preventing demand projections; finally, higher education institutions had poor data on registration and enrollment.

Eighth, a maldistribution of candidates between programs created difficulties with respect to manpower economics in four ways:

a. The demand was greatest for socially prestigious professions (for example, engineering, medicine, law, economics).

b. In some of these prestigious professions—namely engineering and medicine—there was a substantial disproportion between candidates and places available.

c. In other high status professions (for example, law), although the demand was great, the disproportion was less severe. These professions, however, were overcrowded and employment was modest.

d. For certain areas (for example, agronomy, veterinary medicine), candidate demand was low; these professions were not considered socially prestigious, even though employment demand—although not salaries—was good.

Ninth, the lack of a guidance program, either on the secondary or higher level, meant that candidates were denied educational, vocational, social, and psychological orientation. The absence of such vital information made the exam competition and admission to higher education institutions all the more harrowing and very much impersonal.

As we shall see, the federal government took into account the process and problems of admission in its policy to reform the system of access to higher education.

NOTES

1. U.S., Agency for International Development, Brazil: Education Sector Analysis, p. 52; Ministério da Educação e Cultura, Catálogo Geral das Instituições de Ensino Superior: 1973 (Brasília: Departamento de Assuntos Universitários, MEC, 1973), p. 13

2. William A. Harrell, The Brazilian Education System: A Summary (Washington, D.C.: U.S. Office of Education, 1970), p. 14.

3. U.S., Agency for International Development, Brazil: Education Sector Analysis, pp. 66-67.

4. Ibid., p. 64.

5. Ministério da Educação e Cultura, Catálogo Geral, p. 24.

6. Brazil, Decreto-lei no. 66.258 de 1970, Diário Oficial, 25 February 1971.

7. Magda Prates Coelho and Elisa Maria Pereira, O Emprêgo no Brasil de Profissionais Treinados no Exterior, Projeto Retorno, Documento no. 4 (Rio de Janeiro: Fundação Getúlio Vargas, 1971), p. 7.

8. U.S., Agency for International Development, Brazil: Education Sector Analysis, p. 55.

9. Ministério da Educação e Cultura, Caracterização Sócio-Econômica do Estudante Universitário (Rio de Janeiro: Centro Brasileiro de Pesquisas Educacionais, Instituto Nacional de Estudos Pedagógicos, 1968).

10. Fundação CESGRANRIO, Analise do Questionário de Informações sobre o Candidato (1972) (Rio de Janeiro: Departamento de Pesquisas, Fundação CESGRANRIO, n.d.).

11. Robert O. Myhr, "Student Activism and Development," in Contemporary Brazil: Issues in Economic and Political Development, eds. H. Jon Rosenbaum and William G. Tyler (New York: Praeger, 1972), pp. 349-50.
12. Ibid., p. 350.
13. Ministério da Educação e Cultura, Relatório da Equipe de Assessoria ao Planejamento do Ensino Superior: Acôrdo MEC-USAID (Rio de Janeiro: MEC, 1969). See also Arthur José Poerner, O Poder Jovem (Rio de Janeiro: Editôra Civilização Brasileira, 1968).
14. Jornal do Brasil, 28 May 1968.
15. Myhr, "Student Activism and Development," p. 363.
16. Roberto do Valle, "Os 'cursinhos,' mal crônico," Educação Hoje, July/August 1970.
17. Anexo III, "Interview with Prof. Edília Coelho Garcia," in O Acesso à Universidade, IVa Conferência Nacional de Educação, ed. Nádia Franco da Cunha (Rio de Janeiro: INEP, 1967), pp. 1-2.
18. Anexo II, "Interview with Prof. Norbertino Bahiense," in O Acesso à Universidade, ed. Nádia Franco da Cunha, pp. 1-2.
19. Ministry of Education and Culture, Education in Brazil (Brasília: Commission for International Affairs, MEC, 1971), pp. 33-34.
20. U.S., Agency for International Development, Brazil: Education Sector Analysis, pp. 71-73. However, even before Projeto Rondon there were several university-sponsored community development projects in operation, such as CRUTAC (a student-based technical assistance program for rural communities) and MUDES (a private foundation cooperating with the MEC and offering work-study, community action, and scholarly activities).
21. Ministry of Education and Culture, Sector Plan for Education and Culture, 1972/1974 (Brasília: General Secretariat, MEC, 1971.
22. Samuel Levy, The Demand for Higher-Education and the Labour Market for Professionals in Brazil, Contract no. AID-12-692 (Rio de Janeiro: Human Resources Office, USAID, 1972), p. 1. We shall use Levy's definition of demand as being a function of the private rate of return to higher education.
23. Ibid., p. 4.
24. This conclusion is substantiated in Fundação Carlos Chagas, Estudo de Algumas Características Sócio-culturais de Candidatos ao Ingresso em Escolas de Nivel Superior (São Paulo: Fundação Carlos Chagas, 1969).
25. Levy, The Demand for Higher-Education, p. 15.
26. Ibid.
27. Levy, The Demand for Higher-Education, p. 24. Another indicator of the pattern of expansion of higher education is provided

by Estatísticas da Educação Nacional, 1960-1971, published by the MEC in 1972. Data are provided on the growth of enrollment in universities (public and private) and isolated colleges (public and private). Since the former are largely public and the latter overwhelmingly private, we are given yet another indicator of the pattern of higher education expansion. From 1964-1971 university enrollment grew by 296 percent while the rate for isolated colleges was 572 percent.

28. Levy, The Demand for Higher-Education, p. 24.
29. Ibid., p. 24.
30. Ibid., p. 36.
31. Ibid., pp. 57-63.
32. Ibid., p. 66.
33. Ibid., pp. 68-70.
34. Benno Sander, "Educational Law and Practice in a Developing Country: Empirical Study of the Impact Made by Brazilian Federal Law No. 4024 on Secondary Education in the State of Rio Grande do Sul" (Ph.D. diss., Catholic University of America, 1970), pp. 44-45. During the Empire and Republican Periods, Brazil had, at different times, "preparatory exams" and "maturity exams" for higher education. For more information on the subject, see the lengthy and detailed history of Brazilian education by Primitivo Moacir, A Instrução e o Império (São Paulo: Cia. Editôra Nacional, 1936).
35. Nádia Franco da Cunha, Vestibular na Guanabara, pp. 57-58.
36. Ibid., p. 58.
37. Anísio Teixeira, "Access to Higher Education: Brazil," in Access to Higher Education, Vol. 2, by United Nations (Liège, Belgium: UNESCO and the International Association of Universities, 1965), p. 26.
38. Ibid., p. 24.
39. Teixeira, "Access to Higher Education: Brazil," p. 24.
40. Further diagnosis along with recommendations for improvement can be found in Nádia Franco da Cunha, Vestibular na Guanabara; Valnir Chagas, "A seleção e o vestibular na reforma universitária," Revista Brasileira de Estudos Pedagógicos 53 (April/June 1970); Ernest W. Hamburger, "O exame vestibular e os desajustes no sistema de ensino," Educação Hoje, January/February 1971.

CHAPTER

7

THE SEQUENCE OF POLICY DEVELOPMENT

The purpose of this chapter is to present in detail the course of policy development on access to higher education: government action and reaction to those initiatives on the part of interested parties.

The sequence of policy development on access to higher education may be examined in three stages: planning the first experiment and reaction to planning initiatives; modifications for the second experiment and reaction to the first one; and preparations for the third experiment and reaction to the second experiment.

One will note that reactions to policy implementation have been grouped with the planning of subsequent experiments. The rationale for categorizing phenomena this way is to convey the fact that the reactions to policy implementation and the planning of subsequent experiments often proceed independent of one another. That is, the federal government does not always wait for reactions to its previous initiatives in order to plan or initiate future policy actions; nor, for that matter, do those who react to federal policy always wait until programs have been implemented before responding.

STAGE ONE: PLANNING THE FIRST EXPERIMENT AND REACTION TO PLANNING INITIATIVES

Higher education, as already noted, was not a high priority for government policy makers immediately following the March 1964 Revolution. When the government did finally turn its attention to dealing with postsecondary education, as embodied in Decree-Law no. 53 (November 18, 1966), no attention was paid to the issue of access.[1]

Planning the First Experiment

With the ascension of Tarso Dutra to the post of Minister of Education in 1967, concurrent with mounting antigovernment student demonstrations, steps were taken to reevaluate the system of access to higher education. Minister Dutra decreed a single entrance examination for each subject area for all universities—private as well as public—to take place simultaneously in January 1968.[2] This move, however, was considered too ambitious and, thus, was not implemented: regional authorities complained about the examination timetable, and private institutions challenged the legality of federal regulation. The time was not yet ripe for such an innovation.

A broader, less ambitious, and more fundamental approach to the access problem was the policy paper issued by the Council of Rectors of Brazilian Universities in October 1967.[3] This important document was the inspiration for, and harbinger of, subsequent public policy on access to higher education. The Council of Rectors asserted that the access issue was intertwined with the issues of university reform and expansion of higher learning. Moreover, the establishment of a new policy on the exame vestibular was, according to them, of national significance in light of its economic, social, political, and pedagogical aspects. The Council advocated adoption of the following measures within feasible time sequences: promotion of more adequate articulation between secondary and higher education; expansion and rational distribution of places in the university based upon manpower requirements; student orientation to dissuade candidates from applying for admission to socially prestigious programs in overcrowded career areas; and modernization and improvement of testing and measurement procedures.

Following the report by the Council of Rectors, government activity to reform the mechanisms of access to postsecondary education increased. In December 1967, the Federal Education Council approved a plan to improve articulation between secondary and higher education. As proposed by Valnir Chagas, the plan comprised instituting a first cycle (one or two years) of university general education; creating new entities of higher education, some offering only the first cycle and others only a professional cycle; and creating technical courses of first cycle duration in existing institutions.* The intention of the plan, with regard to access, was to absorb a good portion of

---

*Chagas' plan for first-cycles of liberal and technical education outside the university suggests a Brazilian variant of the American community college idea.

the excedentes, defer career choice away from the overcrowded professions, and furnish Brazil with much needed middle-level technical manpower.

The Chagas Plan did not come into fruition, however. The traditional attitudes toward both social status and the organizational pattern of higher education blocked such innovation.

During this time, student dissent was intense. While isolated as well as coordinated disruptions centered on political repression, there was, at its base, vociferous protest for expanding and reforming higher education and abolishing the system which created excedentes.*

In July 1968, President Costa e Silva appointed a task force to reexamine the system of higher education in Brazil and come up with a plan for university reform that would be broader than the 1966 Law. Concerning access to higher learning, the task force proposed in their final report (August 16, 1968) that the college entrance exams should be revamped to cover the instruction common to the various forms of secondary education without exceeding that level. At the same time, secondary education (for the most part college preparatory in nature) would have to expand its curriculum to offer specialized and professional education jointly with college preparatory studies so that those who did not enter the university would at least have a marketable, technical skill when they finished high school.[4]

The task force went on to endorse the expansion of places in the university, focusing exclusively on the "priority careers" of medicine and allied health professions; engineering (specifically, industrial) and related technological professions. Furthermore, the report called for graduated unification of college entrance examinations, initially by groups of courses of study, and later including all courses in the university. Unification would then encompass various universities and isolated schools, eventually leading to regional unification of exams. One important result would be an end to multiple inscriptions and, subsequently, the achievement of a far more accurate picture of demand for higher education.[5]

The recommendations of the task force were incorporated into a set of laws, the most notable being University Reform Law no. 5,540 (November 28, 1968). Particular attention was given to unification of entrance examinations in article 21:

---

*See the "Political Charter" of the outlawed National Union of Brazilian Students as outlined in the <u>Correio da Manhã</u>, 5 August 1967. The original charter of 1938 addressed the same issues.

THE SEQUENCE OF POLICY DEVELOPMENT 89

> Within three years from the date of enactment of this
> law, the entrance examination competition will be
> fully identical in content for all courses of study or
> subject matter areas and unified in its execution, in
> the same university or federation of schools or the
> same isolated establishment of pluricurricular organi-
> zation, in accordance with the statutes and by-laws. [6]

The most important document in the historical development of
Brazilian higher education, the 1968 Law, was a fundamental, far-
reaching, yet overly ambitious piece of legislation. The ills of
Brazilian higher education were candidly and accurately diagnosed,
but the prescriptions were very often ambiguous, contradictory, or
naive.

Furthermore, implementing university reform was but one of
many challenging, pressing, and formidable tasks on the Ministry of
Education's administrative agenda (for instance, literacy training,
cooperative education, technical education, teacher recruitment,
primary school expansion); and it was by no means the top priority.

In addition, the period 1968-69 was a most difficult one for
both the military government and politicized Brazilians. As cited
earlier, the intensification of antigovernment student riots; terrorist
bombings; government repression of the press, artists, writers,
professors, and even initial supporters of the regime—all this meant
that internal security would be the military government's immediate
concern.

On August 31, 1969, President Costa e Silva was incapacitated
by a stroke. A military triumvirate assumed power and shortly thereafter chose General Emílio Garrastazú Médici to serve as president.
As his new Education Minister, Médici chose Jarbas Gonçalves Passarinho, Costa e Silva's Minister of Labor. It was under Passarinho's
tenure as Minister of Education that access to higher education received the greatest attention of the federal government, including both
civilian and military governments prior to 1964.

Addressing the Council of Rectors on January 27, 1970, Passarinho called the type of college entrance examination held in Brazil
"an intentionally erected barrier to make the candidates stumble" and
defended the creation of a unified entrance examination for Brazil.
The minister added that excedentes would disappear only after some
time, with the initiation of diversified middle-level education and the
rational growth of university places. [7]

Passarinho seriously intended to concentrate on the plans for
implementing a unified exam in 1971, in which tests would be given
simultaneously as to date and time. For in addition to preventing
multiple inscriptions, such a system would provide MEC with an

accurate accounting of real demand for higher education. However, the time-consuming problem of the excedentes diverted the Ministry of Education's attention and efforts away from an overall solution to the problem of access to higher education.

Following the 1970 entrance examination competition, Minister Passarinho took measures to stop colleges from reducing places, while at the same time announcing MEC's refusal to approve students beyond an institution's capacity. He asserted that through university reform (for example, departmentalization, recruitment of professors), MEC was engaged in increasing places in the university. Passarinho stated that the Ministry of Education was in the process of undertaking a survey of universities' physical utilization to determine if institutions were making full use of their physical plant.[8]

The minister pledged to do everything possible to expand educational opportunity within existing institutions and along national manpower requirements. He stressed that he would not contribute to the proliferation of private "weekend colleges" that had sprung up overnight to absorb the overflow of students, since most of these colleges were of dubious academic quality. He mentioned that Brazil was not unique in facing a demand for higher schooling, and that the roots of the problem lay in reforming primary, secondary, and secondary technical education, as well.

For the next several months, a unit of the Ministry of Education vigorously worked to provide places for the largest possible number of excedentes. MEC's influence did produce some positive results. As late as August, Minister Passarinho met with 130 excedentes of the Faculty of Medicine of the Federal Fluminense University (UFF): he approved admission for them and blasted UFF for not planning adequately and at least providing as many freshman places as the year before.[9]

Finally, in October 1970, the Director of the Department of University Affairs (DAU) in the Ministry of Education, Newton Sucupira, announced that beginning with the 1971 examination competition excedentes would "technically" disappear. This would be done by making the exams "classifying" rather than eliminatory.[10] For example, instead of an arbitrary cutoff point, the twenty places available for study in a certain program would be filled by the candidates with the twenty highest marks on the exams. Sucupira also announced simultaneous examinations in the federal universities throughout the country. Proposed by the MEC and approved by the Council of Rectors, the simultaneous examinations would not apply to state or private institutions of higher education, although they would hopefully join on their own volition at some future time.

Newton Sucupira explained the three types of unification that were brought up in conversations at the MEC. The first entailed uniform content and centralized execution within the university—not based on faculdades (schools or colleges within a university), but áreas de conhecimento (subject matter areas), such as the humanities, biomedical sciences, and technological sciences. The second encompassed unification, not within the university, but by region. The third consisted of one series of examinations for the entire nation. The director of DAU stated the first type would be the preferred one, since the second was a desired goal but one which would not be viable logistically, educationally, or politically for 1971. The third proposal was deemed highly impractical and never given serious consideration.

Within a week after Sucupira's remarks, Minister Passarinho issued Regulation no. 3,585 (October 27, 1970) authorizing the Director of DAU to reach agreements with universities and isolated establishments for the purpose of holding unified examinations by subject matter areas in each educational region at some future time.[11] The Ministry of Education had paved the way for the desired goal of unification on a regional basis. Although this could not be operationalized immediately, the MEC pronouncement was a smoke signal for the benefit of the educational community.

During 1971, the MEC's efforts to deal with the problem of access to higher education gained momentum. On January 5, 1971, the ministry lauded the "notable increase" in freshman places during the past few years and hailed the 30 percent increase in places from 1970 as a proud accomplishment.[12] MEC added, however, that due to the shortcomings of social and educational systems which encouraged students to enter the university, only 165,000 students of the 270,000 candidates for admission could be accommodated. The MEC pointed out that the development of higher education could not be assessed solely in terms of available places; for it was also evident in increased salary benefits for professors and greater reliance upon full-time faculty—two notable Ministry accomplishments. The government clearly felt that a haphazard expansion of higher education, subsequently inflating places in the university, would prejudice both the country and students by bringing about poor quality education and producing manpower not geared to the national development priorities established by the Médici Government.

Newton Sucupira, director of DAU, speaking for Minister Passarinho, stated his satisfaction with the vestibular simultâneo (simultaneous exam competition) held recently in federal universities (6,669 places were involved), and he announced his intention to direct preliminary planning of unified entrance examinations by region for 1972.

With regard to excedentes, Sucupira asserted that the MEC's decision to adopt a classifying exam for federal institutions—and recommend that private, state, and municipal colleges do the same—meant that the juridical figure of the excedente had ceased to exist:

There is no way in which to discuss excedentes.
There are not now, nor will there be, excedentes.
What actually exists are students who were not
classified in the entrance exam competition; and
for this reason, they have no right whatsoever to
matriculate.[13]

The MEC, however, would see to it that, under the classifying system of examination, institutions publish a notice beforehand establishing the number of freshman places that would be available. Requests relating to matriculation of "non-classified" candidates would not be handled by the MEC.

In February 1971, Newton Sucupira designated a national commission to examine the problem of the exame vestibular: Comissão Nacional de Vestibular Unificado (CONVESU). The commission was chaired by Carlos Alberto Serpa, the young Vice-Rector of the Pontifical Catholic University (PUC) of Rio de Janeiro. Other members included Adolpho Ribeiro Netto of the University of São Paulo (USP) and President of the Carlos Chagas Foundation, a nonprofit organization responsible for handling the unified science exams in São Paulo; Bruno Alípio Lobo of the Federal University of Rio de Janeiro; Manoel Luiz Leão of the Federal University of Rio Grande do Sul; Valnir Chagas and Padre José Vasconcellos, both of the Federal Education Council.

CONVESU held its first meeting on March 22. The purpose of the meeting was to trace along general lines the unification of college entrance examinations for the entire country, by subject matter area and geo-educational district for 1972.[14] (A detailed agenda was pre-established by DAU.) They agreed to periodic meetings and the initiation of feasibility studies on various aspects of admission.[15] The following day, Minister Passarinho announced that plans were being formulated for the 1972 exam competition and that President Médici would follow with a decree regulating procedures for all federal universities.[16]

Passarinho further stated that although the MEC could not order all colleges—namely, private ones—to also hold their entrance examinations on the same days as the public colleges and universities, he would, nevertheless, extend an "invitation" to them to join. With the "invitation" would go the reminder that for the current year these institutions had received approximately twice the amount of federal aid as the year before; furthermore, should they decide not to accept the MEC "invitation," they should no longer count on government financial assistance with which to face their internal difficulties.[17] At the same time, Minister Passarinho mentioned that the MEC was studying the possibility of requiring that inscription fees for the exams—a major source of revenue for private colleges—correspond exactly to the cost of mounting the examination competition.

CONVESU terminated its preliminary study on March 27, 1971, five days after its first meeting. It recommended the following:

1. College entrance examinations should be regionalized.
2. Regional exams should be planned within various states for 1972.
3. The creation of nonprofit foundations to coordinate higher education institutions' participation in a regional examination system should be encouraged.
4. Multiple choice, objective tests should be constructed for the entrance exams.
5. Computers should be utilized for correcting tests, classifying candidates, and general management.
6. The exam competition should be a nonprofit operation with fees collected by the executive body; any profits will be used only for subsidiary activities related to the selection process (for example, research, development).
7. In addition to subject matter tests, a test of intellectual ability should be introduced.
8. Preventive measures should be taken to assure the administration of a just examination: careful screening of examiners, guaranteeing objective tests, training reviewers for each examination commission in methods of testing and measurement, standardizing scores.
9. Implementation of a regionally unified exam for 1972 with regard to date and time should be considered.
10. Exams should be grouped in three areas, encompassing all career programs: biological sciences, exact sciences and technology, and human sciences.
11. Whether university admission is to first-cycle studies or directly to a career program, the process should be, nevertheless, classifying—not eliminatory.[18]

A month later, speaking for CONVESU, Newton Sucupira announced that all universities would be required to follow a classifying system of examination. However, only state, municipal, and federal universities would have to hold their examination competition on the same date.[19]

Professor Sucupira presented Minister Passarinho on June 28 with a draft of a proposal to regulate the exam competition for 1972. The Minister submitted the proposal to President Médici, and on July 13, Decree 68,908 was signed. Minister Passarinho viewed those provisions of the decree which did away with excedentes and eliminated multiple exam registration as the most important. The other articles of the decree comprised the following:

a. Prior to the competition institutions will be required to announce the number of places available for the corresponding academic period.
b. Registration for the test will be granted only upon proof of completion of high school and payment of the registration fee.
c. The amount of the registration fee will be regulated by the Commission on Educational Fees together with the Federal Education Council.
d. The tests must be limited in content to cover the compulsory disciplines of middle-level education, eventually increased to include a modern foreign language; the complexity of the test material will not exceed the secondary school level; the tests will be identical for an entire institution or group of institutions.
e. Elaboration, application, and evaluation of tests, as well as the classification of candidates, will be centralized within the institution; the MEC, at the same time, will gradually work to unify the exam competition regionally.
f. The planning and execution of the examination competition may be turned over to special organizations (public or private), permanent in nature, concerned with research and development to improve the competition.
g. Results of the competition will be valid only for the academic year for which it is held.[20]

The government wasted no time in seeking to operationalize the presidential decree. On July 26, 1971, the Director of DAU issued Regulation no. 96 creating a special commission which, besides studying and interpreting the recent presidential decree, would propose complementary legislation and apply the decree throughout the land. Acting in the name of DAU, the commission was to bring about, by way of cooperation with public and private institutions, jointly held examinations in various localities. The regulation specifically stated that the process of unification should be done "within the spirit of gradualism."[21]

The members of the special commission were as follows: Carlos Alberto Serpa (chairman), Adolpho Ribeiro Netto, and Manoel Luiz Leão. They were given two weeks to conclude their initial studies. Originally the commission was to investigate the implementation of unified exams in Rio Grande do Sul, São Paulo, and Greater Rio de Janeiro (Guanabara State and Rio de Janeiro State). Because of the constraints of time, however, the commission proposed to Sucupira and Minister Passarinho that Greater Rio de Janeiro be selected as an experimental laboratory for the new system of regionally unified examinations by subject area; and that efforts would be concentrated in the bottleneck areas of science, technology and biomedical sciences.[22] The Ministry of Education accepted the commission's proposal; and for the next fifty days, members of the commission feverishly worked, uninterrupted, contacting all institutions—public and private—in Greater Rio in preparation for a unified examination for that area in 1972.

The portarias (regulations) following the presidential decree of July 1971 were vague and abstract, raising doubts and questions of interpretation. Candidates were worried and perplexed as to which subjects would be covered on the tests. After all, they would need sufficient time to prepare for the examinations. The DAU Commission no. 96 set a limit of nine subjects which could be offered within the various divisions of study (science and technology, biomedical sciences, and human sciences). The subjects were: mathematics, geography, history, Portuguese, foreign language, physics, chemistry, biology, and natural history. Not wishing to infringe upon university autonomy, Serpa left the number of tests and content matter up to the council of each university, with the hope that they would use good sense. (The foreign language would automatically be English or French, the ones most commonly taught.)*

Serpa candidly admitted that all the other administrative matters were as yet unresolved; however, he assured the public that within 15 days a decision would be made.[23]

Five days later, in a communication between Serpa and Sucupira, the date of January 9, 1972, and the time, 8:00 A.M., were set for commencement of the examination competition.

Shortly thereafter, Serpa announced that higher educational institutions were generally very receptive to the plans for unification of the entrance exam competition; in fact, almost all public and private universities in Greater Rio de Janeiro would participate in the 1972 competition in the areas of biomedical sciences and science/technology. Those institutions not participating in the competition

---

*These guidelines were incorporated into Ministerial Regulation No. 524, BSB, of 27 August 1971, published in the Diário Oficial, 1 September 1971.

were: the Medical College of Vassouras (they were linked to the exam competition held in the São Paulo area); Civil Engineering College of Barra do Piraí; Roberto Lisboa Engineering College; the Superior School of Industrial Design; and the National School of Statistical Science. These last two schools, according to Serpa, due to their own peculiarities, offered tests and programs of study totally different than those proposed by CONVESU.[24]

The directors of cursinhos made three suggestions to Commission No. 96: no introduction of new material; if anything, delete; assign different weights to the tests, the most weight given to the more important tests in each specialty area; and extension of unification to the humanities and social sciences, at least in public universities.[25] Serpa responded that the only change in the exam material would be in Sector A of the science/technology area: in the language test series 50 percent of the items would comprise questions on geography (see Table 7.1). As to weights of tests, the new system of standardized scores would assure equitable grading of the tests. With regard to the third suggestion, Serpa said that there was simply not enough time to extend the unified examination to cover other areas (that is, humanities and social sciences). He candidly admitted, in fact, that his commission could not maintain contact with all the colleges and isolated schools in biomedical science and technology in Greater Rio because they were so numerous; consequently, he had to concentrate on the most popular ones.[26]

In terms of operationalizing the new college entrance examination system, the period from the middle of September to the middle of October 1971 was the most significant so far. It was one of intensive planning and sustained effort to sensitize and mobilize institutions to participate in the unified examination scheduled for Greater Rio.

Minister Passarinho announced that the MEC was considering a system of pre-option for the unified exam by which a candidate would select two career programs before the tests and, if classified, would gain admission to one. On September 22, 1971, the Commission on Educational Fees of the Federal Education Council enacted a regulation based on authority of article 4 of Decree 68,908 of July 13, 1971. The regulation set a limit of CR$120 (US$20) on test registration fees, required a full accounting within ninety days from higher educational institutions, and required profits from the exam competition to be spent for educational research on the selection process or for scholarships.[27]

Several days later, responding to a request from CONVESU, the Pontifical Catholic University of Rio de Janeiro and the Federal Fluminense University of the State of Rio de Janeiro agreed to unify their examinations in nontechnical areas: the former in human sciences, social sciences, and theology, and the latter in human

TABLE 7.1

Proposed Format of Test Requirements by Subject Matter
Areas and Course of Study: Greater Rio de Janeiro
College Entrance Examinations, 1972

Area	
Science and Technology	Biomedical Sciences
Courses of study	
Sector A: engineering, physics, mathematics, earth sciences, chemistry, chemical engineering, astronomy, meteorology, architecture, operational engineering, cartography	Psychology, biological sciences, nursing, pharmacy, medicine, dentistry, nutrition, veterinary medicine
Sector B: geography, biology	
Tests	
Sector A: Portuguese, physics, mathematics, chemistry, foreign language (50% language, 50% geography)	Portuguese, foreign language, biology, physics, chemistry
Section B: Portuguese, physics, chemistry, mathematics, foreign language, geography (for geography programs at the State University of Guanabara and Federal University of Rio de Janeiro), biology (for biology at the Federal University of Rio de Janeiro)	

Source: Comissão Nacional de Vestibular Unificado (CONVESU), 1971.

sciences. The tests they would require were Portuguese, general history, history of Brazil, and English or French.[28]

Meanwhile, the Ministry of Education stated that the major thrust of the 1973 exam competition would be unified exams in Rio Grande do Sul and São Paulo, in addition to Rio de Janeiro.[29]

The MEC issued the following pronouncements as objectives for regionally unified examinations in the biomedical sciences and science/technological areas: guarantee the equilibrium of the tests in relation to programs of study; furnish the commission of test development with a reviewer from secondary education; provide the commission with assistance of specialists in objective testing and measurement; encourage the standardization of scores in test correction; consider in the classification criteria for candidates—within the areas of science and biomedical science—the options made by the candidate at the time of inscription; permit candidates two career options in order of preference and institutional choice; and base classification on the score of the candidate in terms of his first choice career: Unfilled places for a first option career would go to those who designated it as second choice.[30]

On September 29, 1971, in an official note to the Ministry of Education, Serpa reported on the status of CONVESU's invitation to the higher educational establishments in Greater Rio de Janeiro to join in a unified system of exams. The note revealed that not all the responses to the invitation were positive, particularly among the isolated colleges. For example, the Medical College of Petrópolis was undecided (eventually it agreed to join), as was the College of Medical Sciences of Volta Redonda (it finally decided not to join). The Civil Engineering College of Volta Redonda agreed to adopt the tests and programs of the unified exam system, but decided nevertheless, not to join for "private" reasons, chiefly its interest in attending to the needs of local candidates. The Roberto Lisboa Engineering College also agreed to follow the examination program divulged by CONVESU but declined from joining, as the Department Council of the College had already planned their own system for admission by examination. The Federal Rural University of Rio de Janeiro State (UFRRJ) refused to join the regional unification system or even adopt the published program. The University made the following arguments: they already planned and set up an examination program, and it was too late to change; programs in humanities and social sciences needed examinations anyway; there were hundreds of poor candidates who were interested in UFRRJ because of scholarships, transportation grants, and free housing; for many students in the local community who could not afford to live away from home, the University was their only way of obtaining a higher education; and

THE SEQUENCE OF POLICY DEVELOPMENT

these candidates would help the university because UFRRJ would not have to worry about housing for them.[31]

A major step was taken on October 13, 1971 to consolidate previous gains and further reform the system of access to higher education. In the presence of Newton Sucupira and Carlos Serpa, the rectors of the universities of Greater Rio de Janeiro signed an agreement with the Ministry of Education in which norms were established for the 1972 examination competition in the science/technology and biomedical areas. The agreement also created a center to take charge of coordinating and administering the unified examination, and all participating faculties were to be subordinate to this unit.[32]

Several provisions of the agreement are worth mentioning here; for they are important to the understanding of both external and internal political relationships. Under the agreement, the center created to coordinate and administer the examination competition in Greater Rio was given the name Center for the Selection of Candidates to Higher Education in Greater Rio de Janeiro (CESGRANRIO). The higher education institutions would participate via a Central Commission in CESGRANRIO; each of the 11 member institutions would send a representative (to be named by the director of the Department of University Affairs of the MEC) who would participate in the Central Commission as a spokesman for his respective institution.[33]

The general responsibilities of CESGRANRIO would consist of the following: announcing the materials and programs of the competition; publishing registration and test information and collecting registration fees; examining and approving accounting procedures for the competition; approving the plan for utilizing the profits from the collected fees; determining the statistical treatment and evaluation of the results of the competition; divulging the results and conclusions with respect to the competition and developing related research on systems of selection, educational measurement, and human resources; promoting the improvement of the adopted methods and emitting general norms to be followed by each subject matter area; and providing an accounting of all its actions to the Department of University Affairs of the Ministry of Education.[34]

Article 9 of the agreement provides for the creation of three Coordinated Sectoral Commissions subordinate to CESGRANRIO: COMCITEC (science and technology), COMBIMED (biomedical and health sciences), and COMSART (social sciences, arts, and letters). The three commissions would be composed of representatives of those institutions which offered programs in each sector (for example, the Pontifical Catholic University of Rio de Janeiro would participate in the COMSART and COMCITEC sectors but not in COMBIMED, since it did not have a medical school); the representatives would be selected by the director of DAU—one representative for each institution. Paragraph 5 lists the specific duties of the Coordinated Sectoral Commissions. Generally, each commission would be responsible for the following: planning, administering and supervising the execution of the examination competition within its respective area—this would include naming a banca examinadora (examining bench); assigning the candidates to available freshman places in accordance with the adopted classifying system; and furnishing a complete report of the competition in its area to CESGRANRIO, and afterward to the participating institutions.[35]

The last section of the agreement spells out the obligations of both the Department of University Affairs of the Ministry of Education and the participating institutions. With regard to the former, the DAU would be obliged to assist CESGRANRIO "in any way necessary," designate a president, and select three coordinators (for each sectoral commission); the role of the president would be defined based upon proposals of CESGRANRIO, and the duties of Coordinators would be deferred to them based upon the approval of CESGRANRIO.[36] The DAU would also assure financial assistance to nonfederal participating institutions in 1972, recognizing the loss of income to them from inscription fees due to regional unification. Participating federal institutions would be assured priority with regard to solicitation of monies for special projects (for example, research) for the same reason.[37]

For their part, the institutions would agree as follows: participate in CESGRANRIO by way of the Central Commission and Coordinated Sectoral Commissions; establish beforehand the freshman places offered in each sector in which they participate; furnish for distribution to the candidates, by registration time, information on courses of study offered; matriculate the candidates sent by CESGRANRIO, following the criteria for classification; and contribute their inscription fees, by sector, to CESGRANRIO.[38]

The agreement would have a duration of one year, according to article 12, and any major doubts regarding the execution of the agreement would have to be referred to the director of the Department of University Affairs.[39]

Speaking at the ceremony in which the agreement was signed, Newton Sucupira asserted that Greater Rio de Janeiro would be the laboratory for testing the new system of access to higher education; and if successful, it would be the model for the rest of the country to follow.[40]

Reaction to Planning Initiatives

Initiatives of the federal government in planning a unified exam competition produced various reactions among interested parties.* Initial reaction came from the press. Focusing on Minister Passarinho's intention to adopt unified college entrance examinations, given on the same day and same time throughout Brazil, the press was originally wary about such a venture. In fact, Rio de Janeiro's Jornal do Brasil issued a scathing editorial on the subject:

> It is a shame such innovative measures reflect an obsessive desire for uniformity. . . . The spirit of current legislation, beginning with the reforms that have been carried out during the last few years, is of exactly the opposite mold—namely, one of flexibility which begins by respecting university autonomy. Examinations on the same day and at the same time, with tests elaborated upon by an all-powerful central body, capable of imposing the same questions covering the same material—all this does not escape being an old specter which awakens totalitarian spirits. . . . To unify means to suffocate. And universities need to breathe in the open air.[41]

As the Ministry of Education sought to provide public information on its intentions, elaborating and clarifying the details, the reaction of the press became more supportive. Just three months after issuing this critical editorial, the Jornal do Brasil hailed the MEC's change in orientation towards the entrance exams as "praiseworthy" and asserted that, in principle, the classifying and unifying entrance examination was "grounded in realism."[42]

Following the 1971 examinations, the need to revamp the examination system became even more apparent. Support grew among educators for a unified exam, one with few administrative difficulties. Even educators who shared an elitist philosophy of education largely agreed that the level of the exams far exceeded the ability of the secondary school graduates and, therefore, violated University Reform Law no. 5,540 (November 1968). To reiterate, the traditional

---

*Interest groups, including their positions on access to higher education, reactions to the experiments with a unified entrance examination system, and their role in policy formation, are discussed in Stages Two and Three of this chapter.

aim had been to eliminate as many as possible, passing only the "best of the best," due to lack of both freshman places and professors in the university. To illustrate, in the Portuguese tests for the Faculty of Letters of Federal University of Rio de Janeiro, the test organizers asked the candidates to make a stylistic analysis of the Brazilian literary giant Guimarães Rosa, based on an excerpt from one of his stories. Of 1,222 students, 464 received a zero and only 38 managed a grade above 5 (out of a possible 8).[43]

The cursinho directors and teachers were almost unanimous in their support of the idea of a unified entrance examination. Besides making it easier for the student, unified exam material would make the instructional job of the cursinho a lot easier, as well. However, while the idea of a unified examination met with their approval, they strongly disapproved of certain aspects of the process.

For example, Victor Maurício Nótrica, Director of Curso Miguel Couto, expressed reservations concerning the introduction of the system of pre-option. He felt students in the biomedical area should have the option of pursuing study in all of the programs in that area, not just two as stipulated in the regulation. The director of Curso Vetor, Antônio José de Vries, strongly opposed the introduction three months before the exam competition of a foreign language and geography as required materials. According to him, this greatly complicated the work of the cursinhos, necessitating an increase of approximately 20 percent in their operating budget to contract teachers for the new subjects and make arrangements for instruction. De Vries also stated that, although the commission organizing the exam competition asked the directors of cursinhos for suggestions, their recommendations were disregarded.[44]

Candidates for the 1972 examination competition were apprehensive and divided on the issue of a unified, classifying college entrance examination. A number of students did not like the fact that a zero on any test would disqualify a candidate from the competition. Other students applauded the idea of unification as a measure which could possibly lead to improved organization and administration of the college entrance exams. On one point all candidates agreed: the number of freshman places in the university had to be increased.[45]

All during the time that the federal government was planning and initiating change in the system of access to higher education, one aspect of the problem received considerable attention of concerned parties and was the focus of major controversy—the issue of excedentes.

According to many, including the press, excedentes would not disappear with the stroke of a magic wand: the problem was a structural one; and although the MEC had banished the word from its vocabulary, the problem would not be resolved until the ratio between places and candidates greatly decreased.[46]

Also vocal, however, were the educational conservatives—mostly tenured, full professors—who were unsympathetic to the cause of excedentes and supported the status quo. Representative of this group was Raimundo Moniz de Aragão, Vice-President of the Federal Education Council, former Minister of Education, and former Rector of the Federal University of Rio de Janeiro. In a speech before officer candidates at the Superior War College, Aragão asserted that the nation did not need to matriculate excedentes since higher education should be selective, and only those who show a talent for higher studies should continue their education.[47] Professor Aragão did mention, however, that he opposed multiple inscriptions for the examinations as giving an unfair advantage to the candidates of means who could afford to pay several registration fees.

The students naturally were the ones most concerned about the problem of excedentes. Medical school excedentes organized in 1971 in an effort to secure more places in the medical schools. They criticized the MEC for not expanding higher education and accused authorities of actually cutting back places, thereby violating Decree-Law no. 405 (December 31, 1968). The government responded that the decree-law referred to increasing places only for 1969 and did not require a 15 percent annual increase in matriculations, as claimed by the medical excedentes. Also, the government claimed that the problem of physicians in Brazil was not one of numbers, but distribution.[48]

In what could be considered a peace offering to the excedentes and a step toward defusing the controversy surrounding the issue, the Federal Education Council issued Regulation no. 6 (March 1, 1971), making it difficult for colleges to limit places. According to this, colleges were required to submit information of an administrative nature, including the amount of federal aid received during the past five years for the purpose of admitting excedentes to study, by specific program. It also required valid reasons for cutting back places. In addition, institutions had to supply the Council, through the Department of University Affairs, with any other information it requested.[49]

Nevertheless, the government's efforts to provide public information and offer juridical gestures of its good intentions did not obscure the fact, in the minds of many concerned parties, that much more had to be done. The Association of Guanabara Medical Students (AEMEG), meeting in July 1971, expressed the sentiments of a great many university students and candidates for admission when they declared in an official note:

> The unification of college entrance examinations has been a student demand of long standing . . . however,

if the number of places in universities will not be increased proportionate to the number of candidates registered, it will be possible to eliminate "legally and technically the figure of the excedente," but he will continue to exist. . . . Moreover if funds for the universities are not increased, if conditions of work and research are not improved, if the number of professors, administrators, and staff in the universities is not increased, the problem of university education will merely have been touched upon in one of its facets, without resolving the great structural problems afflicting the Brazilian university.[50]

To summarize the situation at the end of 1971: the Ministry of Education was definitely moving towards reforming the system of access to higher education (for example, unification, classification, and—to some extent—excedentes); and while the reform ideas which shaped government policy were generally applauded—the interested parties would be satisfied only with results. The results, however, which would have completely satisfied many in this constituency, in some instances, would necessitate policies which the government considered either unfeasible or undesirable.

STAGE TWO: MODIFICATIONS FOR THE SECOND EXPERIMENT AND REACTION TO THE FIRST EXPERIMENT

As elucidated in the previous section, the period 1968-71 was one of increasing and intensive governmental activity in the realm of policy development on the issue of access to higher education: drafting major legislation, legal sanctioning, dispensing public information, and program planning. Preparations made, it was not time to initiate the experiment.

The Ministry of Education maintained strict control over federal, state, and municipal institutions with regard to the January 9, 1972 starting date. Other major provisions of Decree no. 68,908 were also implemented, including a limit of CR$120 for inscription fees, single registrations for the examination competition, and the classifying method of selection. Both official and public attention, however, were focused on the pilot project in Greater Rio de Janeiro, where in addition to a regionally unified examination for the biomedical and science/technology areas, another innovation—the pre-option—was introduced.[51]

From the time that the examination competition terminated through the end of March, there were no significant policy initiatives, actions, or developments on the part of the federal government. During that period, the college entrance exams were graded; candidates were classified and registered in college; and the unique and wonderful madness of the <u>carnaval</u> (pre-Lenten festivities) precluded, as usual, serious business of any kind until the beginning of classes in mid-March.

Modifications for the Second Experiment

Finally, CONVESU and Heitor Gurgulino de Souza, the new Director of DAU (Newton Sucupira was appointed President of the Commission of International Affairs of the MEC), met on April 18 in Rio de Janeiro to assess the past exams—particularly with regard to Greater Rio—and plan for the 1973 competition. Professors Serpa and Lobo stressed the virtues of the system of pre-option and revealed CESGRANRIO's plans to assess the socioeconomic background of candidates and measure the fairness of the tests. Serpa proudly noted that 80 percent of the science, technological, and biomedical institutions in Greater Rio were integrated into CESGRANRIO; the fact that only two universities participated in humanities, social sciences, arts and letters was the only real weakness.[52] Finally, Serpa suggested that a representative of the cursinhos be named to CONVESU.

During this time, the Superior Council of CESGRANRIO (eleven representatives of the founding institutions, formerly called the Central Commission) met to discuss the program and tests for the 1973 examination competition.

It was also during the middle of April that CESGRANRIO completed its report and evaluation of the 1972 entrance examination competition and presented a full report to the Department of University Affairs. Table 7.2 presents a statistical summary of data compiled by each coordinating sectoral commission.[53]

The report stated that the coordinated sectoral commissions were satisfied with the exam competition; however, there were suggestions for improvement.[54] COMBIMED did not see the necessity of having each of the tests for each area scheduled for the same date and time; it felt that only the first test for each area need adhere to that provision. Both COMBIMED and COMSART mentioned the factor of candidates who registered for the examinations but failed to show. They felt this was due to candidates taking exams in private institutions at the same time or having already taken the exams and been admitted to one of these establishments.

TABLE 7.2

CESGRANRIO Statistical Report: General Summary, 1972

	Total	COMBIMED	COMCITEC	COMSART
Number of inscriptions	28,657	12,791	8,954	6,912
Number of places	8,801	2,431	4,110	2,260
Number of fee exemptions (total/partial)*	1,566 186	539 49	568 90	459 47
Number of absentees	884	235	278	371

*Granted to candidates who could not afford the CR$120 test registration fee.

Source: CESGRANRIO, Relatório: Concurso Vestibular de 1972 (Rio de Janeiro: Centro de Seleção de Candidatos ao Ensino Superior do Grande Rio, 1972).

It was COMSART alone, however, which criticized one of the fundamental tenets of the unified exam system—the system of pre-option. COMSART asserted that it was unfair for a student with the second best score to be classified in place of one with the best score, only because of the sequence in which these candidates rank their career options.

COMCITEC did not offer any criticisms or suggestions for change. The General Coordinator of COMCITEC was Carlos Serpa.

On the national level, CONVESU, meeting twice during the first week in May, decided to maintain the spirit of the new entrance exam policy for the following year; few significant changes would be made. CONVESU passed a resolution to continually strive to make the tests less rigorous; and, for the time being, they agreed to maintain the career pre-option system and sent a memo to Minister Passarinho asking for a final opinion on the matter.

Professor Serpa indicated that no radical change would take effect until 1975. By that time, students who have come out of institutions complying with the Primary and Secondary Education Reform Law no. 5,692 (August 11, 1971) would be ready to sit for the examinations; and the tests would reflect this situation accordingly.[55]

In short, CONVESU had decided to consolidate the gains of the past exam competition and avoid brisk changes.

On May 9, 1972, Minister Jarbas Passarinho met with CONVESU, and the decision was reached to classify students by pre-option only. As explained by Professor Serpa, the system of pre-option is:

> one of the principal points of the reform. . . . If the student is mature enough to decide on a profession at the end of secondary schooling, the same holds for his selecting an option of study for higher education.56

Serpa added that with a mandatory pre-option procedure, universities would not have to deal with a potentially dangerous situation of internal excedentes. One can readily see, however, that if a student passes the exams in the biomedical area and the university to which he is admitted follows a system of first-cycle studies (general education), the student will have to decide on a major in his second year. Since medicine is the course of study most in demand in that area, there would not be sufficient places available for all who want that major— hence, he becomes an internal excedente.

As for CESGRANRIO's second experiment, the program for the 1973 competition was divulged on May 24, 1972 (see Table 7.3). In the biomedical area no new tests of any kind were added and the courses of study were increased to include physical education and programs in psychology. Later added were agricultural sciences, natural history, animal husbandry, and special education/physical therapy.

COMCITEC moved towards greater uniformity by eliminating sectors for courses of study and tests. All candidates would be required to take the same tests. Added to the list of courses of study were the following: agricultural engineering, forestry, and mechanical engineering (for Naval Officer School candidates). The major in biology (in actuality a program to prepare primary and secondary school science teachers) was deleted since COMBIMED offered a major in biomedical sciences.

The areas of human and social sciences and arts and letters, which participated in a limited fashion in 1972 (that is, PUC and UFF), were expanded to include for 1973 most of the major universities in Greater Rio de Janeiro. Two sectors were set up for career groups, with the more quantitatively based courses of study assigned to Sector B.

Meanwhile, CESGRANRIO was vigorously pursuing contacts with higher educational institutions in the area to encourage them to join in the 1973 unified examinations.

On May 27, 1972, Minister Passarinho signed Regulation no. 413 BSB establishing the rules for the 1973 examination competition.

TABLE 7.3

CESGRANRIO Program Plan for the 1973
Entrance Examinations

	Area	
Science and Technology (COMCITEC)	Biomedical Sciences (COMBIMED)	Human and Social Sciences, Arts, and Letters (COMSART)
Courses of study Engineering; earth sciences; chemistry; geography; physics; chemical engineering; astronomy; meteorology; mathematics; architecture; operational engineering; cartography; agricultural engineering; forestry; mechanical engineering (for Naval Officer School candidates)	Biological sciences; medicine; dentistry; psychology; physical education; pharmacy; nutrition; nursing; veterinary medicine; natural history; animal husbandry; special education/ physical therapy; agricultural sciences (for secondary school teaching)	Sector A: art; communications; library science; law; industrial design; philosophy; history; letters; music; theater; religion; tourism Sector B: management; accounting; economics; statistics; pedagogy; public relations; social service; social sciences; home and family life
Tests Mathematics, physics, chemistry, Portuguese, foreign language	Physics, chemistry, biology, Portuguese, foreign language	Sector A: Portuguese, history, geography, foreign language Sector B: Portuguese, history, mathematics, foreign language

Source: CESGRANRIO (Centro de Seleção de Candidatos ao Ensino Superior do Grande Rio), 1972.

THE SEQUENCE OF POLICY DEVELOPMENT 109

The Regulation authorized the extension of the previous year's regulation on the exam competition, with several alterations. Each exam series had to consist of at least four tests with preferably no less than 50 objective questions per test (article 5). As a step towards the gradual unification of the competition throughout the nation, the DAU was authorized to technically assist institutions in the larger regions in applying the techniques of standardizing scores and making available the test results (article 4).

Most important, however, was the provision in article 3, permitting options for one or more areas of first-cycle studies (for example, the arts, the sciences), one or more courses of study (for example, biology, mathematics), or one or more careers (for example, medicine, pharmacy). Also permitted were several options by institution. Classification, however, would always proceed in descending order by the following: course of study, career, or cycle; and institutional preference.[57]

In what can be considered an audacious and blunt gesture, Minister Passarinho incorporated into article 6 the following: in the Ministry of Education's examination of requests from private institutions for financial assistance, preference would be given to those establishments which held their exam competition on the same date and at the same time; and special preference would be given to those institutions which join one of the already existing systems of regional unification.[58]

Serpa hailed the Minister's Regulation as "another step in the gradual process of implanting the new college entrance examination system" and also viewed it as acclaim of the CESGRANRIO experiment.[59] Regarding pre-options, Serpa stated that this procedure selected both the best students and the most interested ones. He pointed out that universities were pleased with the students they received who were selected by career option; to support his argument, he cited a dropout rate of 40 percent for students selected by test scores alone instead of by pre-option. (However, he did not offer a comparative figure for those selected by pre-option who drop out, nor did he mention student transfers to other courses of study or institutions.)

Several months later, CESGRANRIO added another innovation to college entrance examinations by publishing several brochures to help candidates for admission. A <u>Roteiro do Candidato</u> (Handbook for Candidates) was published for each of the three sector areas. It contained general information on the competition as well as detailed information on the exams themselves. The publication covered clearly and concisely all stages of the competition, from exam registration through matriculation. In addition to this, a <u>Roteiro de Profissões</u> (Handbook of Careers) was distributed to all candidates and also made available to secondary school students who were thinking about going to college. Arranged by sector areas (COMBIMED, COMCITEC, COMSART), the booklet briefly described each course of study, career possibilities, job skills, present and projected labor market conditions (both regionally and nationally) and the types of organizations in which employment could be found.

With only three months remaining until the entrance examination competition, CESGRANRIO's attention turned exclusively to logistical and administrative concerns, including selection of facilities for the 1973 competition in which approximately 52,000 candidates would be competing. Because of the number of students involved, Carlos Serpa acknowledged that sites would be selected on the basis of physical size and suitability for holding tests there.[60]

As in 1972, there would be both full and partial exemptions from the inscription fee, based upon interviews by social assistance representatives of CESGRANRIO; in some cases, visits to the candidate's residence would be made (approximately 10 percent of the candidates asked for a fee exemption).[61] At the same time, the Commission on Educational Fees of the Federal Education Council renewed the regulation setting a limit of CR$120 for the inscription fee. They deemed this amount sufficient to cover the expenses of mounting an entrance exam competition and observed that any deficits which occurred could only be due to poor management.

In a very candid remark, Serpa stated the Minister's desire to create a foundation out of CESGRANRIO would increase the status of the organization legally and operationally (for example, full-time staff, donations from various sources, authority to sign agreements, expansion of research and development activities) and thereby give Serpa, in his words, more power to pursue "appropriate courses of action."[62]

With regard to the nature of the tests themselves, the director of the Department of Research of CESGRANRIO, Aroldo Rodrigues, announced that in two years a different type of entrance examination— one based on aptitudes—would probably be operationalized. Although not ideal, Rodrigues felt it would nevertheless make the selection process better organized and the exams less susceptible to error of interpretation and judgment. He viewed the College Entrance Examination Board (CEEB) in the United States as the best type of organization for coordinating access to higher education, and he asserted that he would like to see a Brazilian variant of that model adopted.[63]

The 1973 unified exam registration data reveal an increase, compared with 1972, of 114 percent in the number of places available and a growth of 81 percent in the candidates taking the unified examinations (see Table 7.4). Although the overall candidate/place ratio decreased from 3.25 to 2.76, with decreases in each sector area,

TABLE 7.4

CESGRANRIO Comparative Statistical Report:
General Summary

	CESGRANRIO 1972	CESGRANRIO 1973	COMBIMED 1972	COMBIMED 1973	COMCITEC 1972	COMCITEC 1973	COMSART 1972	COMSART 1973
Total number of inscriptions	28,657	51,900	12,791	20,051	8,954	13,672	6,912	18,177
Total number of places	8,801	18,779	2,421	4,249	4,110	7,220	2,260	7,310
Percentage increase in places	—	213	—	174	—	175	—	323
Percentage increase in candidates	—	181	—	156	—	152	—	262
Candidate/place ratio	3.25	2.76	5.26	4.71	2.17	1.89	3.05	2.48

Source: Diário de Notícias, Rio de Janeiro, 26 November 1972.

the assumption that participating institutions were expanding freshman places, thereby making classification in the competition much easier, is false. Actually, the principal reason the ratio improved for the candidates was the inclusion in the competition of various institutions which did not participate in 1972, rather than a real increase in opportunity for study. Furthermore, of the 49 careers included in the competition, 16 were new, and 18 others registered increases in the proportion of candidates to places.

Nevertheless, it is important to note that the careers of law, medicine, economics, engineering, and architecture—those traditionally most coveted for reasons of prestige, social status, and income—all showed ratios which would improve the candidates' chances, as compared with the 1972 exam competition (see Tables 7.5, 7.6, and 7.7). In addition, those tables reveal that for majors in the arts, music, social sciences, licentiate in sciences, astronomy, meteorology, geography, agricultural sciences, and home and family life—the ratios produced less than one candidate per place available. Candidates for these courses of study had only to show up for all the exams, not make a zero on any one of the tests, and they were automatically classified!

TABLE 7.5

CESGRANRIO Comparative Statistical Report: COMBIMED

	Places Offered		Candidates		Candidate/Place Ratio	
Career	1972	1973	1972	1973	1972	1973
Agricultural sciences	—	50	—	32	—	0.64
Biological sciences	150	290	345	961	2.3	3.31
Physical education (M)	—	100	—	354	—	3.54
Physical education (F)	—	100	—	262	—	2.62
Nursing	260	300	315	919	1.2	3.06
Pharmacy	240	240	418	867	1.7	3.61
Medicine	1,311	1,679	10,048	9,665	7.6	5.75
Nutrition	150	190	420	872	2.8	4.58
Dentistry	240	455	914	2,073	3.8	4.55
Psychology	40	490	181	2,531	4.5	5.16
Special education	—	110	—	433	—	3.93
Veterinary medicine	120	220	260	1,043	2.1	4.74
Animal husbandry	—	25	—	39	—	1.56
Total	2,511	4,249	12,901	20,051	5.14	4.71

Source: CESGRANRIO, Office of the Executive Secretary, 1973.

Finally, with preparations complete for the 1973 exam competition in Greater Rio de Janeiro, the federal government, in an eleventh-hour gesture, acted to prevent any complications regarding matriculation numbers. On December 7, 1972, Law no. 5,850 was passed stipulating the following: available places announced for the college entrance examinations could not be reduced afterward; these places, however, could be redistributed by areas or courses of study, independent of the Federal Education Council, provided the total number of places remained the same; and any increase in the number of places, due to ties in the classification procedure, could not be computed along with the places available for the next exam competition.[64]

Great care having been taken, the stage was now set for the second experiment with a unified examination.

Reaction to the First Experiment

The reactions to and assessments of the first experiment with a unified examination in Greater Rio de Janeiro—and unified exams in general—became manifest concurrent with (and therefore inclusive of) the planning for the second experiment.
If we accept Eckstein's view that "policy creates politically active groups"[65] and include government as a group along with

TABLE 7.6

CESGRANRIO Comparative Statistical Report: COMCITEC

Career	Places Offered 1972	Places Offered 1973	Candidates 1972	Candidates 1973	Candidate/Place Ratio 1972	Candidate/Place Ratio 1973
Architecture	60	575	155	927	2.5	1.61
Astronomy	70	70	37	67	0.5	0.95
Engineering	2,120	3,450	6,403	6,853	3.0	1.98
Agricultural engineering	—	150	—	353	—	2.35
Cartography	50	50	60	239	1.2	4.78
Forestry	—	50	—	96	—	1.92
Operational engineering	580	1,020	757	2,123	1.3	2.08
Chemical engineering	330	440	468	1,123	1.4	2.55
Physics	230	360	182	444	0.7	1.23
Geography	220	230	170	56	0.77	0.24
Geology	40	65	110	272	2.7	4.18
Mathematics	290	465	432	662	1.4	1.42
Meteorology	30	30	20	22	0.6	0.73
Naval officer	—	20	—	82	—	4.10
Chemistry	140	245	134	352	0.9	1.43
Total	4,160	7,220	8,928	13,671	2.15	1.89

Source: CESGRANRIO, Office of the Executive Secretary, 1973.

TABLE 7.7

CESGRANRIO Comparative Statistical Report: COMSART

	Places Offered 1972	Places Offered 1973	Candidates 1972	Candidates 1973	Candidate/Place Ratio 1972	Candidate/Place Ratio 1973
Section A						
Arts	70	380	40	338	0.5	0.88
Library science	80	270	156	856	1.9	3.17
Communications	250	320	826	1,823	3.3	5.69
Industrial design	—	30	—	228	—	7.60
Law	420	1,200	1,244	2,919	2.9	2.43
Philosophy	30	150	40	207	1.3	1.38
History	150	460	295	920	1.9	2.00
Letters	330	1,620	1,049	3,270	3.1	2.01
Music	20	260	6	151	0.3	0.58
Theater	—	40	—	42	—	1.05
Tourism	—	80	—	99	—	1.23
Total	1,350	4,810	3,656	10,853	2.71	2.25
Section B						
Management	40	610	260	2,604	6.5	4.26
Social sciences	120	250	163	195	1.3	0.78
Accounting	—	150	—	429	—	2.86
Economics	260	530	1,330	2,349	5.1	4.43
Education	160	550	745	755	4.6	1.37
Home and family life	—	50	—	17	—	0.34
Statistics	—	40	—	173	—	4.32
Licentiate in sciences	—	30	—	6	—	0.20
Public relations	—	30	—	39	—	1.30
Social service	140	260	680	757	4.8	2.91
Total	720	2,500	3,178	7,324	4.41	2.92

Source: CESGRANRIO, Office of the Executive Secretary, 1973.

nonofficial groups, as Latham suggests[66]—the interest group provides a useful way in which to examine reaction to the experiment and reform of the system of access to higher education.*

Press

The press, a long-time supporter of higher education reform, reported that most concerned parties expressed general satisfaction with the new system of entrance to the university. In a piece entitled "A Good Mark for the Tests," Veja (the Brazilian equivalent of Time or Newsweek) captured the overall reaction to the 1972 examinations.[67] The article reported that negative aspects of examination competitions had been overshadowed by several positive lessons of the recent examinations—the main one being the quality of the test items. The test

---

*It is essential, however, to note that in the case of Brazil the only interest group which had the power to significantly influence public policy outcomes was the government. In his definitive work on associations and interest group politics, Philippe C. Schmitter ascertains that "the structural transformation of Brazilian society has not led to the formation of autonomous, aggressive, and highly interactive interest groups articulating competitive, alternative demands . . . [in addition] despite the conclusive evidence on the general increase in associability, there is no such evidence of an increase in the influence these groups have upon policy-making. In short, 'pressure group predominance' may not be the inevitable component of political modernity it is often thought to be." Interest Conflict and Political Change in Brazil, pp. 366-67.
With respect to the issue of access to higher education, students, professors, rectors, secondary schoolteachers, the press, cursinho directors, and officials of isolated colleges had neither strong bargaining positions nor significant influence on policy formation. They were either coopted, manipulated, repressed, or ignored by the government. (On several occasions, however, students were successful in exerting influence on the federal government, such as the case of the 1968 student demonstrations and the protests of medical school excedentes. Nevertheless, the government's response to these pressures was always compatible with federal interests, as well.) The point is that a discussion of the relative importance of nongovernmental interest groups is irrelevant because the amount of influence they maintain and exert in the policy-making process is not particularly significant.

questions were considered easier and much more reasonable than those of previous exams. Consequently, there was a surprising air of tranquility surrounding the 1972 competition, with fewer protests about the difficulty concerning the level of the questions. Furthermore, the opinions were identical regarding the pilot experiment in Greater Rio de Janeiro.

Most newspapers had comments on the new entrance exam system, and most of their editorials were very positive. Indicative of this was the editorial issued by the Jornal do Brasil. Calling the classifying system "one of the most legitimate renovations" of Brazilian education, the editorial stated: "The new entrance examination competition realized this year in the area of Greater Rio de Janeiro in an experimental character . . . should be extended to other geo-economic regions.68

The prestigious Estado de São Paulo, however, the most anti-federalist, independent, and outspoken major newspaper, criticized the proposal of unified entrance examinations. Although recognizing the positive aspects of reforming access and unifying the exams, the editorial expressed the opinion that the MEC, through its Department of University Affairs, had misconstrued the true meaning of the law sanctioning regionally unified exams:

> We have serious doubts concerning the advantage of the imposed centralization which far exceeds the spirit of university reform. . . . It does not seem reasonable to us, in any form, that public higher education should be at the mercy of competing private organizations for the selection of its students. . . . How would one organization be chosen over another? In function of the fees it would charge to candidates? Or the exams they constructed? And it is worth remembering that different universities can prefer different kinds of examinations. . . . And if various private organizations can compete in the "exam market," with or without declared intention of profit, cannot the universities themselves do the same thing?69

In essence, the Estado de São Paulo was asserting that good sense and the public interest dictated that public universities either be given the right to construct and administer their own examinations—each one by itself—or be subject to a State examination under the supervision of an official organ.

The 1972 exams also received foreign press coverage. Illustrative is the article written in the London Times' "Higher Education Supplement" by Fay Haussman, a research associate of the Institut d'Etudes sur l'Education in Brussels, Belgium, and a well-respected authority on Brazilian education. She reported on the simultaneity of the exams, the fee limit, the classifying system, and the fairness of the exam content. Although acknowledging that some educators were concerned about the concept of the unified examination competition vis-a-vis university autonomy, "reactions were positive . . . the usual protests and demonstrations were completely absent."[70]

Finally, acknowledging the timelessness and importance of the unified exams in Greater Rio de Janeiro, the widely-read daily O Globo published a weekly supplement on college entrance examinations; it ran from the first week in October 1972 to January 1973, when the competition was held.

Secondary Schoolteachers

Secondary schoolteachers were critical of the new system implanted in Greater Rio. Before presenting their criticisms, however, it is imperative to consider the reality in which secondary education operates. Secondary education is deprecated by students; belittled and depreciated by university professors, administrators, and other academicians; and pedagogically emasculated by the cursinhos. It is also held in low esteem by the MEC from which it receives a pittance in financial aid, as compared with budgetary outlays for higher education.

Therefore, a feeling of inferiority, coupled with anger and resentment, have conditioned a collective urge among secondary schoolteachers to strike back. The policies and programs formulated by critics of secondary education provide such an outlet.

In assessing the pilot experiment in Greater Rio, representatives of secondary education felt that the topics covered in each test should have been divulged at least a year ahead of time. They argued that teachers cannot change methods and materials halfway through the academic year. They also stated that the secondary schools were not consulted in the elaboration of the entrance exam program; and it was, therefore, not surprising that some topics included exceeded the secondary school level.

Secondary schoolteachers were upset that written expression and essay writing were prohibited from the tests. The exclusive reliance on multiple-choice items, in their opinion, meant that candidates would be evaluated merely on the capacity for storing facts. Antônio Fernandes Rodrigues, director of the Colegio Cinco-Integração Comunitária, remarked:

> The number of candidates increased tremendously, and they used the computer as an emergency solution. So,

the university professor will receive a freshman who
is addicted to answering questions with an "x" mark.
He [the student] will really have enormous difficulty
reasoning.[71]

Padre Francisco José de Silveira Lobo, rector of the Colégio
Zaccaria, thought it would have been better to have a longer test
series, consisting of tests and retests (to verify the results of the
first tests). He, too, was especially opposed to multiple-choice tests
for Portuguese Language and Literature:

In Portuguese, the fundamental principle is correct
expression, so that a person may be correctly understood in society. I do not see how it is possible to
evaluate capacity for expression, which also reveals
much in terms of reasoning, by simply presenting the
student with a series of alternatives to choose from.
The same holds true for interpretation. In the interpretation of a multiple-choice test, for example, what
passes for objectivity is many times the subjective
interpretation of the professor who constructed the
test. The result is the absence of any objectivity
whatsoever.[72]

While they endorsed the system of classification and supported
the idea of a group of tests for various areas, secondary schoolteachers felt the college entrance examinations needed much improvement.

Cursinhos

Immediate reaction to the first experience with the unified
examinations came from the larger, more prestigious cursinhos
and was essentially laudatory in nature.
Giuseppe Nobilioni of São Paulo's Curso Objetivo—Brazil's
largest, and one of the most profitable cursinhos—asserted that "this
was the first clean examination competition, without errors, with
original questions, and within the program."[73]
Antônio de Vries, director of the Curso Vetor, and Victor
Maurício Nótrica, director of Curso Miguel Couto, commented on
the exams in the technological and biomedical areas, respectively.
They both felt that the tests were geared to the secondary school
curriculum, with good questions, excellent organization, and fine
execution. Moreover, Nótrica and de Vries praised the system of
unification by areas and suggested its adoption throughout Brazil.

Their only criticism was that publication of the exam program (topics to be covered in each subject) and norms of the competition should have come much earlier. When asked about the expansion of higher education in the medical and technological areas, neither Nótrica nor de Vries believed that the opening of new colleges or the increase in places in existing schools would dilute the quality of professional education:

> The greater the number of specialists, the better. The competition [among them] will be greater, and this will improve the level of the professionals. The Government should open up higher education instead of stifling it.[74]

Focusing on the Greater Rio de Janeiro experiment, twelve cursinho directors and teachers met to discuss the unified entrance examinations. Reaction was mixed, however. Some thought the 1972 competition was very fair, while others thought it needed much improvement. According to José Gualda, the exam program should follow a more structural and scientific line of inquiry. As for the tests, he argued that they depended upon the capacity of the examining boards; so, at times the exam program could be excellent and the tests terrible.

Many cursinho directors argued that a more exact definition of "secondary education level" was needed in order to discuss intelligently, let alone judge, whether or not tests were excessively difficult. Norbertino Bahiense asserted that those who criticized the exams should know that there have to be some difficult questions on the tests because if all items were on the level of secondary education—scores on the tests would be much too high (that is, a candidate who misses 3 items out of 100 on a test could, hypothetically, not be classified).[75]

As for the organization of the forthcoming unified exams, the cursinhos were very pleased. The only real complaint regarding the planning of the 1973 competition in Greater Rio was the introduction of a major in psychology in the COMBIMED area in June. Echoing the verbal protests of many candidates, Victor Nótrica, while supporting the assignment of psychology to the COMBIMED area, stated:

> We, too, do not agree with that alteration, practically in the middle of the year. . . . We always seek to be on the side of the candidates in any circumstances. . . . [therefore] we were obliged to open up full-time classes for psychology candidates who were knocking on our door.[76]

Arnaldo Struzberg, Director of the Curso AESSE, vehemently criticized the assignment of psychology to the biomedical area, particularly in light of the fact that most candidates in psychology come from classical and normal high schools where physics, chemistry, and biology are not curriculum requirements. He added that his cursinho would have to restructure its schedule and hours, contract additional teachers, and hold classes on Sundays. In his opinion, the only beneficiaries of this last minute change would be the cursinhos which prepare candidates for medicine and related fields, since they were already prepared to handle the change (for example, Victor Nótrica's Curso Miguel Couto).

All agreed that similar modifications of major importance should be done well before the examination competition.

University Professors and Rectors

The reaction of most professors of universities participating in the 1972 unified examinations in Greater Rio was very positive. They praised the excellent organization and execution of the CESGRANRIO experiment.

In a meeting of professors in the biomedical area, their praise was unanimous. In the words of Professor Roberto Alcântara Gomes of the College of Medical Sciences, State University of Guanabara:

> No important modifications need be made in the entrance exam competition. . . . The unification marks enormous progress, and the results are satisfactory both for the candidates, regarding the general structure of the competition, as well as for the universities.[77]

Even the isolated colleges that voluntarily joined the unification commented positively. George Doyle Maia, representing both Souza Marques College and the Medical College of Campos, expressed the opinion that the benefits of unification, such as deferring to a central body the time-consuming and costly business of setting up an exam competition, outweighed the disadvantages (that is, loss of revenue from student inscription fees). Newton Castro, director of the Institute of Biomedical Sciences of UFRJ, expressed great satisfaction with the CESGRANRIO experiment but suggested a system of financial aid for students who are classified for study in a private institution but cannot afford the tuition and fees.

Professors in the science and technology area echoed the laudatory comments made concerning the 1972 examinations. Jorge Kubrusly of the Celso Suckow da Fonseca Federal Technical School and the Santa Úrsula University Association praised the organization of the examinations but added that only time would tell whether major changes would have to be made. Aderson Moreira da Rocha, dean of the College of Engineering at UFRJ, concurred and suggested that since the techniques of exam construction had improved considerably, they should be used as an incentive to encourage high schools to improve the educational level of their students.[78]

When asked if the level of the candidate improved with the unified exams, the professors felt that generally there was very little change: in some instances candidate level improved; in others it declined. They asserted that a classifying examination, as compared with an eliminating one in which only the "cream of the crop" is selected, inherently meant a small group of less able candidates would be admitted. This, they added, was particularly true in areas where the candidate/place ratio favored the candidate.

The only real area of controversy, and one in which only those professors affected voiced strong criticism of CESGRANRIO, had to do with the addition of psychology to the COMBIMED sector for the 1973 examination competition. Psychology professors met in May to discuss the change and its implications. Carlos Pas de Barros, director of the psychology program at PUC, captured the essence of the problem, ascertaining that:

> In the short-run the measure is entirely prejudicial. . . . These measures are valid in the long-run and should have been approved only for the 1974 competition. CESGRANRIO should have either published the examination program early enough or they should not have made the change for this year. After all, what they are really doing is changing the rules of play during the middle of the ball-game.[79]

Previously the examination for majors in psychology was offered in several areas, depending upon the institution. For example, UFRJ offered it in human sciences, PUC in social sciences and arts, and the Federal Fluminense University in biomedical sciences. The question the psychology professors asked at the meetings was, "Which area does psychology belong in—biomedical (clinical psychology), social sciences (social psychology), or technology (industrial psychology)?"

In the opinion of Elso Arruda, director of the Institute of Psychology at UFRJ, it was apparent that the field of psychology requires a broad training in which biology, physics, chemistry, and languages are essential, and mathematics is a very necessary tool for the curriculum, as well as for working in psychology (for example, psychometrics).[80]

Eliezer Schneider, director of the Institute of Psychology and Social Communication of UEG, did not argue that psychology's assignment to the biomedical area was unsuitable, but asserted that his colleagues should not neglect the humanistic aspect of the field: "the psychologist must be a person who is capable of working directly with human beings," without precise models and diagrams. 81

Most professors were of the opinion that there was no ideal solution: psychology has biological, social, philosophical, and mathematical components and, therefore, could be assigned to any one of the designated areas.

Professor Arruda and the psychology department at UFRJ enthusiastically hailed the move to put psychology in the biomedical area rather than in the arts, social and human sciences areas. (The fact that UFRJ would offer 120 of the 490 places in psychology for the 1973 unified exams—more than any other institution—probably had something to do with CESGRANRIO's decision.) Even those who had reservations about the decision—particularly concerning timing—acknowledged that COMSART was very weak in terms of the subjects it offered. More fundamental, however, according to the psychology professors, was the problem of the curriculum: it had to be modified to coincide with the educational exigencies of psychologists. In other words, the curriculum, more than the examinations, needed change.

With regard to the university rectors, Miguel Reale, Rector of the University of São Paulo, summarized the consensus of opinion at a rectors symposium in which he declared that a unified examination "infringes on university autonomy" and that each educational center should maintain its "functional and cultural peculiarities" and, therefore, set its own norms for admission. 82

However, the rectors of the public universities in Greater Rio either voiced their approval of a unified examination system or else remained silent, since they were politically appointed. No doubt some of them heartily endorsed the idea; but because of their politically sensitive position, it was not possible to obtain anything from them but noncommittal verbosity.

Isolated Colleges

Approximately thirty faculdades isoladas in Rio de Janeiro, offering 5,000 places (mostly in arts, letters, and social sciences), remained outside the unified examination system. Their reasons for doing so varied.

Some representatives of these colleges frankly admitted that private colleges that participated in the unification wound up with the less able and poorer students (since bright candidates prefer the large, academically prestigious and free public universities). By staying out of unification, isolated colleges could select their own candidates, choosing students who were both academically and financially able.

Although participating in COMCITEC and COMBIMED, Gama Filho University declined from joining COMSART. According to spokesman Peralva Delgado Miranda, UGF had a well-defined plan which was developed and operationalized in the area of human sciences even before the creation of CESGRANRIO. The university preferred to stay with this format, which allegedly worked so well; and he made it clear that the question was simply one of tradition and should not be taken as disapproval of CESGRANRIO.

A similar reason was given by Carlos Potsch, director of the Souza Marques Faculty of Philosophy. His institution, too, participated in the unified examination competition in engineering and medicine.

However, Rui Octávio Domingues, director of the Estácio de Sá Integrated Colleges, spoke for most isolated colleges when he said:

> We have at the present time a pluralist system of higher education in which there are units which pertain to the Government and others which pertain to private entities. Within that pluralist spirit it is interesting to note that we have, on the one hand, a mass college entrance examination—or rather a massive one—such as that conducted by CESGRANRIO, and, on the other, entrance exams on a small scale such as those given by private institutions. This gives the student another option: if he does not want to participate in a massive exam competition, in which students are treated like computer cards, he can enter another competition in which he will have more material comfort and receive instructions more easily because he will have contact with the actual organizers of the competition. [83]

The isolated colleges all stated that their exam programs and tests differed slightly from those of CESGRANRIO; furthermore, they claimed that the level of their tests faithfully corresponded to that which could be expected of secondary school graduates. Some of them felt that the tests were so accurate in this sense that candidates need not have bothered going to a cursinho.

It should be noted that the isolated colleges offered the same number, or less, tests per area, never more. In addition, almost every isolated college scheduled its examination competition before or after the unified entrance examinations—not during.

Students

Most students felt that the unified examinations had increased their chances for admission. Although many of them believed that the 1972 exams had not yet fully obeyed the criteria laid down by Minister of Education Passarinho for keeping the level of the questions to fair academic levels, they were convinced that the 1972 experience would serve to refine the system for 1973.

Typical was the comment by Ana Maria Lima, a COMCITEC candidate, who stated that "the tests were easy and entirely different from last year's nightmare when I tried the entrance exams for the first time."[84]

For the most part, the students liked many of the features of the entrance exam competition; and, at the same time, disliked others. For example, although students felt that Maracanã Stadium (the giant Rio soccer arena) was an uncomfortable and disagreeable place for test-taking, they nevertheless admitted that no other place was better in terms of centralization and the number of candidates that could be accommodated.

Regarding the tests themselves, students felt that the multiple-choice tests brought some disadvantages (for example, in questions regarding interpretation), but all agreed that multiple-choice tests were the only way to make the competition fair for all students and attend to the great number of candidates. The students generally felt that questions which required a good deal of reasoning should be maintained; but they believed questions designed to confuse, in which the choices were very similar—differentiated only by minute details—should be kept out of the exam. The candidates all asked that the entire exam program be divided equally with each test having approximately the same number of questions spread equally among the various topics. Even if the tests were perfect, the candidates added, students would still have to attend the cursinho since public secondary education was so bad.[85]

Many students liked the system of pre-option, but others concurred with Dalmer Pacheco de Almeida who stated:

> I think the second option is totally full of crap because most persons select as their first option the course of study they really want to pursue. For the second option, they put down any old career. If you really want to pursue a career and you do not get your first choice, you will take the tests over next year—but you are not going to take advantage of the second option.[86]

THE SEQUENCE OF POLICY DEVELOPMENT 125

Concerning other features of the Greater Rio entrance exams, all candidates thought that psychology should never have been moved from COMSART to COMBIMED at such a late date; in fact students opposed change of any kind in the entrance examination program once it was initially divulged. Regarding COMSART, candidates suggested that more be done to bring isolated colleges into the unified system since most of them did not participate in it. One student felt that COMSART's problem actually was due to the absence of vocational orientation materials for candidates in this area. The students praised the handbook published by CESGRANRIO but thought the part dealing with vocational information should have been more specific; they also suggested distributing these booklets at the earliest possible date and sending people from CESGRANRIO to the cursinhos during the year to provide further information.

Generally speaking, students were satisfied with the 1972 unified examinations and quite pleased with CESGRANRIO's plan for the organization of the 1973 competition in Greater Rio. It was not uncommon to find many students like Mara Lúcia Carvalho Brilhante, a medical candidate for the 1973 competition, who enthusiastically asserted:

> In my opinion, the unified examinations are the best thing they ever did because it gives everyone the same chance. As it is now, it is very good, and I do not think anything should be changed.[87]

Government

Reaction of the federal government (that is, the MEC, related agencies, and Minister Passarinho) was very positive, indeed. Nevertheless, this did not prevent a self-evaluation in which the shortcomings of the unified examination experiment were openly discussed.

The first comment on the pilot project in Great Rio was made—not surprisingly—by Carlos Serpa. He explained that the shortcomings of the 1972 examinations were due to late planning of the competition (CONVESU was created only 11 months before) and a lack of statistical data on the number of college applicants, preferred courses of study, and so on. Also, as a consequence of late planning, a complete unification was not possible since the exam program was not finally defined until September. The only institutions unified in the COMSART area were PUC and UFF.

Serpa pointed out, however, that many institutions which did not join the unified exam, nevertheless, adopted the uniform, established examination program.

As far as logistical problems were concerned, CESGRANRIO erred in projecting the number of students who would take the exams: they estimated 25,000, and 28,000 actually registered. Serpa felt this was positive, in a way. For it was his opinion that the classifying rather than eliminatory nature of the examinations attracted students who would not have otherwise registered for the tests. Also, the fact that CESGRANRIO was offering 2,000 grants for exemption from the inscription fee could explain the additional 3,000 student registrations. Another problem stemming from this under-projection was a shortage of 3,000 computerized registration cards, thus delaying registration by one week. The computer system, however, functioned well, according to Serpa, and the test results were made available before the scheduled date.

Lack of time also prevented a thorough preparation of exam monitors and officials, and Serpa's communication with them was possible only through the sector chiefs.

On the positive side, Carlos Serpa believed that the test questions were certainly on par with the secondary school level, based upon student comments and the overall results of the exams. In addition, he mentioned that it was to CESGRANRIO's credit that in designing the exam programs the established test series of universities was respected (for example, for geography majors, CESGRANRIO substituted a test in geography in place of history because UFRJ included a geography test in its program).

Also, Professor Serpa asserted that one of the great glories of the competition was the fact that there was no breach in secrecy surrounding the tests. "Underground" test makers were allegedly selling exact replicas of the exams; the price varied from US$50 to US$500, depending upon the proximity to the test date. When the candidates opened their test packets on the day of the exams, however, there were many long faces in Maracanã Stadium—the pirate copies of the tests had nothing in common with the real thing. CESGRANRIO had established a viable security system.

Finally, Carlos Serpa ascertained that for the 1973 exams there would be very little major change, except for the fact that CESGRANRIO would consider utilizing large university campuses for holding the examinations.[88]

In addition to the evaluation they submitted, each coordinating commission of the sector areas (COMBIMED, COMCITEC, COMSART) offered additional opinions on the unified examination experiment. Herman Jankowitz, the new coordinator of COMCITEC and other members of COMCITEC, expressed great satisfaction with the 1972 competition and stated that CESGRANRIO would seek to improve the exams year after year. They indicated, also, that a number of non-participating institutions and recently organized colleges had written

THE SEQUENCE OF POLICY DEVELOPMENT   127

to CESGRANRIO with respect to participation in future exam competitions. Jankowitz asserted that the organization wanted to dissuade candidates from seeking careers in the fashionable fields of medicine, engineering, and psychology and was distributing to the high schools a publication much more elaborate than Handbook of Careers, containing employment outlook, salaries, and so on.[89]

The COMBIMED members expressed equal satisfaction with the 1972 exams. Bruno Lobo, coordinator, reiterated the need to take great care in the delicate business of preparing the tests: fair questions, rigorously obeying the ministerial regulations, and an equal distribution of questions per topic. The COMBIMED professors agreed with COMCITEC that candidates must receive a pre-examination career orientation to adequately understand the wide possibilities in the particular exam area in which they were registering. COMBIMED frankly admitted wanting to reduce the total number of students seeking admission in medicine.

The only significant problem was elucidated by Professor Bruno Polito, representative of the Medical College of Valença in CESGRANRIO. While clearly attesting to the many positive aspects of the unified examination system, he asserted that, for private colleges such as his, the 1972 unified exam brought a serious problem. Many students who opted for medicine and were classified, and assigned to Valença—their seventh choice institution—invariably asked the college for financial aid to pay the tuition they simply could not afford. Consequently, as Professor Polito pointed out, the Medical College nearly ran a huge deficit because of this; consequently, they decided not to offer any scholarships for 1973.[90]

COMSART, which, in actuality, would be entering for the first time in 1973, believed the unified examination system represented a policy which benefited both students and institutions—one which could furnish a healthy bond between middle and higher education. (COMSART had made every effort to request that universities name to the examining board professors who had experience teaching in secondary schools.) Altair Gomes, representative of UEG, pointed to his institution's choice to enter COMSART (they participated in COMBIMED and COMCITEC in 1972) only because it thought unification was a good thing.

The representatives of COMSART explained the reason for assigning communications to sector A and public relations to sector B. The two courses of study pertained respectively to UFRJ and UEG. Since, traditionally, one had required a mathematics test and the other did not, COMSART decided to respect that tradition; also, there was no time to come up with another type of arrangement.[91]

The response of the MEC officials to the Greater Rio experiment was, indeed, positive. The government felt that a classifying exam was a fair examination and, therefore, the MEC "would not permit, to the detriment of instruction and out of baseless paternalism, an increase in freshman places in the university . . ."[92] Heitor Gurgulino de Souza, the director of DAU, expressed the view that private institutions would eventually join unification to obtain financial assistance; for the complex and onerous task of mounting an exam competition, from which profits could be used only for scholarships, simply would not be worth it.

Minister Passarinho was direct. He said he preferred persuasion, but if needed he would use coercion to get colleges to join unification. He lauded the 1972 exams and stated that it was his natural tendency not to change anything in the 1973 and 1974 examinations, but instead allow time for the new experiment to mature—especially since the core curriculum of secondary education subjects (as outlined in Law no. 5,692) was just beginning to be applied. The Minister was also pleased with the improved ratio of candidates to places and the greater opportunity for poor students, due to the simultaneity of the exams.

This, then, was the reaction to the first experiment with a unified examination system in Greater Rio de Janeiro. On the whole, interest groups were generally satisfied with the results, and all admitted that a refinement of the process was necessary. Certain groups, however, viewed the government's unified examination policy as counter to their interests and, in some instances, a threat to their survival.

STAGE THREE: PREPARATIONS FOR THE THIRD EXPERIMENT AND REACTION TO THE SECOND EXPERIMENT

The preparations for the third experiment differed from the previous planning experience. The reaction to the second experiment, however, was not significantly different.

Preparations for the Third Experiment

Planning for the 1974 unified entrance examinations proceeded in a manner somewhat more isolated than previously and brought fewer innovations as well. This can be attributed to several factors.

First, most interest groups reacted positively to the first experiment with a unified examination. The federal government was extremely pleased with the 1972 exam competition; and their assessment of the 1973 test series, immediately following the conclusion of

THE SEQUENCE OF POLICY DEVELOPMENT

the exams, gave them even greater satisfaction. Therefore, since they felt they were on the right track—politically, educationally, administratively—there would be less need to rely on consultation.

Second, there would be less need to plan innovations for the 1974 exams since what had been operationalized in the past had obviously worked well.

Third, CESGRANRIO was involved with two other, related, planning and administrative concerns: the transition of the organization from a commission to a foundation; and an international symposium on access to higher education, to be held in Rio de Janeiro during the month of March.

On January 4, 1973, CESGRANRIO became a foundation. The Ministry of Education and Culture turned over to the new foundation all property and effects jointly acquired by the entities which established and originally constituted CESGRANRIO. This donation was valued at CR$4,867,708.90 (approximately US$811,300.00).[93] The Statute of the CESGRANRIO Foundation establishes a semiautonomous, nonprofit foundation regulated by the MEC. Organizationally it provides for a Directorate (formerly known as the Superior Council), responsible for broad policy making and major decisions, and a president whose concerns are administration and policy execution, although other powers may be conferred on him if the bylaws so state (see Appendix B).[94]

The bylaws, in fact, do provide for a strong presidency and create an organizational structure through which the executive can operationalize his powers (see Appendix C).[95] In addition to naming all personnel, excluding the directorate, the president is assisted by a Departmental Council comprising the administrative, research, finance, and examination departments; furthermore, he has the authority to delegate any executive functions he chooses to them. Moreover, letter "e" of article 17 (naming presidential functions and responsibilities) grants the president authority (in ambiguous terms) to "administer the Foundation and direct its activities."[96]

Presidential power touches the directorate as well. For according to article 10, section II, the directorate shall comprise former presidents of the Foundation in addition to institutional representatives. Also, the directorate elects a chairman from among itself to a three-year term; however, the term can be extended for an additional three years, even for a chairman who no longer represents his institution in the Directorate.

Minister Passarinho, speaking at the inauguration ceremony of the CESGRANRIO Foundation, asserted that the CESGRANRIO pilot project symbolized the thinking of the MEC regarding higher education access policies in Brazil. Consequently, the creation of foundations in geo-educational districts, comprising one or more states, would be the way in which the government would seek to unify entrance examinations.[97]

Following the minister's remarks, Serpa reiterated the government's opposition to one unified entrance exam for the entire nation. According to him, this could not come about until the reform of secondary education was complete and successful. As CONVESU pointed out, it would be impossible for the test subjects to be based exclusively on the core curriculum of primary and secondary education: only after 1975 would students be graduating from this new system (and at that, only those from the better school systems); and only after 1980 could an evaluation be made as to whether or not the new structure had been implemented.

One should note, however, that the ministerial regulation for the 1974 entrance exams suggested that those responsible for entrance exam competitions consider the core curriculum of secondary school subjects, gradually incorporating it into the exams. CESGRANRIO would use "good judgment," according to Serpa, and only make slight alterations to partially include the core curriculum subjects and material in the competition; and all these alterations would be announced by March 12, 1973.

The ministerial order which regulated the 1974 entrance examination competition represented a reaffirmation of the course being followed by CONVESU and CESGRANRIO in reforming the system of access to higher education nationwide. Although Regulation no. 113 BSB (February 21, 1973) largely restated the major provisions of previous laws, decrees, and regulations, it offered several revisions, clarifications, and minor innovations suggested by Professor Serpa and CESGRANRIO. These were as follows:

   a. To guarantee that the entrance exams do not exceed the level of secondary schooling, there must be present a professionally recognized (locally or regionally) secondary school teacher who will serve in an advisory capacity for the purpose of evaluating the tests before they are given;
   b. Institutions which divide their exam competition by subject matter areas, with different tests for different programs, should move towards a system by which all candidates are given the same tests— tests which are identical in content; depending upon the student's intended major, different weights should be applied to the different tests; the tests should tend to cover all the disciplines and material of the core curriculum of secondary education;

THE SEQUENCE OF POLICY DEVELOPMENT

c. The tests should be developed with qualitative rather than quantitative aspects prevailing: this means tests which predominantly verify reasoning capacity, critical thought, comprehension, analysis and synthesis;
d. It is recommended that the examination series include, in addition, an aptitude test;
e. Institutions responsible for exam competitions should, in all earnestness, seek to give the tests in classrooms or enclosed halls;
f. It is recommended that the objective questions on the tests eliminate, as much as possible, the margin of subjective judgment;
g. All higher education institutions, public and private must present the Department of University Affairs (DAU), within 60 days after registering students, complete information on the numbers of places, candidates, approvals, matriculations, names of candidates and identity card numbers, and candidates' first choice careers;
  1. In the case of regionally unified exams, all the aforementioned information will be presented by the central administrative body;
  2. Institutions which fail to supply their reports by the specified time shall have their requests for funds or their subsidies suspended until they comply;
h. As foreseen in Decree Law 464 (February 11, 1969) which complements the 1968 University Reform Law, it is recommended that institutions seek to unify their exam competitions on a regional basis;
i. Regionally unified exam systems, organized by subject matter areas, should seek to integrate related courses of study in the appropriate area; in this way, candidates will not be limited in their career choices and, therefore, in the number of freshman places for which they can compete;
j. Entities responsible for entrance examination competitions must present the Commission on Educational Fees of the Federal Education Council, within sixty days, with an accounting of inscription fees collected, expenses in conducting the competition, and cash surpluses.
  1. Failure to present this information or to have it approved by the Commission on Educational

Fees shall result in a suspension of any financial assistance furnished by the MEC until the delinquent institution complies.[98]

Carlos Serpa announced that test specialists were already working on the program and tests for the 1974 exams and would complete their work within a week. He mentioned, too, that COMSART would attempt to eliminate its division into two sectors (A and B), perhaps combining mathematics and geography into one test for all candidates. COMCITEC would keep the same tests and eliminate some of the topics from the test program. Serpa admitted that an aptitude test for all three areas was "very probable."[99]

Commenting on the new ministerial regulation, Heitor Gurgulino de Souza, director of DAU, said that universities and isolated colleges not participating in regionally unified examinations would most likely seek to have their tests developed by institutions specialized in developing the methodology needed to test reasoning capacity, comprehension, and analytical ability. He cited the CESGRANRIO Foundation, the Carlos Chagas Foundation, Mapofei, and Cescea as examples of organizations specialized in constructing such tests.[100]

Further exposure and recognition of the government's efforts to reform the system of access to higher education came in March 1973. The Department of University Affairs of the Ministry of Education and Culture and the CESGRANRIO Foundation sponsored the First International Symposium on Access to Higher Education, held in Rio de Janeiro, from March 26 to March 30.

In a press interview with CONVESU members, following one of the conference sessions, Heitor Gurgulino admitted the need for "an intermediate solution for the system of pre-option, taking into account not just career choice but also the number of points obtained, in order to take advantage of the best candidates."[101] Manoel Luiz Leão, another CONVESU member, was even more vociferous: he was diametrically opposed to the preoption idea altogether.

The members of CONVESU also acknowledged that candidates for admission to careers in which places outnumbered candidates had, in reality, "direct access" rather than access via competitive examinations. Several members suggested that a method of selection for such candidates could additionally include an evaluation of the secondary school transcript; but, they finally admitted that this was not feasible since legally selection for higher education could only be done by way of an entrance exam competition.

The success of the regionally unified examinations in Greater Rio de Janeiro moved Minister Passarinho to call on Serpa to do the same for other regions. Consequently, in April, 1973, he traveled to Belo Horizonte, capital of the State of Minas Gerais, where he discussed with university rectors the creation of a Center for the Selection of Candidates to Higher Education in Greater Belo Horizonte. He clearly stated that CESGRANRIO's intention was not to accept invitations to manage exam competitions in other regions, but to provide technical assistance to local specialists so that they could create their own teams, taking into account the resources and problems of each region. Serpa acknowledged that after leaving Belo Horizonte, he would meet with educators and university rectors to discuss unification in the states of Pernambuco and Paraíba (primarily the university centers of Recife, João Pessoa, and Campina Grande) as well as in Paraná (specifically Ponta Grossa, Maringá, and Londrina).[102]

The following month, Aroldo Rodrigues, director of research for CESGRANRIO, announced that with the directorate's approval, three aptitude tests would be administered to all candidates for the 1974 competition. The tests would assess verbal and mathematical abilities as well as abstract reasoning. With the intention of modeling the tests after those of the Educational Testing Service (ETS), Princeton, New Jersey, Professor Rodrigues confirmed his plans to travel to the United States in July for the purpose of establishing an agreement with that organization. The CESGRANRIO research director asserted, also, that the aptitude tests would not be used for classification purposes in the 1974 competition but would serve, rather, to "refine the instrument" so that aptitude tests could be used for classification purposes in the future.[103]

During the second week in May, three cursinhos held simulated entrance exams—even including the pre-option system—to prepare their students for the real thing in January 1974. In the "Biomedical Area" at Curso Miguel Couto, 75.1 percent of the students picked medicine as their first option and UFRJ as their first institutional preference. According to Victor Nótrica, Director of Curso Miguel Couto, the tendency was probably due to the fact that students were unfamiliar with other professions, lacked information about various fields of study, and were captivated by the social prestige of a career in medicine.[104]

At the same time, Herman Jankowitz, COMCITEC director, announced that he was in contact with the Military Institute of Engineering (IME) and the Nuno Lisboa Engineering College; if they agreed to join unification, this would complete the technological area in Greater Rio. (These institutions, however, later decided not to join.) COMBIMED was attempting to obtain the participation of the medical colleges of Teresopolis and Vassouras.[105] (Only the former agreed to unify its exam competition.)

In a major announcement on May 31, Serpa communicated that on June 14 CESGRANRIO would launch its "Campaign to Demystify the Entrance Exams." The campaign would last until the date of the exam competition. By way of television, radio, newspapers, movie theaters, and visits to schools, CESGRANRIO would seek to clarify the selection process and provide sound guidance and counseling to students.[106]

He said that students were prejudiced by not having professional orientation (in a study conducted by CESGRANRIO on the 1973 candidates, 50 percent of the candidates made their career decisions based on the first information they received). He added that this was extremely unpractical since students should reach career decisions through honest, self-evaluation rather than from family and other external influences. CESGRANRIO would try its best to remove the mystery, anxiety, and fear which surrounded test taking. Towards these ends, CESGRANRIO intended to distribute, daily, copies of the Handbook of Careers and the exam programs to all high schools and cursinhos. In addition, high schools and cursinhos could gather questions from students to forward to CESGRANRIO, and these would be answered in the newspapers and on radio. Furthermore, CESGRANRIO would send its president and a team of coordinators and directors to the secondary schools and cursinhos, upon request, to give talks along with an audiovisual presentation.

In a surprising development, the Jornal dos Sports, a student-run Rio daily newspaper, reported on June 13 that three colleges (Souza Marques' engineering and medical schools and the Bennett Integrated Colleges) were pulling out of CESGRANRIO's unified exam system. Although CESGRANRIO remained optimistic, confident that this would not happen, José de Souza Marques, the elderly president of the Souza Marques Technical Educational Foundation, stated that the decision had already been made to withdraw the College of Engineering and the College of Medicine from the unified examinations. His reason for doing so was that "juridically, the foundation cannot be governed by another foundation in its entrance examination competition."[107] This would mean a loss of 192 places in COMBIMED and 300 in COMCITEC. Professor Souza Marques indicated that his institution was awaiting CESGRANRIO's formal invitation to join unification in COMSART, as well, before officially communicating the legal problem which prevented his institution's participation altogether.

The Bennett Integrated Colleges cited administrative problems as their reason for withdrawing from unification in the COMSART area. Internal growth generated some "administrative difficulties" which led the institution to believe that participating in unification would be disadvantageous. The Bennett spokesman added, however, that there was no disagreement over CESGRANRIO's philosophy or criteria adopted for the unified examinations.

THE SEQUENCE OF POLICY DEVELOPMENT   135

The Jornal dos Sports reported that they found out that private colleges resented the pre-option system. Candidates generally opted for public colleges and universities, leaving private colleges as their last institutional options. Consequently, according to private college professors and administrators, this generated difficulties relating to the level or quality of private higher education.[108]

CESGRANRIO divulged on July 6, however, that all the colleges of Bennett would be participating in the 1974 competition as well as the engineering and medical colleges of Souza Marques—and possibly other divisions of Souza Marques which would come under COMSART![109] (See Appendix D for a complete listing of the institutional members of CESGRANRIO.)

Serpa announced on July 7 that the Commission on Educational Fees of the Federal Education Council had granted CESGRANRIO an increase in the exam inscription fee from CR$120 to CR$134.40. Furthermore, CESGRANRIO would plead its case before the Commission for higher inscription fees than isolated colleges starting in 1975—the reason being, its exams were more sophisticated than others (and, therefore, costlier).

At the same time, CONVESU announced that it was completing its analysis and evaluation of the unification plans for the regions of Rio Grande do Sul, Pernambuco, Paraíba, Paraná, and Santa Catarina. If higher education institutions in these regions, as well as those already unified in Greater Rio and São Paulo, were unified by 1975— they would offer between 70 percent and 80 percent of all freshman places in higher education.[110] Serpa mentioned that the National Book Institute was completing the editing for the new Handbook of Careers. The publication would bring together data which would serve to orient all students, not just those in Greater Rio, for careers throughout the land; therefore, approximately 500,000 copies would be printed for the first edition.

Finally, the president of CESGRANRIO admitted that aptitude tests might not be used for the 1974 exams after all; instead, only a small sample of high school and cursinho students would be tested in order to determine the validity of the tests for use on a broader scale the following year.

Reaction to the Second Experiment

Assessments of the second experiment by the various interest groups did not differ significantly from those made following the 1972 examinations. However, the aggregate response was somewhat more favorable than the year before.

Secondary Schoolteachers

There was very little comment from the representatives of secondary schools. They had stated their opinions at the time of the first unified examinations the year before, and very little had occurred to prompt them to offer additional comments. The course of entrance examination development was already determined by the MEC; therefore, secondary teachers would have to continue structuring their teaching to the tests—tests which assessed, in their view, only one type of intelligence and at the same time were impersonal and dehumanizing.

Further comments came from professors of teacher education. Lauro de Oliveira Lima, organizer of the School of Education at the University of Brasília and a respected authority on teaching methods, asserted that the multiple choice tests in the entrance exams lead to "intellectual stifling."[111] He claimed that the objective tests were almost completely based on memory utilization rather than reasoning. Furthermore, he suggested that even the national destiny was at stake because young people were "unlearning how to think." The tests, in his opinion, did not require the formulation of broad intellectual operations and were devoid of creativity. The result was students who were incapable of sustaining a discussion or developing certain points of view.

A noted researcher on secondary education, Nádia Franco da Cunha of the National Institute of Pedagogical Research, stated that the entrance exams were an "educational anomalie" and that unified or not they created excedentes, since the only solution was an expansion in the number of places.[112]

Her solution regarding the tests consisted of intelligence and aptitude tests in which assessments of general culture were made, based upon the candidate's real life experiences and what he learned from them. In general she believed the higher education policies of the federal government—based upon an unfounded fear of diluting quality—did not support expansion.[113]

Cursinhos

The cursinhos were quite satisfied with the exams (they even sent some of their people to Maracanã Stadium to take the tests!). They voiced no major criticism of the 1973 competition, and the opinions of most of the students with whom they spoke regarding CESGRANRIO's examinations were also favorable. While some students felt the exam system was not a panacea, they admitted, nevertheless, that they were more confident in the selection process and its fairness now than before.[114]

THE SEQUENCE OF POLICY DEVELOPMENT   137

The fact that CESGRANRIO published the 1974 exam program sufficiently beforehand pleased the cursinho directors very much. Except for some minor criticism of the mathematics program for 1974, they were very satisfied with the planning arrangements for the forthcoming exam competition. In particular, they applauded CESGRANRIO's campaign to demystify the competition, even though they believed tensions would still exist due to the very fact that candidates outnumbered places.[115]

University Professors and Rectors

University professors who commented on the 1973 exams expressed satisfaction with the organization of the tests and the administration of the exam competition. Even the executive-secretary of the Council of Rectors, Emanoel Campos, indicated that university rectors were manifesting less apprehension concerning unified exams, and that rectors in Greater Rio admitted that a unified exam competition brought less administrative problems. The PUC and UFRJ administrators and professors noticed an effect of the unified exam competition which brought them particular satisfaction: the substantial decrease in the numbers of freshman "no shows" (students who register but either fail to show or drop out shortly after the beginning of classes). In the words of Fernando Pereira of the UFRJ Registrar's Office: "The present mechanism of the entrance exams changed everything."[116] His counterpart at PUC, Professor Paez, stated:

> Before, the student who did not show took away a space that could have gone to another candidate. With the new system of entrance examinations, the problem disappears.[117]

Essentially, it would seem that this was brought about by both the prohibition of multiple registrations and the system of pre-option. The candidate could no longer take exams and file pre-registration forms at half a dozen universities, and either show up at one or go to all of them and make his final selection after a week or two of classes. In addition, the system of pre-option meant the candidate was encouraged to think carefully about a second option—to either fill it in and be able to live with it, or else leave it blank and try again the following year for the first choice career.

Isolated Colleges

Isolated institutions, as could best be determined, did not deviate from their previous position: although every medical school and every engineering school but two in Guanabara State were unified. In the COMSART area, CESGRANRIO was also successful in bringing about the participation of a number of institutions. Nevertheless, following the unified exam competition, most isolated colleges opened their own competitions offering more than 6,624 places (mostly in arts, humanities and social sciences) in Rio de Janeiro alone.[118]

Testimony to the fact that the opposition to unified exams from isolated colleges was political and structural rather than pedagogical, the Gama Filho University used the CESGRANRIO experience in their COMSART competition. In the words of a UGF senior administrator:

> Since everything went so well in CESGRANRIO's examination, there is nothing more natural than adopting the same scheme for our competition.[119]

Gama Filho University, consequently, had a classifying competition with fifty questions per test, classification by computer, pre-option, and many of the other aspects of the unified competition administered by CESGRANRIO.

Nevertheless, scathing criticism was voiced by Antônio Luis Mendes de Almeida, Dean of the Cândido Mendes University Group. Speaking for a number of private colleges opposed to unification he asserted:

> Private colleges are not interested in unification because they know they would always get stuck with the worst students, since the better candidates by way of the classification format choose and obtain admission to, public institutions.[120]

Professor Mendes de Almeida, however, did use an educational argument in attacking the system of pre-option. He asserted that for the candidates who select medicine as first choice but obtain admission to nursing, their second choice, the result is unaccomplished nurses and frustrated doctors. He called on public higher education to concern itself with bringing up its quality to the level of that of private institutions.

Press

In its editorials, the press manifested considerable support of CESGRANRIO and the overall higher education development policies of the Médici government. The media recognized, however, that although higher education had expanded, a classifying system had been set up, and computers used to mark tests (eliminating

THE SEQUENCE OF POLICY DEVELOPMENT   139

manipulation of the results)—one undesirable aspect still remained:
the tense atmosphere which has traditionally surrounded the examinations. Therefore, the press lauded CESGRANRIO's efforts to
initiate a public information campaign to clarify the selection process
for students and their families and change the attitude of many who
still believed the exams were potentially a virtual massacre. In a
true sense, CESGRANRIO sought to personalize what was for many
a dehumanizing experience in mass examination.
    The media felt, at the same time, that CESGRANRIO should
also emphasize the economic aspects of higher education:

> Each area of activity and all professions should be
> the object of data which will allow each candidate to
> examine for himself the objective and social character
> of his calling. In this way only will the entrance ex-
> amination competition truly cease to be the socially
> negative myth which it has come to be.[121]

Having called for higher education expansion in the past on many
occasions, it was also interesting to see prestigious newspapers
such as Jornal do Brasil now espousing a cautious and moderately
conservative position very similar to that of Minister Passarinho,
DAU Director Gurgulino, and former DAU Director Sucupira. Ascertaining that one million students in higher education was a "re-
spectable university population," the Rio daily went on to assert
that:

> As a sign of its growth, among other things, the
> country has come to consume education on a wide
> scale. . . . In view of growing demand, the MEC
> will urgently have to expand the teaching body, lest
> its credibility be questioned regarding the quality of
> the education administered. At the same time, it is
> up to them to contain the proliferation of colleges
> that . . . contribute to the decline of educational quality
> and dump into the labor market the excedentes of various
> professions.[122]

    The newspaper criticized the excessive number of freshman
places in social sciences, law, philosophy, and communications,
which it attributed to the so-called benevolent policy of officially
accrediting colleges which were created haphazardly. CESGRANRIO,
however, was cited as a case where the formation of human resources
did not dispense with a sound educational policy. The vocational
handbooks of CESGRANRIO were praised, and the press called for a

more rigid inspection of colleges by the Federal Education Council and the consideration of geoeconomic and manpower needs as an important factor in their decisions.

Students

Student reaction to the 1973 tests was mixed, although a clear majority of students (particularly those who spent many hours preparing for the exams) thought the tests were very fair.

In COMSART, for example, students found the English test to be the only one that was very difficult; in COMCITEC, chemistry. In COMBIMED, medical and biology candidates thought the test series was fair with the exception of chemistry; while psychology, nursing, and nutrition candidates found a number of the tests generally difficult.[123]

For students taking the tests in Maracanã Stadium, the traditional problems of heat (approximately 105°F) and nervousness plagued the candidates once again.

Government

The federal government and related agencies displayed tremendous satisfaction with the recent exam competition. Calling it a "marvel," Carlos Serpa was joined in his enthusiastic appraisal of the 1973 competition by MEC officials and the functionaires connected with CESGRANRIO. Serpa pointed out that in all areas the timetable was rigorously being obeyed. Nevertheless, the competition was not ideal, mainly because of the need to use Maracanã Stadium with its hard, hot, and rough benches.

Serpa expressed the view that the only shortcoming regarding the tests was the absence of questions dealing with maturity, culture, and aptitudes. The exclusion of stadiums and the inclusion of these kinds of test items would make the exam competition ideal.

The area coordinators of the unified exam were all very satisfied with the competition, and they did not see the necessity for fundamental modifications in the entrance examination policy. COMSART coordinator, Professor Alexandre Sérgio da Rocha, considered the competition in his area a "complete success" and stated that the 1974 exams should be carried out within the same mold.[124] He admitted that there was a possibility that sectors A and B of COMSART would be merged; whatever the decision, however, the solution would be an educational rather than an administrative one.

Professor Bruno Lobo, Coordinator of COMBIMED, was of the opinion that the organization of the 1973 exam competition was not superior to that of 1972: "both transpired with the greatest normalcy."[125] He said that his team's experiences from the 1972 competition along with student cooperation were the prime factors in the success of both exam competitions; in his opinion, COMBIMED's test questions were within ministerial recommendations. He added, however,

> Naturally about 10 percent of the questions on each of the four tests were deliberately formulated on a level slightly more complex than on previous occasions to allow students who took great pains in preparing for the test to distinguish themselves.[126]

The COMBIMED coordinator was particularly pleased with the "decongestion" of traditional sectors, such as medicine. He attributed this to the introduction of new courses of study and career programs in the competition and improved information furnished to students. Consequently, he expressed the opinion that paramedical professions, as soon as they were regulated by the government, should be incorporated into the unified examination system.

COMCITEC was the area which received the greatest praise for the elaboration and development of its tests. Herman Jankowitz, Coordinator, stated that a number of cursinho directors had called to congratulate him on such fine examination questions. Jankowitz attributed the success of the COMCITEC exam competition to four factors: far more adequate time for planning the exams, as compared with 1972; the effective contribution of the press in providing candidates with information on all aspects of the competition; the examining board's thorough analysis of the past year's test questions, thus permitting the establishment of more perfect criteria for the 1973 test items; and the COMCITEC team's ability to carefully consider and learn from the experience of the last unified exam competition.

Regarding future changes in the exam competition, Herman Jankowitz asserted that Maracanã Stadium was ideal for his area; and that although uncomfortable for candidates, the centralization which the stadium afforded was the most important consideration. Ironically, the only real problem which COMCITEC had during the 1973 exams had to do with Marcanã Stadium. In the middle of the COMCITEC tests, construction workers began renovation on parts of the stadium. Using hammers, electric saws, cement mixers, air hammers, and an assortment of foundry equipment, the ADEG Engineering Company laborers worked without a letup, and the noise greatly irritated the candidates. Jankowitz and Serpa spoke with the president of the engineering firm who explained that his company had a timetable to follow; an interruption, he asserted, would result in a large fine. Serpa offered to pay the fine but was turned down.

Finally, Herman Jankowitz endorsed the application of the same test material in each subject to all the sector areas, or at least COMCITEC and COMBIMED. He saw no reason why the same Portuguese test could not be given to all candidates and the same chemistry test to all COMBIMED and COMCITEC candidates.[127]

Because of the lengthy, detailed, and complex nature of this chapter, the author has chosen to present a synopsis of the more significant aspects pertaining to the development of, and reaction to, federal policy actions on access to higher education. A summary of this chapter is as follows:

First, federal initiatives to reform access to higher education initially dealt with correcting distortions in the system of selection (for example, excedentes, multiple inscriptions). The drafting of legislation, the creation of legal frameworks, and the signing of presidential and ministerial decrees and regulations served to define and shape a broad policy of reform. A national commission (CONVESU) was created to assist the minister in planning and policy formation, particularly with regard to the regional unification of entrance examinations. The Minister of Education moved ahead hurriedly to implement changes for the 1972 college entrance exam competition in public institutions. Due to the limitation of time, the scope of program innovation had to be narrowed: the prime experiment would be confined to Greater Rio de Janeiro; a network (CESGRANRIO) was created for this purpose.

The reaction to government planning initiatives was guardedly optimistic. Some offered a mild endorsement of federal intentions, while others maintained a wait-and-see attitude. All were concerned about the issue of excedentes, viewing it as the most pressing problem of selection for higher education.

Once the 1972 entrance exam competition was concluded, the reaction of concerned parties became more clearly defined. The press, including major newspapers (except the Estado de São Paulo), praised the unified entrance examination system. Endorsement also came from professors whose institutions participated in unification and students. Although self-critical of the administrative shortcomings in implementing the new system, the federal government was very satisfied with what had transpired—particularly in Greater Rio. CESGRANRIO was quite pleased, but recognized the need, as did students, for orientation materials and the addition of many more colleges in the COMSART area.

The reaction of the cursinhos was mixed, although most— particularly the large, more prestigious ones—applauded the new system. The main complaint was that the publication of the exam program and norms of the competition should have come earlier. Secondary schoolteachers were critical of the unified exam system.

They believed that the topics covered on the tests should have been divulged much earlier, and they opposed the exclusion of essay questions from the exam competition. Nevertheless, they did agree with grouping the tests by subject matter areas and supported the system of classifying candidates. Finally, isolated colleges criticized the new system. They preferred to select their own students, since they believed that in a unified exam system they would receive the least able candidates—both academically and financially. Undoubtedly, they were also very much concerned with the loss of inscription fees in joining unification.

Second, planning for the second experiment did not gain momentum until after federal policy makers had partially evaluated the experience of the 1972 exam competition. CONVESU subsequently concluded that the most prudent policy would be to consolidate past gains and avoid brisk changes; major attention would continue to be focused on CESGRANRIO. In turn, CESGRANRIO devoted its resources to refining the tests and programs, compiling and disseminating testing and occupational information for candidates, and bringing about the participation of more colleges in the unified examination network. At the same time, the federal government acted to hasten and expand unification throughout Brazil: legal and financial means were used in pursuing this goal.

The reaction to the 1973 unified exam competition did not differ significantly from that of the first experiment, although on the whole it was more favorable. A clear majority of students supported the second experiment with a unified exam, as did university professors. The cursinhos were more enthusiastic in their response, as was the press. However, the press warned about diluting the quality of higher education by an excessive expansion of university enrollments. Finally, a number of isolated colleges, while opposed to the idea of unification, joined, nevertheless, for political reasons (that is, fear of harassment from the Ministry of Education and Culture).

Third, the third experiment with a unified examination system was planned in greater isolation than previous experiments. (This was particularly true in the case of CESGRANRIO.) The government was extremely pleased with the way in which unification was progressing and felt little need to innovate or solicit additional advice or assistance. During this time, CESGRANRIO's status changed from a government commission to a federally-regulated foundation. It focused its attention on further improvement of testing and measurement procedures, recruiting additional private colleges for unification, and launching a student-oriented campaign to demystify the entrance exam competition. In a negative and potentially serious development, several private colleges in the CESGRANRIO network became dissatisfied with the unification scheme and announced that they were considering withdrawal. This, however, did not come about.

NOTES

1. Guido Ivan de Carvalho, Ensino Superior: Legislação e Jurisprudência, 2ª edição (Rio de Janeiro, 1969), pp. 63-65.
2. Jornal do Brasil, 24 October 1967.
3. Aluísio Pimenta et al., Estabelecimento de uma Política para Admissao de Alunos no Ensino Superior do Brasil (Rio de Janeiro: Conselho de Reitores das Universidades Brasileiras, 1967).
4. Tarso Dutra et al., Reforma Universitária (Brasília: MEC, 1968), pp. 29-30.
5. Dutra et al., Reforma Universitária, pp. 3, 5.
6. Guido Ivan de Carvalho, Ensino Superior: Legislação e Jurisprudência, p. 78.
7. O Globo, 28 January 1970.
8. Jornal do Brasil, 3 February 1970.
9. Jornal do Brasil, 13 August 1970.
10. O Globo, 21 October 1970.
11. Guido Ivan de Carvalho, Ensino Superior Legislação e Jurisprudência, 3ª edição (Rio de Janeiro, 1971), p. 75.
12. Jornal do Brasil, 6 January 1971. In the states of Rio de Janeiro and Guanabara there were 10,000 freshman places, approximately a 3:1 ratio. The MEC considered this "reasonable," although the priority areas like medicine, exact sciences, and technology showed higher than 3:1 ratios.
13. Correio da Manha, 22 January 1971.
14. Carlos Alberto Serpa de Oliveira, Simpósio para Avaliação da Implantação da Reforma nas Universidades Brasileiras: Concurso Vestibular (Rio de Janeiro: Pontificia Universidade Católica do Rio de Janeiro, 1971), p. 22.
15. Diário de Notícias, 23 March 1971.
16. Estado de São Paulo, 24 March 1971.
17. Estado de São Paulo, 27 March 1971. Ten percent of the MEC higher education funds were set aside for this purpose.
18. Serpa de Oliveira, Simpósio para Avaliação da Implantação da Reforma nas Universidades Brasileiras, pp. 28-37.
19. Correio da Manha, 22 April 1971.
20. Guido Ivan de Carvalho, Ensino Superior: Legislação e Jurisprudência, 4ª edição (Rio de Janeiro, 1973), pp. 110-12.
21. Serpa de Oliveira, Simpósio para Avaliacao da Implantação da Reforma nas Universidades Brasileiras, p. 54.
22. Ibid.

23. Diário de Notícias, 28 August 1971.
24. O Globo, 16 September 1971.
25. Jornal do Brasil, 16 September 1971.
26. Ibid.
27. Jornal do Brasil, 23 September 1971.
28. Jornal do Brasil, 26 September 1971.
29. O Globo, 27 September 1971.
30. Ibid.
31. Correio da Manhã, 19 September 1971.
32. Ministério da Educação e Cultura, Convênio, Departamento de Assuntos Universitários, Rio de Janeiro, 12 October 1971.
33. Ministério da Educação e Cultura, Convênio, article 7. The eleven participating institutions were: UFRJ, UFF, UEG, UGF, FEFIEG, PUC-RJ, PUC-Petrópolis, EN, ETFCSF, FTESM, FMV.
34. Ibid., article 8.
35. Ministério da Educação e Cultura, Convênio, article 9.
36. Ibid., article 10, paragraphs 1 and 2. The juridical language here is not very clear. In actuality, paragraph 1 permits the DAU to grant the President of CESGRANRIO any additional powers and responsibilities he feels he needs or wants, from time to time. Paragraph 2 provides for Coordinated Sectoral Commissions to formulate their own administrative needs, to be approved or rejected by the President of CESGRANRIO.
37. Ministério da Educacao e Cultura, Convênio, article 10, paragraphs 3 and 4.
38. Ibid., article 11.
39. Ibid., article 12.
40. Diário de Notícias, 13 October 1971.
41. Jornal do Brasil, "Unidade sufocante," 15 July 1970.
42. Jornal do Brasil, 22 October 1970.
43. Jornal do Brasil, 17 January 1971.
44. Jornal do Brasil, 26 September 1971.
45. O Globo, 1 December 1971.
46. Osvaldo Barcellos, "Excedente não desaparece como num passe de mágica," Diário de Notícias, 24 January 1971.
47. Raimundo Moniz de Aragão, speech delivered at the Escola Superior de Guerra (Superior War College), Rio de Janeiro, 8 September 1970.
48. Correio da Manhã, 2 February 1971. The government's statistics reveal a national average of 1 physician for every 1,810 inhabitants; in Guanabara State, that ratio is 1 physician for every 308 inhabitants. According to statistics produced by the Fundação Getúlio Vargas the physician/inhabitant ratio in Guanabara is smaller than that of various developed nations: Israel (1/450), France (1/910), West Germany (1/450), Austria (1/560), and the U.S. (1/700).

49. Carvalho, Ensino Superior: Legislação e Jurisprudência, 4ª edição, pp. 595-97.

50. Jornal do Brasil, 15 July 1971.

51. Institut d'Etudes sur l'Education, Brussels, Belgium, El Boletín, January 1972. Under the system of pre-option, the candidate makes two choices for a program of study in one subject matter area and several institutional choices—this is all done at the time of exam registration. To illustrate, in the science/technology area a candidate could do as follows: first choice, career, engineering; institutional choices, PUC, UFRJ, AUSU—second choice, career, mathematics; institutional choices, UEG, UFRJ, AUSU. In the system of pre-option, candidates' first choice option has priority in classification over candidates who choose the same career as second option—even if the latter candidates' scores are higher.

52. Estado de São Paulo, 19 April 1972.

53. CESGRANRIO, Relatório: Concurso Vestibular de 1972 (Rio de Janeiro: Centro de Seleção de Candidatos ao Ensino Superior do Grande Rio, 1972).

54. Ibid.

55. O Globo, 9 May 1972. The law provides for a "common nucleus" of subjects (that is, core curriculum) required of all students: communication and expression, social studies, mathematics, and physical and biological sciences. In addition, the law provides for a "professionalizing cycle," to be offered in conjunction with academic studies. The idea is to assure that all junior high and high school graduates will have occupational skills.

56. O Globo, 9 May 1972.

57. Brasil, Diário Oficial, 2 June 1972.

58. O Globo, 29 May 1972.

59. Ibid.

60. O Globo, 9 October 1972.

61. Ibid.

62. Ibid.

63. Jornal do Brasil, 18 November 1972. Professor Rodrigues, acknowledging the problem of security that has always plagued the exam competitions, endorsed the idea of a data bank or pool of questions, similar to that used by the Educational Testing Service (ETS), Princeton, New Jersey. Under this system, the test format and topics would remain the same, and the statistically reliable test items would consist of both new questions and items used in previous competitions.

64. Brasil, Diário Oficial, 7 December 1972.

65. Harry Eckstein, Pressure Group Politics (London: G. Allen, 1960), p. 27.

66. Earl Latham, The Group Basis of Politics (Ithaca: Cornell University Press, 1952), p. 12.
67. Veja, 19 January 1972.
68. Jornal do Brasil, "Vestibular aprovado," 22 February 1972.
69. Estado de São Paulo, "A propósito dos vestibulares unificados," 8 June 1972.
70. Times (London), "Examination Reform to Make University Entrance Fairer," 11 March 1972.
71. O Globo, "Professôres acusam: o unificado ainda esta muito errado," 17 November 1972.
72. Ibid.
73. Veja, 19 January 1972.
74. Correio da Manhã, 30 January 1972.
75. O Globo, "Programa tem muito êrro e programas exigem demais," 15 December 1972.
76. O Globo, 7 June 1972.
77. O Globo, "Na biomédica é preciso saber escolher certo," 3 November 1972.
78. O Globo, "Área tecnológica tem bom campo em todos os setores," 10 November 1972.
79. O Globo, 29 May 1972.
80. O Globo, "Psicologia é moda ou uma necessidade?" 1 December 1972. Professor Arruda's educational views on the subject are conservative, indeed. The entrance exams for psychology majors at UFRJ were traditionally given in the area of human sciences in which math, Portuguese, physics, chemistry, biology, English, and French were required; in addition, the psychology program gave aptitude and personality tests. When the human sciences area at UFRJ reduced the number of required subjects by eliminating chemistry, physics and mathematics, Professor Arruda had his program placed in the biomedical sciences area where these subjects were still included. Consequently he was very pleased that CESGRANRIO also placed psychology in the biomedical area. However, he was angry that "decisions in high places" prohibited the examination content from exceeding the secondary school level and at the same time abolished aptitude and personality tests.
81. O Globo, "Psicologia é moda ou uma necessidade?" 1 December 1972.
82. Times (London), 11 March 1972.
83. O Globo, "Faculdades isoladas são uma opção para os vestibulandos," 27 October 1972.
84. Veja, 19 January 1972.
85. O Globo, "Estudantes julgam o vestibular unificado," 20 October 1972.

86. Ibid.
87. Ibid.
88. Jornal do Brasil, 30 January 1972.
89. O Globo, 10 November 1972.
90. O Globo, 3 November 1972.
91. O Globo, "1973: Um teste para COMSART," 24 November 1972.
92. Jornal do Brasil, 12 February 1972.
93. Tabelião Balbino, Certidão: Fundação CESGRANRIO, 22º Oficío de Notas, Rio de Janeiro, 4 January 1973.
94. Ibid.
95. Fundação CESGRANRIO, Estatuto e Regimento (Rio de Janeiro: Fundação CESGRANRIO, n.d.).
96. Ibid.
97. Estado de São Paulo, 5 January 1973.
98. Fundação CESGRANRIO, Legislação Atualizada Referente aos Concursos Vestibulares de 1974 (Rio de Janeiro: Fundação CESGRANRIO, 1973).
99. Jornal do Brasil, 22 February 1973.
100. Jornal do Brasil, 25 February 1973.
101. Jornal do Brasil, 31 March 1973.
102. Diário de Notícias, 4 April 1973.
103. O Globo, 24 May 1973.
104. O Globo, 1 June 1973.
105. Ibid.
106. Jornal do Brasil, 31 May 1973.
107. Jornal dos Sports, 13 June 1973.
108. Ibid.
109. Jornal do Brasil, 6 July 1973.
110. Jornal do Brasil, 7 July 1973.
111. Estado de São Paulo, "Acusação: um ensino deformado," 11 January 1973.
112. Jornal do Brasil, "Professôra vê anomalia na educação, 14 January 1973.
113. Interview with Nádia Franco da Cunha, Brazilian Center for Educational Research, Rio de Janeiro, 7 June 1973.
114. Interview with Victor Nótrica, Director of Curso Miguel Couto, Rio de Janeiro, 16 June 1973; interview with Norbertino Bahiense Filho, Director of Curso Bahiense, Rio de Janeiro, 25 June 1973.
115. O Globo, 1 June 1973.
116. Jornal do Brasil, 11 March 1973.
117. Ibid.
118. Jornal do Brasil, 17 January 1973.
119. Ibid.

120. Jornal do Brasil, "Cândido Mendes não adota unificado," 31 March 1973.
121. Jornal do Brasil, "Vestibulares," 15 June 1973.
122. Jornal do Brasil, "Ensino a qualificar," 8 July 1973.
123. Jornal do Brasil, 10 January 1973.
124. Jornal do Brasil, 14 January 1973.
125. Ibid.
126. Jornal do Brasil, 14 January 1973.
127. Ibid.

CHAPTER 8

THEORETICAL ANALYSIS

Having presented the sequence of policy development on access to higher education and selected a theoretical framework for analysis, it is now necessary to determine the efficacy of disjointed incrementalism in explaining higher education access policy in Brazil.

In addition some pertinent observations will be made with regard to the major product of the federal government's reform policies: CESGRANRIO.

THE EIGHT STAGES OF DISJOINTED INCREMENTALISM

Margin-Dependent Choice

Choices under the military governments were made at the margin of the status quo: only incremental changes were planned and operationalized. Value conflicts which arose did, indeed, involve trading one shared value to bring about an incremental increase of another.

To begin with, the very political universe out of which educational policies were fashioned was identified with the status quo. The process by which the military deposed the constitutionally-elected government of President Goulart in 1964 was by no means a "revolution," in the strict sense of the term. According to Alfred Meusel, a revolution brings a recasting of the social order.[1] Erös views it as "sudden, radical changes which take place both in political and social conditions."[2] Robert Hunter states that revolution will produce "basic changes in the social, military and economic position of the several classes."[3]

THEORETICAL ANALYSIS

The military ascension to power in 1964 brought about neither economic nor social upheaval; and political "revolution" (that is, change from democracy to dictatorship) did not truly crystallize until the middle of December 1968, with the Fifth Institutional Act. Moreover, even today Brazil legally has a bipartite political system. There are a number of other indicators which illustrate the point that post-1964 governments did not radically change the status quo:

The Superior War College had been a significant training institution for military personnel and civilians even before the military came to power.

The technocrats had been active and had inherited the administrative machinery and structures introduced by Getúlio Vargas in 1937.

Administrative constraints with regard to the bureaucracy had historically plagued all previous regimes and continued to do so.

Although strained at times, Brazil had always maintained relations and an active dialogue with the United States.

There had been considerable continuity in government planning for over three decades. Goulart's planning chief Celso Furtado and Castelo Branco's Minister of Planning Roberto Campos were central figures in previous regimes. As Daland points out, "differences in strategy were greater than differences in analysis."[4]

If not a "revolution," then what did happen in 1964? A far better explanation can be found by viewing the situation as a conspirational coup d'etat. Defined by Chalmers Johnson:

Conspirational coups are attempts at revolutionary change made by a small, secret association united by a common sense of grievance that may or may not correspond to the objective condition of a social system. These revolutions are always calculated and they do not involve the masses.[5]

Trading ratios were a common feature of policy making. One need only look at the economic planning of the military governments. To cite a few examples, the government of Castelo Branco was faced with two choices: stimulating national economic growth and development or bringing the exorbitant level of inflation under control. Under the tutelage of Planning Minister Campos and Finance Minister Bulhões, an incremental policy was adopted of focusing greater attention on controlling inflation.

However, with a cut in the growth rate of the money supply, decrease in government spending, freeze on the minimum wage, and the subsequent industrial recession—accompanied by a high rate of unemployment—the balance in the trading ratio (economic growth versus inflation control) swung much too far in favor of anti-inflation measures. Consequently, the government decided to trade off some gains made on the inflation stabilization front in favor of measures which would revitalize the economy. Subsequently, labor intensive and capital intensive actions were taken along with a decrease in taxes on consumer items in order to stimulate purchasing.

With the ascension to power of Costa e Silva and the emerging problem of cost-push inflation, the trade-off ratio was kept from going to extremes by the "crawling peg" system of mini-devaluations (also known as indexing): wages and prices were periodically adjusted, taking into account the cost of living and fluctuations in the cruzeiro.

It would logically follow that if margin-dependent choice were a significant feature of policy making in the Brazilian political, economic, and social systems, it would characterize, also, policy formation on the subsystem level. Education—a subsystem of the social system, with ties to the political and economic systems as well—has undeniably undergone varying degrees of transformation under the military governments. Experimentation and innovation have been commonplace; however, they have always been circumscribed and channeled so as not to radically dapart from, and perhaps come into conflict with, basic tenets, objectives, and goals of the federal government.

Policy formation for higher education, a unit of the educational subsystem, was even less inclined to deviate from the status quo; the reason being, as elucidated in Chapter 5, historical tradition. For almost 160 years, Brazilian higher education was as follows: exclusively professional in character; a major source of literary and humanistic ornamentalism and dilettantism for the upper classes; a low or nonexistent priority for federal governments; and (consequently) overwhelmingly offered in private isolated colleges.

Brazil did not have a true university until 1934 (University of São Paulo); and even amidst university development and expansion in the 1940s and postwar modernization, industrialization, and social and economic change—Brazilian universities were intent upon avoiding change in order to develop a tradition, albeit a young one. The need to firmly implant and nurture without interruption a university, per se, along with the orientation of higher educationists and government policy makers (products and often proponents of the traditional educational system), led to a clear, definitive preference for higher education policy choices which would differ only marginally from the status quo.

In sum, margin-dependent choice is an omnipresent feature of the Brazilian educational system. As Agnes Toward cogently observes:

THEORETICAL ANALYSIS 153

changes claimed for the [educational] system are
likely to be bureaucratic rather than structural,
palliative rather than therapeutic, involving new
nomenclature applied to old programs by practiced
administrators.6

Restricted Variety of Policy Alternatives

The policy alternatives available to the Brazilian government
for the issue of access to higher education were restricted by the
fact that only strategies which differed incrementally from the status
quo could be considered. In addition, even certain incremental policy
alternatives were restricted! The fact is bureaucracy—its nature,
structure, vitality, and response capabilities—can determine whether
or not that which is incremental and feasible is also viable.* This is
especially true in the case of Brazil. To quote Minister of Education
Passarinho:

Unfortunately, we do not have the flexibility of the
armed forces ministries which can punish subordinates
or functionaries quickly, in any part of the country.
Consequently, the irregularities found in the various
areas of the MEC's activities are not immediately
remedied, as we would all desire.7

The problems of admission to higher education, as presented
in Chapter VI, were numerous and complex. In fact, so formidable
were these problems that it became apparent to policy makers that
anything short of a great, quantum leap and radical transformation
would be doomed to failure.

Yet, what would be the result? Rapid expansion of public colleges and universities would bring about a great decline in the quality
of higher education; moreover, even if quality were to be sacrificed,
sufficient physical, human, and capital resources were simply not
available. Nor were resources available to readily graft onto secondary education a substantial vocational component, complete with
guidance and counseling services. Abolishing the cursinhos, upon

---

*The point here is that in bureaucracies, senior policy-makers
may be restricted in considering certain feasible policy alternatives
due to the lethargy and/or incompetence at lower levels of bureaucracy. This is true in the case of Brazil.

which so many high school students depended, such an action would
be politically unwise; for among other things it would most likely
lead to strong reactions from college-bound students and their families. Finally, it was not possible, logistically or otherwise (for
example, persuasion, propaganda), to bring about—voluntarily or
involuntarily—a more rational distribution between candidates' career
preferences and economic manpower requirements.

The only realistic alternative was for the government to focus
attention on the development of a policy on college entrance examinations.[8] According to senior policy makers, the problem of the
excedentes was merely the most visible manifestation of a woefully
deficient system of selection for higher education. To resolve the
problem of the excedentes only would be to relieve the symptoms
without curing the illness. It became clear that the exame vestibular
was the centrifugal force, affecting in a profound way, all other problems of access to higher education. Policy makers believed that because of the prime importance of the college entrance exams, a
strategy of incremental change would not only produce multiple effects
in a number of spheres in the short run, but—hopefully—bring about
major change in the long run.

Minister Passarinho announced in December 1969, shortly after
taking office, and again in January 1970, at a meeting of the Council
of Rectors, that the MEC would follow the policy of reforming the
system of access to higher education by way of unification of entrance
examinations. This had been proposed, in general terms, in article
21 of the University Reform Law (1968); however, Minister Passarinho
had intended to see that it was actually operationalized. He made it
known that the exams first had to be given simultaneously as to date
and time, federal institutions being the only ones for which the directive was mandatory.

Although Minister Passarinho hoped to see at least this gradual
step taken for the 1971 exams, the problem of the excedentes, which
had erupted in 1967-68, prevented the initial phase of unification
from fully coming about.

The minister's DAU director, Newton Sucupira, cleverly proposed, however, a simple scheme for technically resolving the
problem of the excedentes—the adoption of a classifying system of
selection to replace the eliminatory one. In terms of politics and
equity, this solution was a brilliant one. It no doubt endeared
Sucupira even more to the Minister, and he soon emerged as the
most powerful higher education policy maker after the Minister of
Education. The influence and power which Newton Sucupira had at
his command cannot be understated. (He was also head of the Higher
Education Chamber of the Federal Education Council.) The single
most important education personality, Sucupira thoroughly dominated

THEORETICAL ANALYSIS 155

the higher education panorama during the Médici government. Minister Passarinho trusted him explicitly and practically gave him carte blanche to deal with the government's higher education affairs. The opening remark the Minister made to his researcher at an audience with him was: "If you have been speaking with Sucupira, you have heard it all—we rarely disagree."[9]

Returning to the policy alternatives decided upon—unification of the entrance examinations—the desired goal was regional unification by core areas (technology and exact sciences; bio-medical sciences; arts, humanities, and social sciences). However, the MEC made it known that logistically, politically, and educationally, unification would have to first take place along these lines within the university. National unification—one exam series for all Brazil—was never considered as an immediate alternative.

It was Sucupira's idea to appoint a national commission to study the unification and reform of the college entrance examinations and report and make recommendations to the Ministry of Education. Sucupira and Minister Passarinho selected six prominent educators— based upon their philosophy and administrative ability—to serve on the commission. In February 1971, CONVESU was created.

If the MEC, through Minister Passarinho and Newton Sucupira, shaped the parameters of policy—CONVESU expedited its realization. The policy agenda, created by the Department of University Affairs, was clearly spelled out: unification of exams by subject matter areas on inter-institutional and geographic levels, standardization of exam programs and matriculation fees, computer applications, testing and measurement procedures, and equity in examination content.

It was up to CONVESU to provide the technical agenda and opine on the feasibility of operationalizing the objectives set forth. In essence, the function of CONVESU was to provide staff work for the minister of education as a basis for subsequent decrees and regulations; it was also, as one member commented, "a vehicle for selling ideas."

The MEC had decided unequivocally which policy alternative would be followed to facilitate change and prescribed the boundaries and directions, as well. Together with input from CONVESU, Minister Passarinho hoped to achieve an optimal accommodation between the <u>political</u> and the <u>technical</u>.

Restricted Variety of Policy Consequences

The MEC senior policy makers did, in fact, arbitrarily choose not to consider remote, imponderable, intangible, uninteresting and poorly understood consequences of policy. They definitely were not the type of men who contemplate that which is theoretically possible (the synoptic ideal) instead of what is operationally feasible. Incidentally, one member of CONVESU did fit that category, however. Not surprisingly, he was often politely ignored and never taken seriously; consequently, his actual leverage was insignificant.

The central policy makers were—except for the individual mentioned above—rational, managerial, and pragmatic, with a keen understanding of realpolitik. Newton Sucupira best expressed the orientation of senior policy makers when he asserted that in reforming the system of access to higher education:

> What we need is a political, rather than exclusively technical decision. . . . Machiavelli was right: the most obvious and direct course of action is not always the wisest one.[10]

Attention was focused exclusively on the important policy consequences of the MEC's unification plans and CONVESU's proposals. The minister was primarily concerned, in the beginning, with the problem of excedentes and the need for simultaneous exams in order to eliminate multiple inscriptions (a practice which he believed prevented an accurate accounting of the demand for higher education and economically discriminated against poor candidates).

The Ministry of Education had a firm commitment to reforming access to higher education along certain lines. Policy makers desired to pursue and implement their plans with dispatch; and there were enough major consequences to be considered without dwelling upon intangible, unclear, and less significant results which could occur. In addition, it was common knowledge that Minister Passarinho was not especially interested in the technical aspects of policy—unless they were aspects which had significant political implications.

One might ask: Does this behavior not reveal short-sightedness, self-assuredness, arrogance, and even recklessness among policy makers? Not necessarily. This type of restricted analysis is a common practice among economists; and, as many environmental and conservation groups will attest, it is a fundamental feature of decision making in corporations and other enterprises.

In the case of access to higher education in Brazil, two important factors intervened to restrict even further the variety of major policy consequences and accelerate the flow of public policy.

First, the federal government was not "breaking new ground," so to speak, with regard to the concept of unified college entrance examinations. This experiment had taken place before, in a number of places, on various levels, and under different arrangements; the kind and degree of success and failure varied. (This will be discussed in the seventh feature of the strategy.) Consequently, the MEC could address its attention to a finite configuration of policy consequences and avoid certain pitfalls.

Second, the Ministry of Education and Culture, by virtue of the Brazilian political system, was insulated from negative reaction resulting from miscalculations of policy consequences. An authoritarian regime faces fewer limitations upon its executive power; hence, it need not display as much caution or moderation in either the formulation or implementation of policy. As a result of cooptation and then domination of the judicial system, emasculation of the legislative system, and the evaporation of active and independent interest groups, the government could choose whether or not to make adjustments and revisions in policy, due to consequences it may not originally have considered. With particular regard to higher education, the federal government had an additional, major instrument of leverage—it controlled the purse strings upon which federal higher education was exclusively dependent, state higher education was significantly dependent, and private higher education was partially dependent.

Be that as it may, given the homogeneous and incrementalist orientation of policy makers, as well as structural features which safeguarded the outputs of policy making, certain important consequences were, nevertheless, neglected. This occurred in spite of the fact that the consequences were, indeed, real, relevant, and well understood.

Two instances of important consequences being neglected occurred in meetings of CONVESU. In its initial report to the Minister of Education in March 1971, the commission recommended that plans for the unification of college entrance examinations make it mandatory for both private as well as public institutions to hold their exame vestibular on the same days and at the same times. The MEC vetoed this for political reasons. (Passarinho and Sucupira confidentially decided beforehand that only public institutions would be obliged to hold their exams simultaneously.)

The government did not want to create the impression that it was imposing reform measures on private higher education institutions. It preferred to pursue a strategy of detente rather than confrontation with the private sector. After all, the expansion of higher education had taken place, for the most part, in the private sector; this thereby freed the government, to a large extent, from the pressures and financial burdens of expansion, allowing it to pursue other courses of action (for example, the qualitative improvement of postsecondary education). Also, by maintaining good relations with private higher education, the government hoped to be able to quietly and selectively intervene, with little interference, to regulate tightly— and even eradicate—those private colleges which it considered academic cesspools. Furthermore, the MEC could hopefully gain additional leverage by mustering the support of the better private colleges in the government's campaign against low-quality private institutions. Finally, as one member of CONVESU pointed out, the MEC feared that, if all private institutions were required to join unification, the financial aid they would demand—mainly to alleviate the deficit from lost inscription fees—would be, collectively, exorbitant.

The second instance where important policy consequences were neglected concerned a CONVESU recommendation dealing with tests and measurement; it, too, was vetoed by the MEC. CONVESU suggested that aptitude tests of verbal and mathematical ability be a required part of the examination competition and that the standardization of test scores be mandatory throughout the entrance examinations. The government responded that the implementation of aptitude tests would be premature: until the great disparity in quality among secondary schools diminished, an exclusive reliance on subject matter-based tests was necessary. In addition, the MEC asserted that Brazil had neither the sophisticated test making resources nor the economic resources necessary to undertake, immediately, either a campaign to adopt a system of aptitude tests or efforts to standardize test scores. The government recognized these as important objectives, ones which should be attained in the immediate future—the latter with greater facility than the former.

According to Newton Sucupira, the first draft of CONVESU's report was somewhat ambitious: it would have regulated more than it should have and would have infringed upon university autonomy.[11]

However, as Manoel Luiz Leão of CONVESU pointed out:

Ninety-nine percent of what we proposed in our final report was eventually adopted, including our recommendations regarding standardized test scores, objective tests, and the consideration of aptitude tests for some future time.[12]

Adjustment of Objectives to Policies

While it is true that policies are sought to attain certain objectives, the reverse also takes place. That is, the ends of public policy are governed by means. Policy objectives are derived largely from an inspection of means. Therefore, a reciprocal relationship exists between means and ends.

This was true in the case of policy making on access to higher education in Brazil. Although policies were initially sought to achieve

THEORETICAL ANALYSIS 159

widespread, comprehensive, and uniform reform of the system of selection, the deep-rooted traditions of Brazilian higher education limited the means actually available to the MEC to mandate and monitor major change; and, consequently, they necessitated a readjustment of policy objectives.

To begin with, as already mentioned, the initial draft of CONVESU's report to the minister of education was too audacious in scope. The MEC simply did not have the means to implement the commission's recommendations. Consequently, the resulting policy objectives primarily concerned excedentes and the simultaneity of exams, as these pertained to public institutions.

Very early in the process of policy formation, the desired objective of one national college entrance examination was put aside: politically, administratively, and educationally it would be impossible to implement. The most obvious and important limitation of this plan was the generally poor quality of secondary education, particularly in the public sector. For the very same reasons, the desired objective of aptitude tests in the exam series was abandoned for immediate consideration. In short, a national college entrance examination system based on aptitude tests would have to wait until the educational quality and performance of primary and secondary education had improved substantially.

In December 1972—more than one year after the passage of the Primary and Secondary Education Reform Law and eleven months after the successful CESGRANRIO experiment—Minister Passarinho remarked that he was opposed to a single college entrance examination in 1974 and that such a system should not be introduced before 1975. Furthermore, he cautiously urged that even material from the core curriculum of secondary school subjects (an innovation of the 1971 Law) not be included in the 1974 competition:

> This is one of the points of the CONVESU report about which I told Professor Gurgulino de Souza I had my doubts and which I wanted to discuss. The natural tendency should be not to modify anything, since the core curriculum is just beginning to be applied throughout Brazil.[13]

Consequently, policy objectives were adjusted to provide for subject matter-based, achievement tests only and for unification to proceed on a regional basis.

Even regional unification plans had to be readjusted in terms of scope. It soon became apparent that multiple regional unification systems would be politically and administratively too difficult to set up, particularly in a short period of time. Therefore, the government decided to confine its efforts to Greater Rio de Janeiro. Both geographically and politically that area was the ideal choice. There were a great many colleges concentrated in a relatively small area. Furthermore, Rio de Janeiro, being the former capital, was quite susceptible to government influence. In addition, there were already plans, at the highest levels of government, to unite the State of Guanabara with the State of Rio de Janeiro economically and politically in the near future.[14]

Finally, it must be stressed that the time factor entered prominently in the decisions of policy makers to adjust their original objectives. Both CONVESU and CESGRANRIO were expected to fulfill arduous missions within a very brief period of time (less than one year). If there was to be any innovation at all in the 1972 examinations, great expectations would have to be lowered. Lacking the authority to take direct measures to force private higher education institutions to join unification, the government initially relied upon good public relations to gain the cooperation of private colleges.

CESGRANRIO, too, had to make adjustments. The time factor prevented unification of exams by the three desired subject matter groups (biomedical sciences; technology; arts, humanities, and social sciences). Consequently, COMSART—the most complex area to coordinate—was temporarily relegated to a lesser position of priority. Only the Pontifical Catholic University of Rio de Janeiro and the Federal Fluminense University participated in COMSART during the first experiment with unification in Greater Rio. CESGRANRIO, therefore, concentrated its major efforts in COMBIMED and COMCITEC. Even so, there was insufficient time to contact all isolated colleges in Greater Rio, and CESGRANRIO thus decided to aim at only the most popular ones.

What emerged, in the aggregate, from the readjustment of objectives mentioned above was an overall reform policy characterized by gradualism. As these readjustments were increasingly made, the Ministry of Education was espousing more and more its intentions to unify the entrance exams gradually. As CESGRANRIO President Serpa remarked:

> Logically, the change from one system of entrance
> examinations to another must be done gradually and
> with careful preparation.[15]

Be that as it may, Braybrooke and Lindblom clearly point out that the relationship between ends and means is reciprocal. It has been shown in the above discussion that, with respect to access to higher education in Brazil, the proximate ends of policy are governed by means. This should not, however, be considered a refutation of the conventional view of policy making in which means are governed by ends. For in the case of Brazil the relationship is, indeed, reciprocal.

Any plan for a true unification of college entrance exams—be it national or regional in scope—would have to include private higher education. For in terms of number of institutions, total enrollments, and rate of expansion, the private sector exceeded the public sector. Although the federal government did not have the authority to compel private higher education to join unification—the ends of public policy were of such crucial importance that the government found the means to indirectly apply leverage in order to attain its objectives.

That leverage was aimed precisely at the very lifeblood of private institutions—the inscription fees they collected from the college entrance examination competition. The profits from the exam competitions were used by the colleges for such purposes as remuneration for those responsible for making, monitoring, and marking the tests; faculty and administrative salaries and bonuses; and investment. Through the Commission on Education Fees of the Federal Education Council, a limit of CR$120 was initially set for inscription fees. Furthermore, profits were required to be used only for scholarships or research on the selection process, and institutions were required to furnish a full accounting of income and expenditures within 90 days from the date of the entrance examinations.

An indication of the results of this action is found in Table 8.1. Listed in the table are the income and expenditures for college entrance examinations of a sample of private higher education institutions in Greater Rio in 1972. The income and profits from the 1972 exam competition held by these colleges dropped considerably as a result of the new regulations, not to mention the fact of competition from CESGRANRIO. (Unfortunately, pre-1972 figures are unavailable for purposes of precise comparisons.)

Only 25 percent of the private colleges showed a substantial financial gain from the exam competition. However, representatives from several of these institutions told this researcher, angrily, that the figures reported to DAU should definitely not be construed as profits. The reason they gave was that these "profits" entailed no more than the redistribution of surplus income to the restricted categories outlined by the Federal Education Council.

Not wishing to create the impression that regulations dealing with inscription fees were coercive measures, Minister Passarinho offered monetary incentives to those private colleges which would accept his "invitation" to join unification in Greater Rio de Janeiro. In reality, this was to compensate them for lost inscription fees. Yet, the nuance of coercion, or at least sanctions, was present when the minister stated further that those institutions not cooperating with

TABLE 8.1

Income and Expenditures for Entrance Examinations of
Selected Private Higher Education Institutions
in Greater Rio de Janeiro, 1972
(in cruzeiros)

Institution	Income	Expenditures
Santa Úrsula University Association	143,760	38,523
Catholic University of Petrópolis	40,000	59,000
Hélio Alonso College of Communications	52,680	20,037
College of Philosophy, Science and Letters of Nova Iguaçu	96,480	96,480
College of Law, Estácio de Sá	510,000	126,900
College of Economics, Estácio de Sá	171,351	65,760
College of Political and Economic Sciences of Rio de Janeiro	181,180	32,400
College of Law of Campos	10,400	7,620
Dom Bosco Educational Association	10,100	3,875
College of Dentistry of Volta Redonda	24,120	24,120
College of Civil Engineering of Volta Redonda	21,840	21,140
School of Medical Sciences of Volta Redonda	94,800	94,800
College of Philosophy, Science and Letters of Volta Redonda	42,480	—
College of Dentistry of Nova Friburgo	19,558	19,080
College of Civil Engineering of Nova Iguaçu	34,750	46,440
Veiga de Almeida University Association	78,720	72,768
College of Medicine of Campos	24,974	83,160
Silva e Souza University Association	14,023	10,100
Souza Marques College of Philosophy	85,560	85,560
College of Dentistry of Campos	16,530	17,160
School of Physical Education of Volta Redonda	12,971	15,480
Roberto Lisboa College of Engineering	150,089	—
College of Philosophy, Science and Letters of Barra do Piraí	48,480	48,480
College of Civil Engineering of Barra do Piraí	54,120	54,120

Source: Department of University Affairs, Ministry of Education and Culture, Brasília, D.F., 1973.

THEORETICAL ANALYSIS 163

the MEC should not expect to have their requests for financial or technical assistance looked upon with great favor.

Actually, an invitation only would probably have achieved very little; for most private college administrators with whom this researcher spoke stated that the MEC had a poor track record for living up to its promises.

Did the MEC keep its word this time? Of the eighteen nonfederal institutions which had joined CESGRANRIO, nine received technical and financial assistance from the Department of University Affairs (see Table 8.2). It must be noted that the DAU disbursements were made in response to <u>specific requests</u> from higher education institutions. Therefore, any number of the ten nonfederal institutions which did not receive funds may or may not have solicited support from the federal government. In addition, there was no evidence that other government sources of assistance, direct or indirect, to private colleges in Greater Rio were curtailed.

Five nonfederal institutions which received no support from the DAU in 1971 did obtain funds in 1972. These institutions, however, along with the Souza Marques Technical Educational Foundation, did not receive <u>any</u> DAU support in 1973! When this observation was posed to DAU Director Sucupira he responded: "We never promised private institutions an equal sum of money to replace income lost from joining unification."[16] Equal compensation for income lost from inscription fees is one thing; a political ploy resulting in a break of faith is quite another. Nevertheless, the MEC had no binding obligation to compensate nonfederal institutions which joined unification.

In addition, the great success and popularity of the first CESGRANRIO experiment enticed participating institutions to stay and prompted many nonparticipating colleges to join. This, combined with the facts that Law 5,540 prohibited unreasonably difficult exams; that an inscription fee limit and conditions were imposed; and that unification reduced the time, effort, and costs of mounting an exam competition, prompted many nonfederal colleges and universities to join CESGRANRIO. These were clear indicators of the intentions and directions of federal educational policy.

In sum, the federal government did not hesitate to utilize both sanctions and rewards to prevent major readjustments of objectives to policies and was, thus, able to pursue its policy goals.

Reconstructive Treatment of Data

An additional feature of disjointed incrementalism is that in the course of exploring new data, problems are transformed, a shift in values occurs, and new policy proposals appear; this process, though, may commence with a shift in values.

TABLE 8.2

Technical and Financial Assistance from the Department of
University Affairs, Ministry of Education and Culture,
to Nonfederal Member Institutions of
CESGRANRIO, 1971-73
(in cruzeiros)

Institution	1971	1972	1973
Pontifical Catholic University of Rio de Janeiro	3,384,000	2,800,000	2,900,000
Catholic University of Petrópolis	940,000	940,000	1,000,000
Souza Marques Technical Educational Foundation	1,199,000	1,110,000	—
College of Medicine of Campos	338,400	338,000	400,000
Gama Filho University	—	300,000	—
Santa Úrsula University Association	—	100,000	—
College of Medicine of Petrópolis	—	100,000	—
State University of Guanabara	—	300,000	—
College of Medicine of Valença	—	100,000	—

Source: ASSEPLAN, Department of University Affairs, Ministry of Education and Culture, Brasília, D.F., 1973.

In the case of policy formation on access to higher education in Brazil, however, the reconstructive treatment of data was not a notable characteristic.

First, there was no significant shift in values among policy makers which served as a motivating force or consequence of policy development. While some of the philosophical positions of the three major education ministers under the military government (Moniz de Aragão, Dutra, and Passarinho) may have differed—they all shared the same values. Among these was the belief in the need for a more equitable system of access to higher education. Multiple inscriptions, excedentes, unfair tests, and exorbitant registration fees were all

THEORETICAL ANALYSIS

distortions which the education ministers believed needed correction. Unification of entrance examinations as a means of correcting these inequities in the system was a welcome innovation.

Second, the exploration of new data available did not actually transform the problems facing policy makers. Long before the military regime came to power, policy makers were cognizant of the historically-rooted structural and functional problems of access to higher education. Project studies, reports, and assessments merely confirmed the existence and seriousness of the problems of access.

Finally, the new policy proposals that emerged did not entail, in any sense, significant new departures; rather, they were incremental steps which, in fact, comprised a gradual progression and amplification of past efforts and experiences at reform.

Serial Analysis and Evaluation

That policy making proceeds by way of long chains of policy steps is a logical outgrowth of the theory of margin-dependent choice. As Braybrooke and Lindblom observe:

> The return of analysts, time after time, to approximately the same values at approximately the same margins of choice and to confrontation of the same analytical and evaluative problems in a highly familiar context, though perhaps implicit in the incremental and exploratory character of analysis, is sufficiently important to merit . . . emphasis. . . . [17]

The problem of access to higher education in Brazil is one that, most definitely, has been analyzed and evaluated serially. As previously stated, the formidable problems of selection, endemic to the Brazilian educational system, were by no means new. Piecemeal efforts were made to remedy the situation long before the military came to power in 1964. And although one would expect a centralized authoritarian regime to fully utilize its capabilities to make quantum leaps in dealing with certain problems—the Brazilian federal government did not do so.

The concept and application of unified college entrance examinations were not new ones, as we shall see in examining the next feature of the theory. Here, let us focus attention upon serial analysis and evaluation concerning the major thrusts of the government's efforts to reform the system of access to higher education. The sequences of policy development, as outlined in Chapter 7, would be sufficient confirmation of the fact that a long chain of incremental policy steps was taken to arrive at present policy situations and positions. Therefore, it will suffice to mention here only those sequences which were especially significant.

To begin with, the position paper issued by the Council of Rectors in October 1967 was of fundamental importance. Although very general in nature, it was exactly this aspect of the report which served as its major virtue and enhanced its credibility. It linked the issue of access to higher education to the issue of university reform and expansion; viewed the whole process as extremely significant to national development (a fundamental tenet of the military power structure); and asserted that the exame vestibular was the fulcrum of the entire machinery. The measures the Council of Rectors proposed with respect to secondary and higher education articulation, manpower factors, distribution of places, and testing and measurement procedures were later evaluated as key areas in which time, money, and effort should be spent.

The 1968 University Reform Law, the next major sequence in policy development, represented a fundamental move to gravitate from the general to the specific. Article 21 provided for the entrance exams to be uniform in content for all courses of study or core areas and unified within the same university or consortia of institutions.

As the situation concerning the excedentes worsened, concurrent with the deteriorating conditions regarding internal security, the government responded. The director of the Department of University Affairs, Newton Sucupira, devised an ingenious plan for abolishing the situation of the excedentes: making the exams classifying rather than eliminatory. As announced in October 1970, this was an incremental step of great consequence. The new grading system thus eliminated the phenomenon of excedentes and its legal definition.

During that same month, Minister Passarinho authorized the DAU to reach agreements with higher education institutions—public and private—to bring about the eventual unification of entrance exams by region. Previously, Decree-Law 464 (February 11, 1969) had recommended that institutions seek to unify their entrance examinations on their own volition.

In February 1971, Regulation no. 36 was issued, thereby creating CONVESU. The commission was assigned the task of furnishing a feasibility study on unification of the entrance exams, as well as the enactment of the measures proposed by the October 1967 Council of Rectors report. The March 1971 CONVESU report presented findings and specific recommendations of the commission, and it served as the basis for the July 1971 presidential decree regulating entrance examinations.

The embodiment of these reform measures was CESGRANRIO, created by Regulation no. 206 in October 1971. This was the culmination of the government's efforts to promulgate reform of the system of access to higher education. Through serial analysis and evaluation, policies were decided upon—including the cautious policy of lowering expectations and pursuing, instead, the modest goal of implementing CONVESU's recommendations in one region (Greater Rio), rather than running the risk of achieving only minimal success or failing miserably in multiple regions.

Subsequent regulations and pronouncements, such as Regulation no. 113 BSB (February 21, 1973), were exclusively concerned with solidifying and refining the enactments cited above.

Finally, it should be pointed out that the August 1971 law reforming primary and secondary education contained provisions which were intended to be compatible with the reform effort already underway on access to higher education. The law's section which required all secondary education to adopt a uniform, core curriculum was a logical and serial step towards attaining several of the objectives and goals set down by policy makers: improved articulation between secondary and higher education; uniformity in exam content; avoidance of unreasonably difficult tests; the eventual incorporation of aptitude tests in the exam competition; and the elimination of unequal opportunity to compete in the exam competition, due to the disparities in quality of secondary education. In addition, by sanctioning a professionalizing cycle of education, the law intended to deflect many students from higher education altogether.

Remedial Orientation of Analysis and Evaluation

Braybrooke and Lindblom maintain that the characteristics of the strategy support and encourage movement away from certain situations rather than movement toward specific goals. That is, the alleviation of a particular social evil instead of the pursuit of a better world.

The initial concerns of Brazilian educational policy makers were in accordance with these features of remedial orientation of analysis and evaluation. A grand design for reform, comprising goals toward which to move, was not the focus of attention. Instead, policy makers concentrated on moving _away_ from or alleviating specific problems which were becoming more acute: excedentes, multiple examination registration, and grossly unfair test questions.

However, this characteristic of the strategy of disjointed incrementalism would seem to describe only the initial phase of policy making on access to higher education. For thereafter, many indicators revealed that policy makers were apparently moving toward specific, well-defined goals and the attainment of stable and concrete long-term aspirations.

In actuality, policy makers did not deviate from an incremental strategy. One must not confuse <u>substance</u> of policy with the <u>flow</u> of policy formation. It is precisely this misinterpretation which may erroneously lead one to believe that Brazilian educational policy makers were pursuing a synoptic approach to problem solving, in which a blueprint was utilized to rationally and scientifically achieve "change," "reform," and "equality." The fact is that the piecemeal, serial, and remedial pursuit of circumscribed objectives and goals does not constantly govern the <u>speed</u> of policy formation.

In the case of access to higher education in Brazil, there were several factors which enabled policy makers to move briskly, although incrementally, in the direction of policy implementation.

To begin with, past experiences and practice with partially unified entrance examinations served as a guiding source for policy makers in their quest for a new system of access to higher education. The first significant crystallization of the idea of unified entrance exams came in 1963, in São Paulo, with the creation of CESCEM (Center for the Selection of Candidates to Schools of Medicine and Biology). However, it became apparent immediately that a more complex organization would be needed to administer CESCEM's tests and to undertake psychological and educational research as well. The need was filled in 1964 with the establishment of the Carlos Chagas Foundation. In 1965 the organization tested 2,465 candidates for admission to one of six medical colleges participating in the system; by 1973 this had grown to 16,007 candidates and 19 medical and medical-related institutions (federal and state, as well as private).[18]

From 1965 to 1966 Guanabara State was the site for an experiment with unified examinations in medicine. Greater Rio medical colleges (UFRJ, UEG, and the School of Medicine and Surgery) plus the Federal University of Juiz de Fora and the Federal University of Espirito Santo, in response to political pressures, sought to unify their examinations. However, Pedro Aleixo, a politician who briefly served as Minister of Education under Castelo Branco, took a number of actions which antagonized medical college professors. He granted permission to a great many medical school excedentes to enroll, used <u>pistõloes</u> (political privilege or "pull") to obtain medical school admission for the sons and daughters of friends, and created new medical colleges. The medical school interest groups eventually became so infuriated with this "demagoguery" that they pulled out of unification.[19]

Guanabara State, however, finally served as the site of a successful experiment in unification with the creation, in 1967, of CICE (Interscholastic Commission for the Qualifying Competition for Engineering Schools). Initially involving the Pontifical Catholic University of Rio de Janeiro and the Federal Fluminense University,

THEORETICAL ANALYSIS

CICE was the forerunner of CESGRANRIO; and its coordinator, Carlos Serpa, was also to become the head of the latter organization.

The year 1967 also saw further development in the concept of unified exams. A successful attempt was made to offer a unified exam competition in economics and administration in São Paulo. CESCEA, a center for such purposes, was created and is still functioning today. Also, initial success marked the experiment with unified exams in the medical schools in the State of Rio Grande do Sul. With assistance from the Chagas Foundation, GESA (Executive Group for the Selection of Students) brought together six medical schools in Rio Grande do Sul. Attempting to copy the Chagas Foundation's system of operations, GESA never succeeded in building its own structure. It relied too much upon professors, overworked them, and failed to pay them.[20] By 1972 GESA had become defunct.

It should be mentioned that the University of Brasília had a unified exam competition by subject matter area, including tests in general knowledge, expression, and aptitudes. The Federal University of Ceará followed these steps in 1969. Also that year, Mapofei was created in São Paulo. It was a selection center for candidates in engineering; however, unlike most organizations, its tests were not objective in structure.

Finally, in 1971, immediately preceding CESGRANRIO, the Federal Fluminense University offered an entrance exam competition in which one series of tests was used for admission to all academic programs.

As one can see, the roots of CESGRANRIO lie in the recent past. From these past endeavors, policy makers were able to draw upon a reservoir of information, avoid serious pitfalls, and direct their efforts towards the most promising strategy by which to confront the problem of access to higher education.

To continue, another factor which allowed and actually encouraged policy makers to swiftly move towards their goals was the nature of the Brazilian political system, along with the political climate at the time policy initiatives gained momentum.

In essence, a military regime, characterized by the centralization of authority, depoliticization, and a small and visible military-technocratic elite determining policy, faces far fewer restrictions and obstacles in formulating and implementing policy than do other systems of government. Consequently, it can move over a wider range of activities and at a faster pace. In the case of Brazil, this was further enhanced by the Fifth Institutional Act and subsequent repressive measures. With the congress having lost even its forum, the press under censorship, and dissent thoroughly stifled, the elite could move with confidence and alacrity towards achieving its objectives.

Nevertheless, it is essential to point out that power is never that monolithic; and in the Brazilian case, although centralization and authoritarianism indeed narrowed the locus of power, it in no way affected the practice of incrementalism.

Finally, in addition to the factors of past precedent and political authoritarianism, there is a third factor which hastened the flow of policy formation. Predetermined goals (which may even be considered a consequence of the first two factors) were a vital feature of policy development on access to higher education. From a careful scrutiny of government publications, newspaper articles, reports, written correspondence, conversations, and interviews, it became evident that many of the fundamental goals as well as specific objectives for reforming the system of access to higher education had been circulating several years before the creation of CONVESU and the presentation, and subsequent acceptance, of that commission's recommendations.

Particularly significant was the fact that the report of the Council of Rectors Seminar held in May 1969 issued conclusions written by Valnir Chagas and Rubens Maciel which were later plainly adopted by the Ministry of Education. The report contained specific recommendations which were in many ways identical to those espoused by CONVESU.[21]

In addition, article 4 of Decree-Law no. 464 (February 11, 1969) encouraged inter-institutional cooperation, preferably via public and private nonprofit foundations, for the purpose of offering joint entrance examinations. Also, the Commission on Educational Fees of the Federal Education Council was given the authority, by virtue of Decree-Law no. 532 (April 16, 1969), to regulate inscription fees.[22]

Going further back in time, one can find some of the seeds of reform in an essay written in 1962 by Valnir Chagas—an essay which later constituted Opinion no. 58/62 of the Federal Education Council. Chagas wrote that the basic cycle of university studies offered a sound way for higher education institutions to structure their entrance exams, since basic cycle studies—and, therefore, entrance exams— could be grouped by social sciences, biological sciences, and human sciences.[23] Even prior to this was the 1956 University Reform Law authored by Raimundo Moniz de Aragão.

It is interesting to note that Newton Sucupira chaired the May 1969 Rectors Seminar and was a member of the Federal Education Council when Opinion no. 58/62 was issued by that body.

In short, it seemed as if the Ministry of Education under Passarinho was following—although incrementally—a cautious plan for reforming the system of access to higher education. Goals and objectives were predetermined based upon earlier discussions and recommendations.

THEORETICAL ANALYSIS 171

In actuality what occurred was the crystallization of many of the ideas and plans which Valnir Chagas and Newton Sucupira had been advocating in the Federal Education Council from the time of the presidency of João Goulart. For Minister Passarinho, these were ideas which were compatible with political considerations and, therefore, ripe for picking.

These three factors, then—past precedent, political authoritarianism, and predetermined goals—prompted policy makers to move swiftly and confidently towards realizing their objectives and goals.

Social Fragmentation of Analysis and Evaluation

The eighth and last feature of Braybrooke and Lindblom's strategy is a problematic one for this study. They assert that analysis and evaluation occur at a great many points throughout society in a fragmented manner. Moreover, the lack of articulation and coordination among analysts denotes a "disjointed" process by which policy is formulated. Using the United States for reference purposes, Braybrooke and Lindblom state:

> A problem as many faceted as national security, for example, is under study in at least hundreds and perhaps in several thousand different centers—government agencies, universities, private organizations, committees, and other institutions. Furthermore, regarding certain notions about efficiency, each of many different approaches is taken simultaneously by dozens or hundreds of centers in imperfect communication with one another.[24]

In the case of Brazil, analysis and evaluation of the problem of access to higher education—and, for that matter, higher education in general—proceeded in just the opposite fashion! The MEC, largely through the Department of University Affairs and its auxiliary units, thoroughly dominated the analytical and evaluative functions.

There are three factors which, taken collectively, offer a rational explanation for this contradiction with the last characteristic of Braybrooke and Lindblom's strategy. First, the authoritarian political system restricts decentralized analysis and evaluation, preferring instead centralized control; moreover, it places constraints on the dissemination of official data. Second, as a developing nation Brazil does not possess the federal financial resources to support or subsidize a multitude of nonfederal centers, institutions, organizations, projects, and studies. Where the government has provided funds for nonfederal research and development, these have been in lifeblood, critical areas which bring a faster and greater economic return (for example, commerce, industry, natural resources exploration, commodities). Third, as noted in Chapter 4, centralized planning and other federalist features of the administrative state have been ever present since Vargas' Estado Nôvo. This obviated either the need or inclination to have the government "contract" work outside federal bureaucratic structures.

It would be erroneous to conclude that there is a major flaw in Braybrooke and Lindblom's theory—namely, that social fragmentation of analysis and evaluation are characteristic of politically open-economically developed nations rather than politically closed-economically less developed ones. True, the former countries (for example, U.S., Great Britain, France, West Germany) are more likely to manifest such a trait. And it is also true that the latter nations (for example, Cuba, North Vietnam, Uganda, Bolivia) are far more inclined not to display that feature. Nevertheless, such distinctions do not hold true in every case.*

There are politically closed-economically less developed countries such as Peru and Argentina where there is social fragmentation of analysis and evaluation. More importantly, to some extent Brazil may be considered one such country! For while it is correct that higher education policy does not fit the description, policy making in a number of other areas (for example, industry, natural resources, agriculture) as well as in other spheres of educational activity, such as adult and technical education, does, indeed.

Moreover, upon close scrutiny one could rightly argue that policy formation on access to higher education was, at least, fragmented to the extent that a number of groups outside the MEC's Department of University Affairs did play a part in its development: the Federal Education Council, Council of Rectors, CONVESU, CESGRANRIO, and the Carlos Chagas Foundation. In addition, secondary contributions were made by students, university professors, private colleges, and cursinhos.

Concerning disjointedness, however, policy formation on access to higher education in Brazil deviated significantly from the strategy. There was definitely a good deal of coordination and articulation among the groups and agencies mentioned above. Moreover, many

---

*One should not overlook countries which are politically open-economically less developed (e.g., Venezuela) and politically closed-economically developed (e.g., Spain) which analyze and evaluate policy in a socially fragmented manner.

of the key personalities involved in the analysis, formulation, and evaluation of policy had multiple roles. For example, Carlos Serpa was the head of both CONVESU and CESGRANRIO, vice-rector of a private university, and full professor.

The presence of an independent, pluralist system of public and private institutions engaged in data collection, analysis, and evaluation was definitely lacking.

Regardless of one's predilection for or abhorrence of disjointedness, what is clear is the fact that in elite political systems, such as Brazil, the rejection of disjointedness is a precarious course of action. For the absence of independent sources to analyze, evaluate, and criticize issues, problems, and actions can often result in a homogenized and sterile assessment of policy. Pitfalls and dangers at times cannot be anticipated; and innovation, experimentation, and sound contingency planning cannot proceed. What protected Brazil from these potential difficulties was the fact that access to higher education was an issue which had long been familiar to all: a number of alternatives had been previously explored and the consequences previously anticipated.

CESGRANRIO: SOME BEHAVIORAL OBSERVATIONS

A glimpse at the internal workings of CESGRANRIO will complement the theoretical analysis offered above and shed additional light on the politics of access to higher education in Brazil.

The structural and functional components of CESGRANRIO were well circumscribed and restricted. The DAU maintained strict control over the commission: it appointed Carlos Serpa as president, named the representatives of the initial member institutions, and selected the three coordinators of the sectoral commissions (COMBIMED, COMCITEC, COMSART).

The clear intention of the MEC was to create an organization to carry out CONVESU's policy recommendations for unifying entrance examinations. By naming Serpa, President of CONVESU, to head CESGRANRIO and structuring the concentration of power almost exclusively in the presidency and the sectoral commissions (the unit responsible for area exams and through which member institutions were obligated to participate)—the government assured the realization of its objectives. Therefore, with the power in the hands of Serpa and the three sectoral coordinators, CONVESU had little contact with CESGRANRIO after that organization was created.

If CONVESU was a policy-making body, CESGRANRIO was a decision-making body. Carlos Serpa shared but a small part of that power with the Directorate of member institutions. The Directorate was more of a forum than a decision-making body. Moreover, when CESGRANRIO was transformed from a government commission to a foundation, the statutes and bylaws preserved, and even amplified, the provisions for a strong president; in fact, the bylaws granted full rights in the Directorate for former presidents of the foundation!

It would seem that with major decisions having been made by CONVESU and delineated further by federal legislation (Regulation 413 BSB, May 1972, even states the number of tests and items), the Directorate would have been dissatisfied with its limited role. This, however, was not the case.

The members of the directorate collectively seemed to be quite content with their role: serving as a forum and deliberating on the technical and mechanical aspects of unification in Greater Rio. They clearly understood that the DAU and Serpa were in charge and were content to leave the administrative decisions to Serpa. (The first decisions, the major ones dealing with preoption, classification, and area tests, had been mandated.)

The meetings of the directorate were described by members as "harmonic," "democratic," and "open." Most members knew each other before, and they shared a common philosophy of education. With similar viewpoints on the issue of access to higher education, there was little divergence of opinion (no more than two or three alternatives were ever discussed). There was ample opportunity for long debates and discussions, and agreements were reached by consensus. Representatives of the member institutions usually confined their participation to subject areas in which they taught or with which they were familiar.

When queried as to the configuration of influence in the directorate, some members stated that there was no over representation of federal university influence; most, however, acknowledged that influence consisted of a combination of the university represented and the representative's personality, although it was hard to distinguish between university weight and personal weight. *

---

*It is interesting to note a science-technology-medicine preponderance of great magnitude among decision makers. To illustrate, at the time CESGRANRIO became a foundation there was only one member of the Directorate (Altair Gomes of UEG) whose field was not science, technology or medicine! Serpa and the three sectoral coordinators were all engineers or scientists. Furthermore, even in CONVESU the three major policy makers were all engineers or scientists.

THEORETICAL ANALYSIS 175

With regard to specific action, the directorate spent time on such matters as psychology's place in one of the three sectoral areas, scholarships for poor students who were admitted to private colleges but could not attend for financial reasons, test content and organization, pre-registration (which it believed should be conducted more smoothly), and problems of reclassification.

Members of the directorate, it should be noted, did not always support Professor Serpa. They vetoed a proposal to include in the bylaws a provision for granting voting rights in the Directorate to the three area coordinators; and they also rejected a motion to grant voting rights to institutions which were not founding members. Serpa supported both these minority proposals.

Moving to the executive and administrative levels of CESGRANRIO, it is essential to mention that Carlos Serpa thoroughly dominated CESGRANRIO: he was CESGRANRIO. With Newton Sucupira and the DAU fully behind him, he could boldly and swiftly implement decisions and dispatch directives. His power increased as CESGRANRIO changed from a commission to a foundation. Under the former arrangement, the agenda and chain of decisions and actions travelled from Minister Passarinho to Newton Sucupira to Carlos Serpa; with the latter arrangement, it went from Serpa to Sucupira—for review—and then to Passarinho.

Administratively, however, Serpa's monopoly on power, decisions, and actions yielded a number of negative consequences. Decision making was so centralized that Serpa's work load was tremendous. He was occupied with tasks which easily could have been delegated to subordinates; and when he was absent from CESGRANRIO headquarters, there was a crisis of authority and little work was accomplished.

Lapses in the administrative timetable of CESGRANRIO were the result of an overworked president and problems of communication and cooperation. A dedicated, bright, hard-working young man, Serpa's awesome responsibilities forced him to become increasingly inaccessible, to both his staff and individuals outside CESGRANRIO.

In defense of Carlos Serpa, it must be mentioned that he was, indeed, overwhelmed by work. In addition to serving as president of both CONVESU and CESGRANRIO, he was also vice-rector for development and professor of industrial and metallurgical engineering at the Pontifical Catholic University, and an engineering consultant. Furthermore, the DAU relied excessively upon him and frequently sent him to Brasília for consultation and to many parts of Brazil to advise educators on the unification of college entrance exams. As Serpa analyzed the evolution of his role: "The president of CESGRANRIO has become less and less an administrator and more and more a politician."[25]

Finally, CESGRANRIO's relations with several important external groups (cursinhos, nonparticipating colleges, and the press) deserve mention. First, the only cursinhos with which CESGRANRIO maintained significant contact were Curso Bahiense and Curso Miguel Couto. While Serpa did not like the cursinhos and viewed them as somewhat of a threat to the reform of secondary education, he did not actually despise them as did Newton Sucupira. Rather than eradicate them, Serpa believed they would eventually disappear once the problems which brought about their creation were solved. Furthermore, Carlos Serpa solicited scholarships from cursinhos for poor but academically promising high school students who wanted to go to college. Minister Passarinho retained a realistic attitude vis-a-vis the cursinhos and even invited several cursinho directors to attend the March 1973 International Symposium on Access to Higher Education.

The director of Curso Bahiense frankly stated that his relations with CESGRANRIO were "cool," but stressed that this was due to a personality conflict with CESGRANRIO's president. He further emphasized that students applauded CESGRANRIO's efforts and that criticism came only from the "misinformed."[26]

Victor Nótrica, director of Curso Miguel Couto, reiterated much of what Professor Bahiense had to say, with the exception that his cursinho had "excellent, although precarious, relations with the government" and good relations with CESGRANRIO (although he acknowledged it was virtually impossible to get to see Professor Serpa).[27] He revealed that the main reason he got along well with the federal government was that he lobbied and looked to them for advice. In addition, the director of Curso Miguel Couto had hired a public relations firm to deal with the MEC. (Nótrica wryly stated that Curso Bahiense did not need to go to this expense, since some of its staff were army colonels!)

Regarding private nonparticipating colleges, Carlos Serpa actively sought to bring them into the CESGRANRIO network through kindness and persistent persuasion. CESGRANRIO shared some of its technical information with several of these colleges before officially inviting them to join unification. These private schools decided to utilize much of CESGRANRIO's know-how but refrained from joining.

Many of the private nonparticipating colleges were large and financially successful, particularly the Estácio de Sá Integrated Colleges, Hélio Alonso College, and Cândido Mendes College. Some private colleges had special reasons for not joining unification. The Superintendent of Instruction of SUESC, Lourival Pinto Cordeiro, asserted that his institution was founded to serve the needs of poor students, and that the May 1973 exame vestibular yielded CR$123,000 for scholarships.[28] He believed that CESGRANRIO was good for public

THEORETICAL ANALYSIS

institutions and for private colleges with less than 1,500 freshman applicants (the minimum number needed, in his opinion, for an exam competition to be profitable).

The unanimous opinion of private nonparticipating colleges was summed up by João Uchôa Cavalcanti of the Estácio de Sá Integrated Colleges. He asserted that besides a loss in inscription fees, there was a high probability that private colleges would get stuck with both poor quality students and students who would be totally or partially dependent on the college for financial aid. Furthermore, according to him, the pre-option and reclassification systems would bring many discontented students to private colleges; and he added, "We don't want students who don't want us!"[29] When asked under what conditions he would join CESGRANRIO, he said: if CESGRANRIO were not CESGRANRIO and Estácio de Sá were not Estácio de Sá.

It is important to note that the movement of Souza Marques College, the Bennett Integrated Colleges, and other private colleges participating in CESGRANRIO to seriously consider leaving the organization can be attributed to most of the reasons outlined by Professor Cavalcanti. Both Joel Sanches of Bennett and Tito Urbano Silveira of Souza Marques confirmed that the classification of candidates not really desiring admission to their respective colleges was a prime consideration in contemplating withdrawal.[30] Also, in the case of Souza Marques College, an institution which had received a great deal of financial assistance from former Minister of Education Tarso Dutra, the college did not obtain any DAU support whatsoever in 1973. This, combined with the fact that Professor Souza Marques, the elderly president of the college, was apparently losing his mental faculties and prone to erratic behavior, most likely had something to do with the institution's decision, as well.

The next question is: Did CESGRANRIO or the Ministry of Education use any means other than persuasion and financial sanctions to encourage private colleges to join unification? Although this was initially difficult to determine, it was discovered that the federal government did, in fact, take subtle steps to coerce some private colleges to join CESGRANRIO. MEC inspectors would continually harass these colleges by inspecting physical facilities, administrative and financial systems, academic programs, and so on. At times they would inspect a college's building construction and plumbing several times in one week. One private college administrator remarked that the MEC wished to instill in them the fear that they could be closed down any minute. To illustrate, the Nuno Lisboa University Association rejected an invitation to join CESGRANRIO. In June 1973, shortly after the inauguration of new facilities—a library, classrooms, laboratories, and pavillion—the MEC revoked Nuno Lisboa's right to hold college entrance examinations.[31] This may have been more than coincidence.

Instead of banding together to confront intimidation from the MEC, private colleges fortified themselves behind their own bastions and engaged in furious competition with each other. By undercutting one another, they believed they could prevent being "swallowed up" by the DAU. Skepticism, fear, and anxiety did, indeed, grip many private nonparticipating colleges.

Concerning the last group, the press, one should be aware of the fact that the news media were practically the only link between CESGRANRIO and the public. Moreover, newspapers had somewhat more freedom in reporting and editorializing on educational concerns than on other matters.

The press unanimously asserted that they had poor access to CESGRANRIO and that the organization put up barriers to the news media. Serpa, according to them, monopolized all information; and neither the area coordinators nor anyone else in CESGRANRIO dispensed information without first gaining the approval of Serpa or his press aide. Journalists claimed that not only was Professor Serpa very inaccessible, but, more crucially, that the press aide provided the greatest obstacles for the media.

The newspapers acknowledged that CESGRANRIO was newsworthy mainly because access to higher education was a prime news issue, and that there was a large increase in circulation at the time of the entrance examination competition. The editorial policy of the newspapers regarding CESGRANRIO did not vary significantly. O Globo, the most pro-government Rio daily, only reported the news, believing that if they took a position regarding CESGRANRIO they would not receive the information they wanted. The Jornal do Brasil mostly reflected a variant of government policy. Serpa, however, once accused one of the Jornal do Brasil's reporters of accepting money to write bad copy on CESGRANRIO.

The Jornal dos Sports was the most independent and critical of the Rio newspapers. Its criticism, however, was confined to the philosophical aspects of college entrance exams as conducted by CESGRANRIO. Editors of that newspaper were aware that if they touched on the political aspects of CESGRANRIO, they would get in trouble. The Jornal dos Sports, because of its independence, resourceful, and determined reporting, and its wide readership among high school and university students, was the newspaper which CESGRANRIO was most concerned about, and at times fearful. Its newspaper editor once accused Carlos Serpa's office of having given results of CESGRANRIO's tests to O Globo four hours before the information was divulged to other newspapers. Finally, all the newspapers understood that CESGRANRIO was a political vehicle for Carlos Serpa.

What was CESGRANRIO's evaluation of its relations with the press? According to Professor Serpa, the press was very accessible and his organization had "excellent relations" with the press. The media were always hungry for news and kept a careful watch on CESGRANRIO's activities.

Serpa, however, accused the press of trying to influence his organization. He went on to say that the press insisted on finding out about activities that were still in the planning stage; when CESGRANRIO refused to divulge these plans, the newspapers considered this as being "uncooperative." Nevertheless, he candidly admitted that in 1972 the secretariat of CESGRANRIO mistakenly often blocked information to the press out of fear.[32]

CESGRANRIO acknowledged that media coverage was definitely in its interest—regardless of what the press reported about their organization. It was believed that publicity—even adverse publicity—would lead to visibility and respectability for CESGRANRIO. And this was a prime objective of federal policy.

NOTES

1. Encyclopedia of Social Science, vol. 7, s.v. "Revolution and Counterrevolution," by Alfred Meusel, p. 367.
2. A Dictionary of the Social Sciences, 1964 ed., s.v. "Revolution," by J.S. Erös, p. 602.
3. Robert Hunter, Revolution: Why, How, When? (New York: Harper, 1940), p. x.
4. Robert Daland, "The Paradox of Planning," in Contemporary Brazil: Issues in Economic and Political Development, eds. H. Jon Rosenbaum and William G. Tyler (New York: Praeger, 1972), p. 31.
5. Chalmers Johnson, Revolution and the Social System (Palo Alto: Hoover Institute of War, Revolution, and Peace, Stanford University, 1964) pp. 49-50.
6. Agnes Toward, "Education: Brazil," in Handbook of Latin American Studies, no. 33, ed. Donald E.J. Stewart (Gainesville: University of Florida Press, 1971), p. 282.
7. Jornal do Brasil, 9 May 1973.
8. Interviews with Minister of Education Jarbas Passarinho, Brasília, 19 June 1973; and Professor Newton Sucupira, former Director, Department of University Affairs, Brasília, 18 June 1973.
9. Interview with Minister of Education Jarbas Passarinho, Brasília, 19 June 1973.
10. Interview with Newton Sucupira, Brasília, 18 June 1973.
11. Interview with Newton Sucupira.
12. Interview with Professor Manoel Luiz Leão, Pôrto Alegre, 4 May 1973.

13. O Globo, "Professôres apóiam Passarinho contra o vestibular uno em 74," 22 December 1972.
14. Jornal do Brasil, "Decisao politíca da integração pode ser tomada em 73," 31 December 1972.
15. O Globo, 22 December 1972.
16. Interview with Newton Sucupira, Brasília, 18 June 1973.
17. David Braybrooke and Charles E. Lindblom, A Strategy of Decision (New York: Free Press, 1963), p. 100.
18. Adolpho Ribeiro Netto, A Fundação Carlos Chagas: Seleção para a Universidade e Pesquisa para a Educacao (Sao Paulo: Fundação Carlos Chagas, 1973.
19. Interview with Professor Bruno Alipio Lobo, Rio de Janeiro, 6 July 1973.
20. Interview with Professor Manoel Luiz Leão, Pôrto Alegre, 4 May 1973.
21. Carlos Alberto Serpa de Oliveira, Simpósio para Avaliação de Reforma nas Universidades Brasileiras: Concurso Vestibular (Rio de Janeiro: Pontificia Universidade Catóĺica do Rio de Janeiro, 1971), pp. 25-28.
22. Ibid., pp. 30; 48.
23. Valnir Chagas, "A admissão à universidade e a Lei de Diretrizes e Bases," Revista Brasileira de Estudos Pedagógicos 37 (January-March 1962): 8-18.
24. Braybrooke and Lindblom, A Strategy of Decision, pp. 104-05.
25. Interview with Professor Carlos Alberto Serpa de Oliveira, President, CONVESU and CESGRANRIO, Rio de Janeiro, 23 July 1973.
26. Interview with Norbertino Bahiense Filho, Rio de Janeiro, 16 June 1973.
27. Interview with Victor Mauricio Nótrica, Director, Curso Miguel Couto, Rio de Janeiro, 16 June 1973.
28. Interview with Lourival Pinto Cordeiro, Superintendent of Instruction, SUESC, Rio de Janeiro, 25 June 1973.
29. Veja, 10 January 1973; interview with Professor João Uchôa Cavalcanti, Director, Estácio de Sá Integrated Colleges, Rio de Janeiro, 22 June 1973.
30. Interview with Professor Joel Sanches, Dean of Instruction, Bennett Integrated Colleges, Rio de Janeiro, 25 June 1973; interview with Professor Tito Urbano Silveira, Dean, School of Engineering, Souza Marques Technical Educational Foundation, Rio de Janeiro, 5 June 1973.
31. Diário de Notícias, 6 June 1973. The DAU contended that Nuno Lisboa had violated the law by offering more freshman places than it was allowed. Technically, this was not true.
32. Interview with Professor Carlos Alberto Serpa, Rio de Janeiro, 23 July 1973.

CHAPTER 9

CONCLUSION

As stated in the Preface, the primary concern and major focus of the study cover the formative years 1964-73. In actuality, that period was the most important and critical one for higher education policy formation. Consequently, the sequence of policy development elucidated and the analysis presented in preceding chapters were confined to the aforementioned time frame.

The conclusions presented here are based on events and developments which occurred during the period 1964-73; although, an epilogue covering 1974 and 1975 is incorporated in this chapter to update information on educational policy and illuminate the expressed conclusions.

The author emphatically states, however, that as of mid-1976 nothing has occurred pertaining to access to higher education in Brazil which would refute or seriously challenge the major theoretical or educational conclusions of the study.

The major findings of the study may be classified under two headings: theoretical, and educational. These categories serve as convenient reference points for interpreting the results of the research.

THEORETICAL FINDINGS

In assessing the applicability of disjointed incrementalism towards explaining the process of policy formation and its outputs, it can clearly be seen that the theory should be neither wholly accepted nor totally rejected. Basically, what does one find at each of the eight stages of the strategy?

The first four stages (or more precisely, features) of the theory explain very well policy formation on access to higher education. First, it is revealed that margin-dependent choice is a reflection of the following: the political characteristics of the regime (ideologically conservative-politically authoritarian); and higher education's traditionally elitist role and its historically low status as a federal priority. The second feature, restricted variety of policy alternatives, is a consequence of the inertia of the federal bureaucracy as well as the complex and formidable nature of the problems of access to higher education. The third feature, the restricted variety of policy consequences, coincides with the behavioral characteristics of the central policy-making groups—cautious, rational, managerial, and pragmatic. In addition, since the problem was not a new one, most consequences were either known or anticipated. Furthermore, the authoritarian powers of the regime insulated the Ministry of Education and Culture from strong reaction from disenchanted individuals and groups. The fourth feature, adjustment of objectives to policies, is an integral part of the policy-making process. The awesome task of reforming the system of access to higher education, due to many deep-rooted obstacles (combined with the limitations of time in initiating change) forced policy makers to adjust their objectives and goals to the means available. As Braybrooke and Lindblom state, however, the ends-means relationship is reciprocal. And it was shown that the federal government did find the means to vigorously pursue certain policy goals by exerting leverage, via regulation of inscription fees and limitations on its uses and financial sanctions.

The fifth characteristic, reconstructive treatment of data, is not, however, a notable aspect of policy formation on access to higher education. First, there was no significant shift in values among policy makers. Second, since the educational problem facing the policy makers were familiar ones—and ones for which a number of remedies had been tried—there was no notable transformation of the general problem nor promulgation of radically new policy proposals.

However, for this second reason—the formidable problems of selection—policy making most definitely adheres to the sixth feature of disjointed incrementalism, serial analysis and evaluation. Piecemeal, serial steps were taken by the federal government to reform the system of access to higher education.

It would appear that remedial orientation of analysis and evaluation, the seventh feature, accurately describes only the initial phase of reform. The fact is, however, that policy makers did not deviate from an incremental strategy. True, the factors of past precedent, political authoritarianism, and predetermined goals, enabled policy makers to move swiftly and undauntedly towards implementing goal-oriented decisions. But these pertained to the flow of policy formation, not the substance or shaping of policy.

CONCLUSION

The eighth and final characteristic of the theory, social fragmentation of analysis and evaluation, is only partially useful in explaining policy formation on access to higher education. Due to centralized control (stemming from political and bureaucratic considerations) and limited financial resources (most acute in developing nations), analysis and evaluation were not disjointed and not entirely fragmented.

Lack of disjointedness poses a potentially serious problem for policy makers: without independent sources of analysis, evaluation, and criticism, there is the definite possibility that obstacles, setbacks, and dangers will be neither anticipated nor resolved swiftly and smoothly. The safeguard in the case of Brazil, of course, was the fact that the policy issue (access to higher education) involved a traditional problem—one for which many alternatives, efforts, and consequences had already been anticipated. As for fragmentation, this did occur, however, under the umbrella of federal agencies or federally-related groups and institutions.

Nevertheless, it was noted that policy making in other spheres and in other areas of education does, in fact, adhere to this feature of Braybrooke and Lindblom's theory.

It may be generally concluded that, for the most part, disjointed incrementalism is a useful theoretical framework for public policy analysis on education. Its limitations in the analysis of access to higher education in Brazil are due to the nature of the political and bureaucratic systems, the homogeneous characteristics of the policy-making elite, and the fact that policy makers had long been familiar with the issue at hand.

EDUCATIONAL FINDINGS

The educational findings of the study may be grouped as follows: technical; institutional; and socioeconomic. They summarize the positive accomplishments of government policy actions, negative aspects of these initiatives, and tasks which are yet to be completed.

First, with respect to the technical findings, the change from an eliminatory to a classifying examination system has done away with excedentes and made the process of selection more just. The simultaneity of the exam competition has improved a candidate's chances for selection by permitting multiple applications to college via a single series of tests.

Objective tests and the standardization of test scores have brought administrative conveniences to those responsible for the tests. The tests have alleviated the dispute over test grading and the controversy concerning political favoritism; at the same time, they have brought about an improvement in the quality of test items. A critical need has emerged, however, for specialists in testing and measurement—one which Brazil is having difficulty meeting.

The distribution of handbooks on careers, dispensing of testing information, and use of media campaigns have been positive steps towards alleviating the anxiety, tension, and misinformation which have traditionally surrounded the exam competition. Moreover, this has helped fill the gap in guidance information which secondary education still is not equipped to provide students.

Grouping the exams by three areas (biomedical sciences; science and technology; and arts, humanities, and social sciences) was administratively convenient. But more importantly, it provided educational policy makers with the means to unify, at some future time, college entrance exams based exclusively on the core curriculum of secondary education. This would supposedly shatter the importance of the cursinhos, and they would disappear. On the other hand, arbitrary assignment of major subjects to one of the three test areas was not particularly rational. (Recall the controversy centering on where psychology rightfully belonged.)

The pre-option system of classification has provided the candidate with two career choices and many institutional choices. While it has selected the most interested candidates, however, it has not always selected the most able ones.* Furthermore, it has limited a candidate's choices to only one of the three subject matter areas. Finally, the career pre-options are inconsistent with the basic cycle of university studies: the former requires career decisions before enrollment; the latter expects career decisions to be made after a year of general education. Taken together, they could conceivably create a system of internal excedentes at the time the student begins study in his major area.

Second, with regard to institutional findings, public higher education, for the most part, has been satisfied with the unified examination system, because of the administrative conveniences and the economy of time and energy which unification has brought. While the secondary education community has been antagonistic towards the higher education establishment, it has, indeed, been pleased that the government has encouraged colleges and universities to follow

---

*As already stated, for careers in which the number of candidates has been less than the number of freshman places available, candidates have been able to gain admission simply by not making a zero on any test in the examination series.

CONCLUSION

CESGRANRIO's example in employing secondary schoolteachers as reviewers in test construction for the exam competition.

Reform and unification of the college entrance examinations have signified a lesser role for the cursinhos; in order to survive financially, a number of cursinhos have begun to merge, and some have even purchased private high schools.

With respect to private colleges, government-mandated unification has exacerbated the already keen competition among them. For a number of these institutions, it has been a matter of survival. Private institutions have been very reluctant to join the unified exam system, believing that the probability of receiving many poor students and less able students would increase considerably. Another serious reservation they have had about participating in a unified exam system is that in the classification process small private colleges whose purpose, almost exclusively, has been to meet the needs of local residents would be saturated with a cosmopolitan student body at the expense of local candidates. This would be especially acute among rural colleges of medicine, engineering, architecture, and other prestigious areas of professional study.

The third group, the socioeconomic aspects of education, also manifests mixed findings. It was found that education determines income, and higher education yields particularly high benefits. To candidates—most of whom are from the middle and upper classes—social prestige has been more important than the economic rewards of a particular career. The simultaneity of entrance exams in public institutions has aided the government in achieving a more accurate accounting of the demand for higher education. Free tuition, however, encourages high enrollment; and despite federal efforts to bring supply and demand into closer equilibrium, the lag between the two is still great.

A noble effort has been made, at least, with the enactment of the 1971 Primary and Secondary Education Reform Law. The "professionalizing" provision of the law requires that every high school student graduate with some vocational-technical training. Should the high school graduate not classify for higher education, he would at least have a marketable skill.

Poor students have, indeed, benefitted from the inscription fee limit and the simultaneity of exams. For a flat fee, they have two career choices and can apply for admission to study at a multitude of institutions. Nevertheless, scholarships are few and modest in amount; and the high tuition and full-time study requirement for certain professional programs (engineering, medicine, architecture, dentistry) at private institutions are tremendous barriers to poor students.

This study leads to a number of conclusions of far-reaching importance concerning the contemporary development of education in Brazil and the system of access to higher education. These are as follows:

1. Selection for higher education continues to be economic in nature: access to higher education is, for the most part, a middle-class phenomenon. Candidates from the higher income families have the highest passing rate on the college entrance examinations. For the children of the poor, selection for higher education begins long before the entrance exam competitions: the shortage of places in public schools, along with the expensive cursinhos, present formidable financial obstacles for lower income groups. While the political and technical decisions made have done much to bring about a more equitable system of access, they have not brought about a more equal one.

2. Articulation between secondary and higher education is slowly improving due to the 1971 Primary and Secondary Education Reform Law. By testing candidates for admission on the core curriculum of secondary education, legitimacy and credibility are thus given to this level of schooling. Also, by providing high school students with a "professionalizing" cycle of studies, the government hopes to offer an alternative to higher education—namely, work—for those who do not really want to continue their studies; and for those who fail to gain admission to the university, it gives them marketable skills geared to national manpower requirements. While these secondary education reforms have been praised by many technocrats and proponents of secondary education,[1] others believe the professionalizing component is unachievable due to the high cost of installing machine shops, laboratories, and other technical facilities for secondary education institutions.[2]

3. The economic aspects of access to higher education (particularly manpower considerations) have been of special importance to the government. The thrust of the federal government's higher education reform efforts has been shifting from quantitative concerns to qualitative ones.* Higher education expansion has occurred largely in the private sector. Expansion in public institutions has taken place in less costly areas of study such as law, philosophy, and arts and

---

*The skeptics and critics of federal policy assert that, in the lexicon of the government, "quality" is a euphemism for a lack of interest in expanding higher education.

CONCLUSION

letters. Yet, these are the very fields in which the labor market is already saturated!

4. Although there has not been a radical transformation of the system of access to higher education in Brazil, the federal government has, nevertheless, made a number of incremental changes which collectively mark the beginning of fundamental progress. This is especially impressive when one considers the awesome and complex educational problems it inherited.

5. The federal government has chosen to reform the system of access to higher education via the exame vestibular. Today, the college entrance exams still remain the exclusive means by which candidates are selected for admission to higher education. It has been decided that unification of college entrance examinations will proceed on a regional basis with the federal government closely monitoring the process[3]—in essence, centralization with decentralized nuclei.

6. The most notable educational, administrative, and technical achievements made in the reform and regional unification of the college entrance exams have occurred in the area of Greater Rio de Janeiro. The CESGRANRIO Foundation has been the exclusive vehicle for this progress. Although it has been a greater quantitative rather than qualitative success, when compared with the privately-sponsored Carlos Chagas Foundation in São Paulo—it is, however, the model which the government has chosen for the regional unification of college entrance exams.

7. For a truly unified network of college entrance exams to exist, private higher education must be brought into the system. Many private colleges are reluctant to join, and several of those which have joined unification are having their misgivings.

8. Brazil is heading towards an entrance examination system similar to that of the United States. The CESGRANRIO Foundation intends to complement its subject matter tests (that is, achievement tests) with aptitude tests, develop a data bank of test items, and continually strive to scientifically refine testing procedures and measurement devices.*

EPILOGUE

While no major changes have occurred in access policy since late 1973, there have been a number of developments that merit attention.

---

*Its research department maintains contact with and seeks advice from the Educational Testing Service (ETS) in Princeton,

1974

The 1974 unified college entrance examination competition in Greater Rio de Janeiro witnessed 66,048 candidates competing for 20,918 places. The programs in most demand were medicine, engineering and business administration; in least demand were communications, social sciences, home economics, and general science.

CESGRANRIO, for the first time, administered a pre-test to randomly selected candidates for the 1974 exams. The tests were designed to measure verbal, mathematical, and abstract ability, and the results would be compared later with the selected candidates' university performance. CESGRANRIO also set up a Commission on Secondary Education to work more closely with secondary schools to disseminate and clarify information on unified entrance examinations in Greater Rio de Janeiro. Financially, CESGRANRIO netted CR$3 million from the 1974 exam competition. The surplus was spent on books, materials, equipment, and other examination-related items— most notably, a CR$250,000 rotating scholarship fund.

Discontent among participating private colleges increased during 1974. They complained that in spite of membership in CESGRANRIO, they received little or no financial support from the federal government. In addition, the vast majority of these private colleges were "affiliated" institutions: they were not founding members of CESGRANRIO and, according to the statutes and bylaws, were not extended an equal role in governing the organization. Consequently, they complained that they had no real voice in CESGRANRIO—in spite of the fact that they comprised 32 of the 43 participating institutions in that organization.

In a somewhat related development, a group of private colleges in Rio de Janeiro announced in November that they planned to hold their own joint examination competition. They criticized Carlos Serpa for pressuring colleges to join CESGRANRIO and acting as if he were the Minister of Education.* In addition, they criticized Serpa's dual role as head of both CESGRANRIO and CONVESU: how, they argued, could a member institution lodge a complaint to CONVESU against CESGRANRIO and expect satisfaction?

New Jersey. Richard S. Levine, late Vice President, Educational Testing Service, Princeton, New Jersey, 22 April 1974, personal letter.

*It is interesting to note that the 1975 entrance exam registration fee was CR$161 for CESGRANRIO's unified competition while nonparticipating (private) colleges were prohibited from charging more than CR$150.

CONCLUSION

As for the examinations, CESGRANRIO announced in mid-1974 that in the 1975 competition COMBIMED, COMCITEC, and COMSART would all offer tests on the same subjects; however, the physics, mathematics, chemistry, and biology material would be different for COMSART. Many students opposed this planned change, claiming it required an "encyclopedic knowledge" from each candidate. Most students strongly preferred to be tested only on those subjects related to their intended major.

There were several federal initiatives pertaining to college entrance examinations. To begin with, a presidential decree was issued authorizing the award of bonus points on the entrance exams to certain groups of candidates: 10 percentage points for those who have successfully completed the professionalizing cycle of secondary education, and 3 percentage points for others with demonstrable technical proficiency.

In late 1974, Minister of Education Ney Braga authorized the use of essay tests in entrance exam competitions. This pleased the University of São Paulo, O Estado de São Paulo, and other institutions and groups which had constantly complained about the growing number of poorly qualified students who were being admitted to higher education. Ney Braga's announcement and its wide acclaim in São Paulo prompted speculation among many that the real motive behind the minister's action was to build a larger, more powerful base to support his aspirations for a higher political office.

The minister of education also permitted aptitude tests as part of the college entrance exams. The aptitude tests, however, would be administered before the regular exam competition; they would be given only to candidates for admission to programs in music, architecture, plastic arts, and physical education; and the grades would not be included in the computation of the candidates' entrance exam scores. The purpose of these tests was to provide a candidate with an assessment of his aptitude for a particular career prior to the actual entrance examinations. Consequently, if the candidate did poorly on the aptitude test, he would have sufficient time to select another career option before the entrance exams began.

It became quite apparent during 1974 that if CESGRANRIO and the federal government wanted to bring about the demise of the cursinhos, many of their actions were producing just the opposite effect. By requiring more and more of candidates (that is, in terms of subjects and material) and initiating yearly changes (although small ones) in the examination competition, students were forced to place even greater reliance upon the cursinhos.

1975

Nationally 897,022 candidates competed for 388,000 freshman places in colleges and universities. Interestingly, the number of freshman places was equal to the number of 1974 secondary school graduates.

In Greater Rio de Janeiro, CESGRANRIO registered 75,348 candidates for an exam competition offering 22,658 places. The areas of study in most demand were medicine and physical education (male and female). In least demand were education, communications, music, and meteorology. No essay questions or special tests were used as part of the examination series; all candidates were tested on the same subjects.

While unified examinations were working well in Greater Rio de Janeiro, the same could not be said of São Paulo. Regional unification in that state was beset by many problems, especially the dislocation of rural candidates from local colleges of medicine, engineering, and other high demand fields by urban candidates who generally score higher on entrance exams. Consequently, a statewide exam unification plan was scrapped.

During most of 1975, the federal government focused its attention on higher education, in general, rather than college entrance examinations and access policy, in particular. The government was deeply concerned about what it considered to be an overexpansion of colleges and universities and a simultaneous decline in the quality of higher education. Isolated colleges were viewed as the principal culprits, and the federal government sought to control the expansion of these institutions. In the words of DAU Director Edson Machado: "A bad university is better than a good isolated college."[4]

For the federal government, improving the quality of faculty and instruction in higher education, not to mention primary and secondary schooling, was far more important than improving the college entrance examinations.

In other developments, the Eighth Seminar of University Affairs was held in Brasília during the first week in May. At that meeting, Padre Vasconcellos of the Federal Education Council spoke to the participants arguing that the classifying system of entrance examinations does not legally prohibit that candidates be required to display a minimum level of understanding of the subject matter on the exams. Vasconcellos advocated the adoption of a dual system of examinations: classifying and eliminatory. His recommendation, while endorsed by such institutions as the University of São Paulo, was not supported by the federal government.

Padre Vasconcellos' idea for resurrecting eliminatory exams was not without foundation. A study issued in June reported that had

CONCLUSION

the 1975 CESGRANRIO entrance exams been eliminatory, only 10 percent of the available freshman places would have been filled![5]

During the last months of 1975, attention turned to final preparations for the 1976 entrance examination competition. It was revealed that less freshman places would be available in medicine, law, engineering, economics, and business administration. This was due to the departure of several isolated institutions from the CESGRANRIO network. These colleges decided that they wanted to use the exam registration fees for their own projects and programs. Consequently, 95,000 candidates planned to compete for 21,573 freshman vacancies— a loss of 1,085 places. Thirty-nine institutions offering 51 programs were scheduled to participate in the 1976 unified exam competition in Greater Rio de Janeiro. Tests on the same subjects for all three areas were retained for 1976, and career options in more than one area were permitted.*

Finally, responding to a critical need, the Ministry of Education and Culture announced late in 1975 that the National Monetary Council would approve an educational loan program (in excess of CR$10,800,000) to benefit between thirty and forty thousand low income students.† A significant number of Brazilian students could not afford the costs of a higher education—be they the direct educational costs of study; room, board, and maintenance; or foregone earnings. It seemed that certain socially conscious federal policy makers recognized that fact and, consequently, an incremental step was taken to increase educational opportunity.

The question was posed in Chapter 1: Can a nation with a traditional educational system depart from past policy practices and initiate reforms commensurate with the exigencies of a modern society?

Although the forces of history, tradition, and custom do circumscribe the scope, intensity, and speed of reform policies and actions, the federal government possesses the fervent belief and the indomitable will to transform Brazil into a developed nation and, eventually, a world power. The centralization of bureaucracy and virtually unlimited executive power aid considerably in introducing and sustaining certain modernizing measures.

---

*An analysis of the 1975 CESGRANRIO Examinations revealed that candidates taking the same tests scored about the same, regardless of their area (COMBIMED, COMCITEC, COMSART).

†The student loan would be reimbursable beginning one year after completion of the course of study, payable in installments over a period equal to the time spent studying.

Yes, Brazil can, indeed, initiate reforms appropriate for the needs of a modern society. This process will most likely occur gradually, through a series of incremental changes.

What remains to be seen is the following: the extent to which the moral values of the political system, policy makers, and society, in general, must change in order for Brazil to become a truly modern nation, as equated with the developed countries of the West; and whether or not Brazil has the capacity to make such a change, by means of reforms in educational policy as well as in other areas of social, economic, political, and cultural concern.

These are important questions for other social scientists to deal with.

NOTES

1. Interview with Cláudio de Moura Castro, Institute of Economic and Social Planning (IPEA), Ministry of Planning and General Coordination, Rio de Janeiro, 12 October 1972.
2. Interview with Deputy Carlos Flexa Ribeiro, Chairman, Education Committee, Federal Chamber of Deputies, Rio de Janeiro, 26 June 1973.
3. Roberto Figueira Santos, "Avaliação da Implantação da Reforma Universitária," II Encontro de Reitores das Universidades Públicas e Directores de Estabelecimentos Públicos Isolados de Ensino Superior (Brasília: Ministério de Educação e Cultura, 1973).
4. Jornal do Brasil, 1 January 1975.
5. O Globo, 14 June 1975.

APPENDIX A

GLOSSARY OF EDUCATIONAL TERMS

áreas de conhecimento: subject matter areas (for example, history, chemistry).

AUSU: Santa Úrsula University Association, a private university in Rio de Janeiro.

banca examinadora: examining board, the educational specialists who construct the tests for the college entrance exams.

"caixeiro viajante": "traveling salesman"; term used to describe candidates (usually of means) who would take several entrance exams around the same time in the same city, other cities, or even in other states.

catedrático: full-professor rank, replaced in 1969 and renamed professor titular; the catedráticos had the power and prestige of an academician who holds an endowed chair.

CBPE: Brazilian Center for Educational Research, part of the National Institute of Pedagogical Studies—the research arm of the Ministry of Education.

CESCEA: a unified entrance examination system followed by some colleges in São Paulo for admission to programs in human sciences, economics, and administration.

CESCEM: a unified entrance examination system followed by some colleges in São Paulo for admission to study in medicine and biological sciences.

CESGRANRIO: a unified entrance examination system followed by the majority of colleges and universities in Greater Rio de Janeiro for admission to programs in arts and letters, science, technology, and biomedical sciences.

CICE: a unified entrance examination system followed by schools of engineering in Rio de Janeiro before the creation of CESGRANRIO.

ciclo básico: basic cycle of one or two years of general education on the post-secondary level.

classificatório: entrance examinations which select candidates in ranking order of their test scores.

colégio: high school.

COMBIMED: Sectoral Commission for the Biomedical Area (CESGRANRIO).

COMCITEC: Sectoral Commission for the Technological Area (CESGRANRIO).
COMSART: Sectoral Commission for the Areas of Human Sciences, Social Sciences, Arts and Letters (CESGRANRIO).
Conselho Federal de Educação: Federal Education Council.
Conselho de Reitores: Council of Rectors of Brazilian Universities.
CONVESU: National Commission on Unified College Entrance Examinations.
cursinho: privately owned and operated preparatory courses for college entrance examinations.
curso: major course of study.
DAU: Department of University Affairs, Ministry of Education and Culture.
director: division director; dean; department chairman.
eliminatório: entrance exams which use an arbitrary, predetermined score as a cut-off point for passing.
EN: Naval School of the Ministry of the Navy, providing post secondary education for naval officer candidates.
ETFCSF: Celso Suckow da Fonseca Federal Technical School, a post secondary technical school in Rio de Janeiro.
exame vestibular: college entrance examinations.
excedente: candidates who passed the entrance exams but were unable to obtain a vacancy because of lack of places; associated with the exame eliminatório.
faculdade: a college or school within a university (for example), School of Medicine of the Federal University of Rio de Janeiro).
faculdades isoladas: isolated colleges; single-purpose incorporated institutions which are usually private and are not connected with a larger institution (for example, College of Economics, School of Design).
FEFIEG: Federation of Federal Isolated Schools of Guanabara State, a higher education institution in Rio de Janeiro.
FIB: Bennett Integrated Colleges, a higher education institution in Rio de Janeiro which grew out of, and still maintains, a secondary school.
FTESM: Souza Marques Technical Education Foundation, a university in Rio de Janeiro.
Fundação Carlos Chagas: São Paulo-based testing and research organization which conducts the examinations for CESCEM.
GESA: a short-lived experiment with a unified entrance exam system in the State of Rio Grande do Sul.
IPEA: Institute of Economic and Social Planning, linked to the Ministry of Planning and Economic Coordination and responsible for research on human resources and the economics of education.

APPENDIX A   195

LDB: Law of Directives and Bases, Brazil's first general education law passed in 1961.
Mapofei: a unified entrance examination system followed by some colleges in São Paulo for admission to programs in the exact sciences.
Maracanã: the huge stadium in Rio de Janeiro where the entrance exams are traditionally held.
MEC: Ministry of Education and Culture.
não classificado: not "classified" (approved) in the entrance examination competition, where institutions use the classificatório method of selection.
núcleo comum: core curriculum of studies set forth in the 1971 Law of Primary and Secondary School Reform.
portaria: government regulation, often announced on the ministerial level.
pre-opção: a candidate's curriculum and institutional choices which may serve as a basis for his selection to higher education.
programa: program; topics covered in each of the subjects on the entrance tests.
prova: test.
PUC: Pontifical Catholic University.
reitor: rector; university president.
UEG: State University of Guanabara, located in the City of Rio de Janeiro.
UFF: Federal Fluminense University, located in the State of Rio de Janeiro.
UFMG: Federal University of Minas Gerais.
UFRGS: Federal University of Rio Grande do Sul.
UFRRJ: Federal Rural University of Rio de Janeiro.
UGF: Gama Filho University, a private institution located in Rio de Janeiro.
USP: University of São Paulo, a state institution.
vaga: freshman place available in a college or university.
FMV: College of Medicine of Valença, a private school in the State of Rio de Janeiro.
vestibular unificado: unified college entrance examinations.

APPENDIX B

STATUTE OF THE CESGRANRIO FOUNDATION

Article 1—The CESGRANRIO Foundation is established and constituted for an indeterminate period of time, serving educational ends and having headquarters and jurisdiction in the City of Rio de Janeiro, State of Guanabara.

Article 2—Among the educational purposes of the CESGRANRIO Foundation are:

a. human resources selection, particularly the selection of candidates for higher education.
b. research in the area of behavioral sciences.
c. training personnel for work in the area of human resources and research in behavioral sciences.
d. supporting research projects judged to be in the public interest by the entities which comprise the organization; notably, critical analyses of the results of the entrance examination competitions.
e. awarding study grants and research grants for persons indicated by the entities which comprise the organization, for use in Brazil or abroad.
f. promoting and encouraging work considered to be of interest to the development of behavioral science as well as translation of foreign works considered to be exceptionally valuable.
g. printing and disseminating scientifically based work conducted by the Foundation and related to its sphere of activities and, also, distributing information which will provide career orientation for young people.
h. promoting and sponsoring, by way of meetings, symposia, congresses, and seminars, contact among scientists, teachers, and researchers dedicated to work in the behavioral sciences.

This is an abridged version of the statute, taken from Tabelião Balbino, Certidão: Fundação CESGRANRIO, 22° Ofício de Notas, Rio de Janeiro, 4 January 1973.

APPENDIX B   197

    i. interchange with public and private entities, national and foreign, for purposes similar to those foreseen under letter "h."

Article 3—The CESGRANRIO Foundation should be able to enter into agreements, accords, settlements, and contracts for providing services to educational establishments, public and private.

Article 4—The property and dues received by the CESGRANRIO Foundation shall be utilized or applied exclusively in accord with its objectives, by way of authorization from its Directorate and in consultation with the Ministry of Education and Culture.

    Paragraph 1. The distribution of profits, dividends, or any other benefits among the participating institutions and the Directorate is strictly prohibited.

    Paragraph 2. The property which constitutes the inheritance of the CESGRANRIO Foundation shall not be transferred or subject to leasing of any type except in special cases, by way of proposal from the Directorate and in consultation with the Ministry of Education and Culture; even in these circumstances, profits and proceeds—although destined for other activities—must serve the same educational ends.

Article 5—The CESGRANRIO Foundation shall be governed by a Directorate composed of one member and one alternate delegate from each one of the entities which founded and constituted the organization; the Directorate shall choose a President from among its members by way of election.

Article 6—The President shall be elected with a mandate for three years.

Article 7—Alternate delegates shall substitute the regular representatives when the latter are unable to attend and shall succeed them in the case of vacancy.

Article 8—The Directorate is responsible for:

    a. developing and approving the by-laws of the CESGRANRIO Foundation.
    b. issuing normative acts necessary for the function of the CESGRANRIO Foundation.

c. considering proposals of agreements, accords, settlements, and contracts for providing services to third parties.
  d. approving staffing arrangements for the CESGRANRIO Foundation.
  e. approving the payment of accounts, presented annually by the President.
  f. annually developing a plan for the application of funds and income of the CESGRANRIO Foundation.
  g. establishing fees.

Article 9—The Directorate shall convene:

  1. ordinarily for:
     a. considering accounts and reports.
     b. approving the detailed budget.
     c. approving the budgetary proposal.
  2. extraordinarily when convened by the President or by an absolute majority of its members for the purposes of dealing with certain issues or for alterations of this Statute—alterations which can occur only by an absolute majority of the Foundation's founding and constituted institutions.

Article 10—The President, delegated the authority to administer the CESGRANRIO Foundation, has, therefore, the power to hire and dismiss personnel; contract professional, technical, or special services; represent the institution in or out of court; and he shall have any other powers which may be conferred on him by the organization's by-laws.

Article 11—Any omission in this Statute shall be resolved by the Directorate, with the exception of the case of the destination of property, upon extinction of the Foundation; this shall be destined for other foundations which propose the same or similar ends.

APPENDIX C

ORGANIZATIONAL CHART OF THE CESGRANRIO FOUNDATION

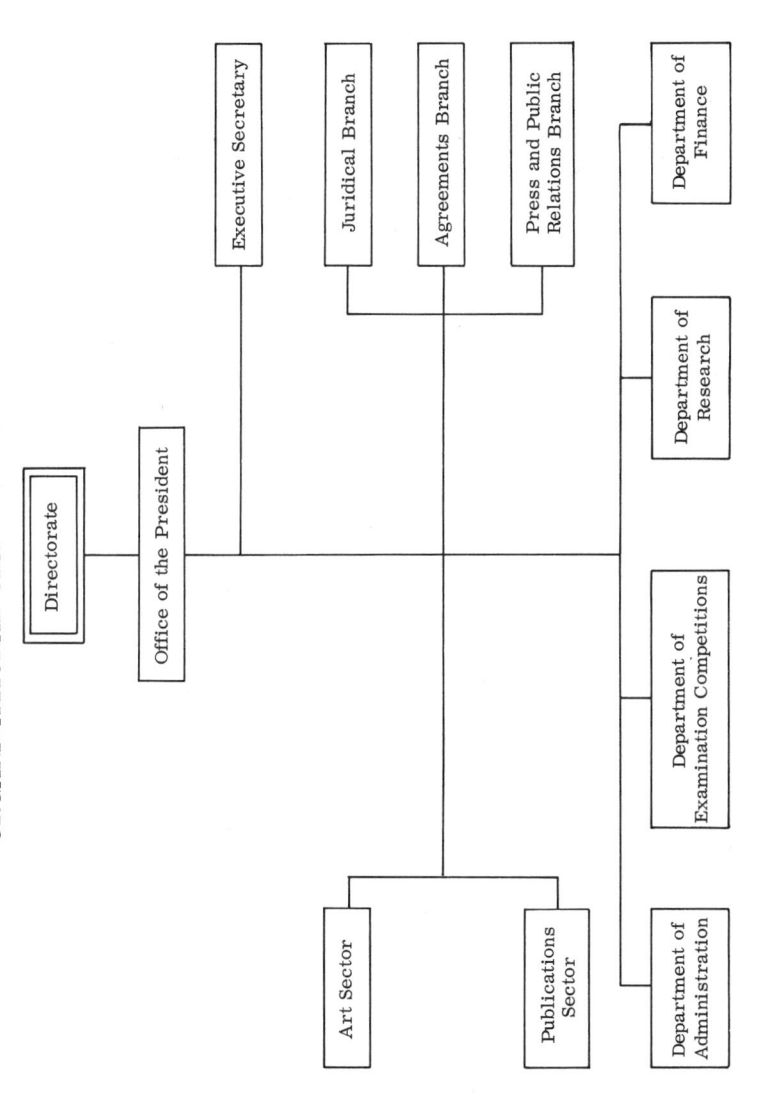

- Directorate
  - Office of the President
    - Executive Secretary
    - Juridical Branch
    - Agreements Branch
    - Press and Public Relations Branch
    - Department of Administration
      - Art Sector
      - Publications Sector
    - Department of Examination Competitions
    - Department of Research
    - Department of Finance

Source: Office of the President, CESGRANRIO Foundation, 1973.

APPENDIX D

CESGRANRIO:
PARTICIPATING HIGHER EDUCATION INSTITUTIONS

Founding Institutions

* 1. Federal University of Rio de Janeiro

* 2. Federal Fluminense University

* 3. Pontifical Catholic University of Rio de Janeiro

* 4. Catholic University of Petrópolis

* 5. Gama Filho University

* 6. Santa Úrsula University Association

* 7. State University of Guanabara

* 8. Celso Suckow da Fonseca Federal Technical School

* 9. College of Medicine of Valença

*10. Federation of Federal Isolated Schools of the State of Guanabara

---

In this list one asterisk indicates initial participation in 1972, two asterisks, 1973, and three asterisks, 1974.

The Naval School was, in fact, a founding member of CESGRANRIO. It cannot, however, enjoy the same rights and privileges as other founding members—particularly with regard to decision making since the Naval School is under the jurisdiction of the Ministry of the Navy, not the Ministry of Education and Culture.

The College of Dentistry of Nova Friburgo participated in the 1973 examination competition but withdrew from CESGRANRIO before the 1974 unified examinations.

APPENDIX D

Other Member Institutions

- **11. Federal Rural University of Rio de Janeiro State
- **12. Veiga de Almeida University Association
- **13. School of Engineering of Volta Redonda
- **14. School of Medical Sciences of Volta Redonda
- **15. School of Dentistry of Volta Redonda
- *16. Naval School of the Ministry of the Navy
- **17. School of Rehabilitation of Rio de Janeiro
- ***18. College of Architecture of Barra do Piraí
- **19. College of Civil Engineering of Barra do Piraí
- **20. College of Civil Engineering of Nova Iguaçu
- **21. Pedro II College of Humanities
- ***22. Hélio Alonso College of Communications
- ***23. Dom Bosco College of Economic Sciences
- **24. Bennett Integrated Colleges
- **25. College of Medicine of the Souza Marques Technical Educational Foundation
- *26. College of Engineering of the Souza Marques Technical Educational Foundation
- ***27. College of Social Service of Rio de Janeiro
- *28. College of Medicine of Petrópolis
- ***29. College of Medicine of Teresópolis
- ***30. Center of Human and Social Sciences, Isabel Institute
- **31. College of Dentistry of Campos

**32. Institute of Nutrition of the State of Guanabara

***33. National Historical Museum

***34. College of Teacher Training of the Niterói Educational Center

**35. Silva e Souza University Association

**36. College of Medicine of Campos

BIBLIOGRAPHY

BOOKS

Abernethy, David B. The Political Dilemma of Popular Education: An African Case. Stanford: Stanford University Press, 1969.

Abranches, Sérgio Henrique; Soares, Gláucio; Fleischer, D.; and Coimbra, M. As Funções do Legislativo. Brasília: Department of Social Sciences, University of Brasília, 1972.

Almond, Gabriel, and Coleman, James. The Politics of the Developing Areas. Princeton: Princeton University Press, 1960.

Altbach, Philip G., ed. Turmoil and Transition: Higher Education and Student Politics in India. New York: Basic Books, 1969.

Altbach, Philip G., and Kelly, Daniel H. Higher Education in Developing Nations: A Selected Bibliography, 1969-1974. New York: Praeger, 1974.

de Azevedo, Fernando. Brazilian Culture. New York: Macmillan, 1950.

Baer, Werner. Industrialization and Economic Development in Brazil. Homewood, Ill.: Irwin, 1965.

Bailey, Stephen K., and Mosher, Edith K. ESEA: The Office of Education Administers a Law. Syracuse: Syracuse University Press, 1968.

Baklanoff, Eric N., ed. The Shaping of Modern Brazil. Baton Rouge: Louisiana State University Press, 1969.

Bauer, Raymond A., and Gergen, Kenneth J., eds. The Study of Policy Formation. New York: Free Press, 1968.

Bauer, Raymond A.; de Sola Pool, Ithiel; and Dexter, Lewis. American Business and Public Policy. New York: Atherton Press, 1963.

Benjamin, Harold. Higher Education in the American Republics.
New York: McGraw-Hill, 1965.

Bereday, George Z. F., and Lauwerys, Joseph A., eds. The World
Year Book of Education, 1965: The Education Explosion. New
York: Harcourt, Brace, and World, 1965.

Blum, Albert A., ed. Teacher Unions and Associations: A Comparative Study. Urbana: University of Illinois Press, 1969.

Bowles, Frank. Access to Higher Education. Vol. 1. Liège, Belgium:
UNESCO and the International Association of Universities, 1963.

Braybrooke, David, and Lindblom, Charles E. A Strategy of Decision.
New York: Free Press, 1963.

Burn, Barbara. Higher Education in Nine Countries. New York:
McGraw-Hill, 1971.

Charlesworth, James C., ed. A Design for Political Science: Scope,
Objectives, and Methods. Philadelphia: American Association
of Political and Social Science, 1966.

Clark, James M. Teachers and Politics in France. Syracuse:
Syracuse University Press, 1967.

Coleman, James S., ed. Education and Political Development.
Princeton: Princeton University Press, 1965.

Coombs, Philip H. The World Educational Crisis. New York: Oxford
University Press, 1968.

da Cunha, Nádia Franco. Vestibular na Guanabara. Rio de Janeiro:
Ministério da Educação e Cultura, 1968.

_____, ed. O Acesso á Universidade. IVa Conferência Nacional de
Educação. Rio de Janeiro: INEP, 1967.

Daland, Robert T. Brazilian Planning: Development Politics and
Administration. Chapel Hill: University of North Carolina
Press, 1967.

Dewey, John. Logic. New York: Henry Holt and Company,
1938.

BIBLIOGRAPHY

Dines, Alberto, ed. Os Idos de Março e a Queda em Abril. Rio de Janeiro: José Alvaro Editor, 1964.

Douglas, Stephen K. Political Socialization and Student Activism in Indonesia. Urbana: University of Illinois Press, 1970.

Dror, Yehezkel. Design for Policy Sciences. New York: American Elsevier, 1971.

_____. Public Policymaking Reexamined. Scranton: Chandler, 1968.

_____. Ventures in Policy Sciences: Concepts and Applications. New York: American Elsevier, 1971.

Easton, David. A Framework for Political Analysis. Englewood Cliffs, N.J.: Prentice-Hall, 1965.

_____, and Dennis, Jack. Children in the Political System: Origins of Political Legitimacy. New York: McGraw-Hill, 1969.

Fagen, Richard R. Transformation of the Political Culture of Cuba. Stanford: Stanford University Press, 1969.

Ferreira, Oliveiros S. As Forças Armadas e o Desafio da Revolução. Rio de Janeiro: Edição GRD, 1964.

Georgeoff, Peter John. The Social Education of Bulgarian Youth. Minneapolis: University of Minnesota Press, 1968.

Grande, Humberto. A Pedagogia no Estado Nôvo. Rio de Janeiro: Gráfica Guarany Ltda, 1941.

Gross, Neil; Mason, W. S.; and McEachern, A. Explorations in Role Analysis. New York: John Wiley, 1958.

Harmon, G. S. The Politics of Education: A Bibliographic Guide. St. Lucia, Queensland, Australia: University of Queensland Press, 1974.

Harris, William, and Levey, Judith S., eds. The New Columbia Encyclopedia. New York: Columbia University Press, 1975.

Haussman, Fay, and Haar, Jerry. Education in Brazil. Hamden, Connecticut: Archon Books, forthcoming.

Havighurst, Robert J., and Moreira, J. Roberto. Society and
Education in Brazil. Pittsburgh: University of Pittsburgh Press,
1965.

Hess, Robert D., and Torney, Judith V. The Development of Political Attitudes in Children. Chicago: Aldine, 1967.

Hodgetts, A. B. What Culture? What Heritage? A Study of Civic
Education in Canada. Toronto: Ontario Institute for Studies
in Education, 1968.

Hunter, Robert. Revolution: Why, How, When? New York: Harper,
1940.

Hyneman, Charles S. Bureaucracy in a Democracy. New York:
Harper, 1950.

Iannacone, Laurence, and Cistone, Peter J. The Politics of Education.
Eugene, Oregon: ERIC Clearinghouse on Educational Management, 1974.

Ianni, Octávio. Estado e Capitalismo. Rio de Janeiro: Civilização
Brasileira, 1965.

Johnson, Chalmers. Revolution and the Social System. Palo Alto:
Hoover Institute of War, Revolution, and Peace, Stanford
University, 1964.

Kazamias, Andreas. Education and the Quest for Modernity in
Turkey. London: George Allen and Unwin, 1966.

Kogan, Maurice. The Government of Education. London: Macmillan,
1971.

Lambert, Jacques. Os Dois Brasís. Rio de Janeiro: Centro
Brasileiro de Pesquisas Educacionais, 1959.

Lane, Frederick S. The Politics of Higher Education: A Selected
Bibliography. New York: Bernard M. Baruch College, City
University of New York, 1974.

Langoni, Carlos Geraldo. Distribuição da Renda e Desenvolvimento
Econômico do Brasil. Rio de Janeiro: Editôra Expressão e
Cultura, 1973.

Lasswell, Harold, and Lerner, Daniel, eds. The Policy Sciences. Stanford: Stanford University Press, 1951.

Latham, Earl. The Group Basis of Politics. Ithaca, N. Y.: Cornell University Press, 1952.

Lauwerys, Joseph A., and Scanlon, David, eds. The World Year Book of Education, 1969. New York: Harcourt, Brace and Jovanovich, 1969.

Liebman, Arthur; Walker, Kenneth; and Glazer, Myron. Latin American University Students: A Six Nation Study. Cambridge: Harvard University Press, 1972.

Lindblom, Charles E. The Policy-Making Process. Englewood Cliffs, N. J.: Prentice-Hall, 1968.

Merelman, Richard M. Political Socialization and Education Climates: A Study of Two School Districts. New York: Holt, Rinehart and Winston, 1971.

Meyerson, Martin, and Banfield, Edward C. Politics, Planning and the Public Interest. Glencoe, Ill.: Free Press, 1955.

Milstein, Mike M., and Jennings, Robert E. Educational Policy-Making and the State Legislature: The New York Experience. New York: Praeger, 1973.

Moacir, Primitivo. A Instrução e o Império. São Paulo: Companhia Editôra Nacional.

Pedreira, Fernando. Março 31: Civis e Militares no Processo de Crise Brasileira. Rio de Janeiro: José Alvaro Editor, 1964.

Poerner, Arthur José. O Poder Jovem. Rio de Janeiro: Editôra Civilização Brasileira, 1968.

Polsby, Nelson; Dentler, Robert; and Smith, Paul. Politics and Social Life: An Introduction to Political Behavior. Boston: Houghton Mifflin, 1963.

Popper, Karl. The Open Society and Its Enemies. Vol. 1. London: George Routledge and Sons, 1945.

Riker, Theodore. *The Theory of Political Coalitions.* New Haven: Yale University Press, 1962.

Robock, Stefan. *Brazil: A Study in Development Progress.* Lexington, Mass.: D. C. Heath and Co., 1975.

Rosenbaum, H. Jon, and Tyler, William G., eds. *Contemporary Brazil: Issues in Economic and Political Development.* New York: Praeger, 1972.

Rosenthal, Alan. *Pedagogues and Power: Teacher Groups in School Politics.* Syracuse: Syracuse University Press, 1969.

Rostow, W. W., and Millikan, Max F. *A Proposal: Key to an Effective Foreign Policy.* New York: Harper, 1957.

Ruddle, K., and Oderman, D., eds. *Statistical Abstract of Latin America, 1971.* Los Angeles: Latin American Center, University of California at Los Angeles, 1972.

Rudman, Herbert C. *The School and the State in the U.S.S.R.* New York: Macmillan, 1967.

Schmitter, Philippe C. *Interest Conflict and Political Change in Brazil.* Palo Alto: Stanford University Press, 1971.

Schneider, Ronald M. *The Political System of Brazil: Emergence of a Modernizing Authoritarian Regime, 1964-1970.* New York: Columbia University Press, 1971.

Sena, Adalberto Corrêa. *Legislação Brasileira do Ensino Secundário.* Rio de Janeiro: Livraria Central, 1929.

Skidmore, Thomas E. *Politics in Brazil, 1930-1964: An Experiment in Democracy.* New York: Oxford University Press, 1967.

Stepan, Alfred. *The Military in Politics: Changing Patterns in Brazil.* Princeton: Princeton University Press, 1971.

_____, ed. *Authoritarian Brazil: Origins, Policies, and Future.* New Haven: Yale University Press, 1973.

Stewart, Donald E. J., ed. *Handbook of Latin American Studies.* No. 33. Gainesville: University of Florida Press, 1971.

Syvrud, Donald E. Foundations of Brazilian Economic Growth. Stanford: Hoover Institution Press, Stanford University, 1974.

Tavares de Miranda, Maria do Carmo. Educação no Brasil. Recife: Imprensa Universitária, 1966.

Webb, Kempton E. The Changing Face of Northeast Brazil. New York: Columbia University Press, 1974.

Wildavsky, Aaron. The Politics of the Budgetary Process. Boston: Little, Brown, 1964.

Wirt, Frederick M., and Kirst, Michael W. The Political Web of American Schools. Boston: Little, Brown, 1972.

Ziegler, Harmon. The Political Life of American Teachers. Englewood Cliffs: Prentice-Hall, 1967.

ARTICLES AND PERIODICALS

Abramson, Paul R., and Inglehart, Ronald. "The Decentralization of Systematic Support in Four Western Systems." Comparative Political Studies 2 (January 1970): 419-42.

Ames, Barry. "Rhetoric and Reality in a Militarized Regime." Sage Professional Paper in Comparative Politics, vol. 4, no. 01-042. Beverly Hills: Sage, 1973.

Bachrach, Peter, and Baratz, Morton. "Decisions and Non-Decisions." American Political Science Review 47 (September 1963): 632-44.

Barcellos, Osvaldo. "Excedente não desaparece como num passe de mágica." Diário de Notícias, 24 January 1971.

Barnes, Samuel H. "Participation, Education and Political Competence: Evidence from a Sample of Italian Socialists." American Political Science Review 60 (June 1966): 348-53.

Bauer, Raymond A. "Social Psychology and the Study of Policy Formation." American Psychologist 21, no. 10 (1966): 933-42.

_____. "The Study of Policy Formation: An Introduction." In The Study of Policy Formation. Edited by Raymond A. Bauer and Kenneth J. Gergen. New York: Free Press, 1968.

Cardoso, Fernando Henrique. "Associated-Dependent Development: Theoretical and Practical Implications." In Authoritarian Brazil: Origins, Policies, and Future. Edited by Alfred Stepan. New Haven: Yale University Press, 1973.

Castello Branco, Carlos. "O emprêgo da técnica." Jornal do Brasil, 19 September 1972.

Chagas, Valnir. "A admissão à universidade e a Lei de Diretrizes e Bases." Revista Brasileira de Estudos Pedagógicos 37 (January-March 1962): 8-20.

_____. "A seleção e o vestibular na reforma universitária." Revista Brasileira de Estudos Pedagógicos 13 (April/June 1970): 292-311.

Comparative Education Review 19 (February 1975).

Correa, Héctor. "Quality of Education and Socioeconomic Development." Comparative Education Review 8 (June 1964): 11-16.

Dahl, Robert. "Critique of the Ruling Elite Model." American Political Science Review 52 (June 1964): 463-69.

Daland, Robert T. "Development Administration in the Brazilian Political System." Western Political Quarterly 21 (June 1968): 325-39.

_____. "The Paradox of Planning." In Contemporary Brazil: Issues in Economic and Political Development. Edited by H. Jon Rosenbaum and William G. Tyler. New York: Praeger, 1972.

Davis, Otto A.; Dempster, M. A. H.; and Wildavsky, Aaron. "A Theory of the Budgetary Process." American Political Science Review 60 (September 1966): 529-47.

A Dictionary of the Social Sciences, 1964 ed. S.v. "Revolution," by J. S. Erös.

Encyclopedia of Social Science, vol. 7. s.v. "Revolution and Counterrevolution," by Alfred Meusel.

BIBLIOGRAPHY

Fishlow, Albert. "Brazilian Size Distribution of Income." American Economic Review 62 (1972): 391-402.

_____. "Some Reflections on Post-1964 Brazilian Economic Policy." In Authoritarian Brazil: Origins, Policies, and Future. Edited by Alfred Stepan. New Haven: Yale University Press, 1973.

Gergen, Kenneth J. "Assessing the Leverage Points in the Process of Policy Formation." In The Study of Policy Formation. Edited by Raymond A. Bauer and Kenneth J. Gergen. New York: Free Press, 1968.

_____. "Methodology in the Study of Policy Formation." In The Study of Policy Formation. Edited by Raymond A. Bauer and Kenneth J. Gergen. New York: Free Press, 1968.

Haar, Jerry. "Higher Education and Public Policy-making: A Theoretical Framework for Analysis." Paper delivered at the annual meeting of the American Educational Research Association, Washington, D.C., March 30, 1975. ERIC Clearinghouse on Higher Education, George Washington University, ERIC Document #ED 104288.

Hamburger, Ernest W. "O exame vestibular e os desajustes do sistema de ensino." Educação Hoje, January/February 1971.

Institut d'Etudes sur l'Education. El Boletín, January 1972.

"Interview with Professor Edília Coelho Garcia." Anexo III, O Acesso à Universidade. IVª Conferência Nacional de Educação. Edited by Nádia Franco da Cunha. Rio de Janeiro: INEP, 1967.

"Interview with Professor Norbertino Bahiense." Anexo II. O Acesso à Universidade. IVª Conferência Nacional de Educação. Edited by Nádia Franco da Cunha. Rio de Janeiro: INEP, 1967.

Jennings, M. Kent, and Niemi, R. G. "The Transmission of Political Values from Parent to Child." American Political Science Review 62 (March 1968): 169-84.

Kirst, Michael W., and Mosher, Edith K. "Politics of Education." Review of Educational Research 39 (December 1969): 623-40.

Langoni, Carlos Geraldo. "A rentabilidade social dos investimentos em educação no Brasil." Ensaios Econômicos, 1972, pp. 343-78.

Langston, K. P., and Jennings, M. Kent. "Political Socialization and the High School Civics Curriculum in the U. S." American Political Science Review 62 (September 1968): 852-67.

Lasswell, Harold. "The Decision Process: Seven Categories of Functional Analysis." In Politics and Social Life: An Introduction to Political Behavior. Edited by Nelson Polsby, Robert Dentler, and Paul Smith. Boston: Houghton Mifflin, 1963.

Lipsey, R. G., and Lancaster, Kevin. "The General Theory of Second Best." Review of Economic Studies 24 (1956-1957): 11-32.

Lowi, Theodore J. "American Business, Public Policy, Case Studies, and Political Theory." World Politics 16 (July 1964): 677-715.

Mascaro, Carlos Corrêa. "Extensão da Escolaridade." Revista Brasileira de Estudos Pedagógicos 47 (April/June 1967).

Mendes de Almeida, Cândido. "Sistema político e modêlos de poder no Brasil." Dados, no. 1 (second semester, 1966), pp. 7-15.

Meyer, John W., and Rubinson, Richard. "Education and Political Development." Review of Research in Education 3 Edited by Fred Kerlinger. Itasca, Illinois: F. E. Peacock Publishers, 1975.

Murphy, Jerome T. "Title I of ESEA: The Politics of Implementing Federal Education Reform." Harvard Educational Review 41 (February 1971): 35-63.

Myhr, Robert O. "Student Activism and Development." In Contemporary Brazil: Issues in Economic and Political Development. Edited by H. Jon Rosenbaum and William G. Tyler. New York: Praeger, 1972.

Novitski, Joseph. "Brazil's Policies Shaped at War College." New York Times, 2 August 1972.

Patchen, Martin. "Decision Theory in the Study of National Action: Problems and a Proposal." Journal of Conflict Resolution 9 (June 1965): 164-76.

BIBLIOGRAPHY

Peterson, Paul E. "The Politics of American Education." Review of Research in Education, 2. Edited by Fred N. Kerlinger and John B. Carroll. Itasca, Illinois: F. E. Peacock, 1974.

Schoettle, Enid Curtis Bok. "The State of the Art in Policy Studies." In The Study of Policy Formation. Edited by Raymond A. Bauer and Kenneth J. Gergen. New York: Free Press, 1968.

Schudson, Michael S. "Organizing the 'Meritocracy': A History of the College Entrance Examination Board." Harvard Educational Review 42 (February 1972): 34-69.

Simon, Herbert A. "Theories of Decision-Making in Economic and Behavioral Science." American Economic Review 49 (June 1959): 253-83.

Skidmore, Thomas E. "Politics and Economic Policy Making." In Authoritarian Brazil: Origins, Policies, and Future. Edited by Alfred Stepan. New Haven: Yale University Press, 1973.

Smith, M. Brewster. "Opinions, Personality, and Political Behavior." American Political Science Review 52 (March 1958): 1-17.

Teixeira, Anísio. "Access to Higher Education: Brazil." In Access to Higher Education. Vol. 2. Edited by the United Nations. Liège, Belgium: United Nations Educational, Scientific and Cultural Organization and the International Association of Universities, 1965.

Toward, Agnes. "Education: Brazil." In Handbook of Latin American Studies. No. 33. Edited by Donald E. J. Stewart. Gainesville: University of Florida Press, 1971.

do Valle, Roberto. "Os 'cursinhos,' mal crônico." Educação Hoje, July/August 1970.

Van de Graaff, John H. "West Germany's Abitur Quota and School Reform." Comparative Education Review 11 (February 1967): 75-86.

Van Dyke, V. "The Optimum Scope of Political Science." In A Design for Political Science: Scope, Objectives, and Methods. Edited by James C. Charlesworth. Philadelphia: American Association of Political and Social Science, 1966.

Webb, Kempton. "The Geography of Brazil's Modernization and Implications for the Years 1980 and 2000 A. D. " In The Shaping of Modern Brazil. Edited by Eric N. Baklanoff. Baton Rouge: Louisiana State University Press, 1969.

Zeckhauser, Richard, and Schaefer, Elmer. "Public Policy and Normative Economic Theory. " In The Study of Policy Formation Edited by Raymond A. Bauer and Kenneth J. Gergen. New York Free Press, 1968.

NEWSPAPERS AND MAGAZINES

Conjuntura Econômica, January 1975.

Correio da Manhã, 1967-75.

Diário das Notícias, 1971-75.

Estado de São Paulo, 1969-75.

Jornal do Brasil, 1968-75.

Jornal dos Sports, 13 June 1973.

New York Times, 2 August 1972.

O Globo, 1969-1975.

Realidade, March 1970.

Times (London), 11 March 1972.

Veja, 19 January 1972; 7 June 1972; 10 January 1973.

DOCUMENTS AND REPORTS

Brazil. Ato Adicional, 6 August 1834.

_____. Constituição da República dos Estados Unidos do Brasil, 24 February 1891.

_____. Decreto-lei no. 66.258 de 1970. Diário Oficial, 25 February 1971.

BIBLIOGRAPHY

_____. Portaria no. 413, BSB. Diário Oficial, 2 June 1972.

_____. Portaria no. 524, BSB. Diário Oficial, 1 September 1971.

_____. I Plano Nacional de Desenvolvimento (PND), 1972/74. Rio de Janeiro: IBGE, 1971.

_____. Projeto da Constituição Política do Império do Brasil, 1 September 1823.

Fundação Carlos Chagas. Estudo de Algumas Características Sócioculturais de Candidatos ao Ingresso em Escolas de Nível Superior. São Paulo: Fundação Carlos Chagas, 1969.

de Carvalho, Guido Ivan. Ensino Superior: Legislação e Jurisprudência, 2ª edição. Rio de Janeiro, 1969.

_____. Ensino Superior: Legislacão e Jurisprudência, 3ª edição. Rio de Janeiro, 1971.

_____. Ensino Superior: Legislação e Jurisprudência, 4ª edição. Rio de Janeiro, 1973.

Castro, Cláudio de Moura. Eficiência e Custos das Escolas de Nível Médio: Um Estudo-Pilôto na Guanabara. Relatório de Pesquisa No. 3. Rio de Janeiro: IPEA/INPES, Ministério do Planejamento e Coordenação Geral, 1971.

CESGRANRIO. Relatório: Concurso Vestibular de 1972. Rio de Janeiro: Centro de Seleção de Candidatos ao Ensino Superior do Grande Rio, 1972.

Fundação CESGRANRIO. Análise do Questionário de Informações sobre o Candidato (1972). Rio de Janeiro: Departamento de Pesquisas, Fundação CESGRANRIO, n. d.

_____. Estatuto e Regimento. Rio de Janeiro: Fundação CESGRANRIO, n. d.

_____. Legislação Atualizada Referente aos Concursos Vestibulares de 1974. Rio de Janeiro: Fundação CESGRANRIO, 1973.

Coelho, Magda Prates, and Pereira, Maria Elisa. O Emprêgo no Brasil de Profissionais Treinados no Exterior. Projeto Retorno, Documento no. 4. Rio de Janeiro: Fundação Getúlio Vargas, 1971.

Dutra, Tarso; dos Reis Velloso, J. P.; Chagas, V.; Sucupira, N.;
do Val, F.; Lyra Filho, J.; Moreira Couceiro, A.; Maciel de
Barros, R. S.; de Avila, Pe. F.; and Peres, L. Reforma
Universitária. Brasília: MEC, 1968.

Harrell, William A. The Brazilian Education System: A Summary.
Washington, D. C.: U. S. Office of Education, 1970.

_____. Educational Reform in Brazil: The Law of 1961. Washington,
D. C.: U. S. Office of Education, 1968.

Instituto Brasileiro de Geografia e Estatística. Resultados Censitários
1970. Rio de Janeiro: IBGE, 1971.

Levy, Samuel. The Demand for Higher-Education and the Labour
Market for Professionals in Brazil. Contract no. AID-12-
692. Rio de Janeiro: Human Resources Office, USAID, 1972.

Ministério da Educação e Cultura. Caracterização Sócio-Econômica
do Estudante Universitário. Rio de Janeiro: Centro Brasileiro
de Pesquisas Educacionais, Instituto Nacional de Estudos
Pedagógicos, 1968.

_____. Catálogo Geral das Instituições de Ensino Superior: 1973.
Brasília: Departamento de Assuntos Universitários, MEC,
1973.

_____. Convênio. Rio de Janeiro: Departamento de Assuntos
Universitários, 1971.

_____. Encontro de Dirigentes. Brasília: MEC, 1974.

_____. Estatísticas da Educação Nacional, 1960-1971. Brasília:
MEC, 1972.

_____. Estatísticas da Educação Nacional, 1971. 2 vols. Brasília:
MEC, 1972.

_____. Relatório da Equipe de Assessoria ao Planejamento do Ensino
Superior: Acôrdo MEC-USAID. Rio de Janeiro: MEC, 1969.

Ministério do Planejamento e Coordenação Econômica. Programa
de Ação Econômica do Govêrno, 1964-66. Rio de Janeiro:
Documentos IPEA, 1964.

BIBLIOGRAPHY

Ministério do Planejamento e Coordenação Geral. Programa Estratégico de Desenvolvimento, 1968-1970. Rio de Janeiro: IBGE, 1967.

_____. Sinopse Estatística do Brasil, 1971. Rio de Janeiro: Fundação IBGE, 1971.

Ministry of Education and Culture. Education in Brazil. Brasília: Commission for International Affairs, MEC, 1971.

_____. Sector Plan for Education and Culture, 1972/1974. Brasília: General Secretariat, MEC, 1971.

Pimenta, Aluísio; dos Santos, Oder José; Guimarães, Magda Soares; and Avelar, Lucia Mercês. Estabelecimento de uma Política para Admissão de Alunos no Ensino Superior do Brasil. Rio de Janeiro: Conselho de Reitores das Universidades Brasileiras, 1967.

Ribeiro Netto, Adolpho. A Fundação Carlos Chagas: Seleção para a Universidade e Pesquisa para a Educação. São Paulo: Fundação Carlos Chagas, 1973.

Santos, Roberto Figueira. "Avaliação da Implantação da Reforma Universitária." II Encontro de Reitores das Universidades Públicas e Diretores de Estabelecimentos Públicos Isolados de Ensino Superior. Brasília: Ministério da Educação e Cultura, 1973.

Serpa de Oliveira, Carlos Alberto. Simpósio para Avaliação de Reforma nas Universidades Brasileiras: Concurso Vestibular. Rio de Janeiro: Pontifícia Universidade Católica do Rio de Janeiro, 1971.

Tabelião Balbino. Certidão: Fundação CESGRANRIO, 22° Ofício de Notas. Rio de Janeiro, 4 January 1973.

United Nations. Demographic Yearbook, 1970. 1971.

_____. Demographic Yearbook, 1972. 1973.

United Nations, ed. Access to Higher Education. Vol. 2. Liège, Belgium: United Nations Educational, Scientific and Cultural Organization and the International Association of Universities, 1965.

United Nations Educational, Scientific and Cultural Organization. Statistical Yearbook, 1970. 1971.

_____. Statistical Yearbook, 1972. 1973.

U. S., Agency for International Development. Brazil: Education Sector Analysis. Rio de Janeiro: Human Resources Office, USAID, 1972.

Webster, Maureen. Three Approaches to Educational Planning. Occasional Paper No. 1. Syracuse: Center for Development Education, Syracuse University, 1970.

UNPUBLISHED MATERIALS

Ames, Barry Charles. "Bureaucratic Policy Making in a Militarized Regime: Brazil After 1964." Ph. D. dissertation, Stanford University, 1972.

Bower, Joseph. "Capital Budgeting Is a Management Problem." Cambridge, Mass.: Harvard Graduate School of Business Administration, 1966. Mimeographed.

Browning, Carol. "The Democratization of Higher Education in France During the DeGaulle Administration of the Fifth French Republic." Ph. D. dissertation, Columbia University, 1971.

Cehelsky, Marta. "Modernizing Authoritarianism and Public Policy: Agrarian Reform in Brazil, 1961-69." Ph. D. dissertation, Columbia University, 1971.

Haar, Jerry. "Access to Higher Education and Public Policy-making: The Brazilian Experience." Ph. D. dissertation, Columbia University, 1974.

Levine, Richard S. Office of the Vice President, Educational Testing Service, Princeton, New Jersey. Personal letter, 22 April 1974.

Moniz de Aragão, Raimundo. Speech delivered at the Escola Superior de Guerra (Superior War College), Rio de Janeiro, 8 September 1970.

BIBLIOGRAPHY

Sander, Benno. "Educational Law and Practice in a Developing Country: An Empirical Study of the Impact Made by Brazilian Law No. 4024 on Secondary Education in the State of Rio Grande do Sul." Ph. D. dissertation, Catholic University of America, 1970.

Serpa de Oliveira, Carlos Alberto. "The College Entrance Examination Competitions." Paper delivered at the Seminar on the Structure and Function of Higher Education, Rio de Janeiro, 12 July 1973.

Stepan, Alfred C. "Patterns of Civil-Military Relations in the Brazilian Political System." Ph. D. dissertation, Columbia University, 1969.

Toward, Agnes. "Some Aspects of the Federal Education Council in the Brazilian Education System." Ph. D. dissertation, University of Texas, 1966.

INTERVIEWS*

Bahiense Filho, Norbertino. Director, Curso Bahiense, Rio de Janeiro, 16 June and 25 June 1973.

Campos, Emanoel. Executive Secretary, Council of Rectors of Brazilian Universities, Rio de Janeiro, 14 June 1973.

Castro, Cláudio de Moura. Institute of Economic and Social Planning (IPEA), Ministry of Planning and General Coordination, Rio de Janeiro, 12 October 1972.

Cavalcanti, João Uchôa. Director, Estácio de Sá Integrated Colleges, Rio de Janeiro, 22 June 1973.

---

*The researcher also had many informal conversations and interviews with more than one-half of the individuals named in this section, as well as with students, teachers, and administrators. In addition, there was extensive contact with the press in Rio de Janeiro and Sao Paulo. However, before granting permission for an interview, members of the press insisted the researcher pledge that their anonymity would be preserved.

Coelho, José Luiz. Director of Support Services, CESGRANRIO Foundation, Rio de Janeiro, 12 July 1973.

Cordeiro da Graça Filho, João Carlos. Dean, Center of Exact Sciences and Technology, Gama Filho University, Rio de Janeiro, 14 June 1973.

Domingues, Rui Octávio. Dean, Estácio de Sá Integrated Colleges, Rio de Janeiro, 22 June 1973.

Flexa Ribeiro, Carlos. Chairman, Education Committee, Federal Chamber of Deputies, Rio de Janeiro, 26 June 1973.

Franco da Cunha, Nádia. Brazilian Center for Educational Research, Rio de Janeiro, 7 June 1973.

Gomes, Altair. Dean, College of Education, Guanabara State University, Rio de Janeiro, 30 May 1973.

Gurgulino de Souza, Heitor. Director, Department of University Affairs, Ministry of Education and Culture, Rio de Janeiro, 10 July 1973.

Jankowitz, Herman, Jr. Coordinator of COMCITEC, CESGRANRIO Foundation, Rio de Janeiro, 13 June 1973.

Kubrusly, Antonio. Chairman, Department of Electronics, Celso Suckow da Fonseca Federal Technical School, Rio de Janeiro, 4 June 1973.

Leao, Manoel Luiz. Member of CONVESU, Pôrto Alegre, 4 May 1973.

Lemos, Delba Guarini. Dean, Center of Applied Social Sciences, Federal Fluminense University, and former Coordinator of COMSART, CESGRANRIO Foundation, Niterói, 4 June 1973.

Lobo, Bruno Alípio. Member of CONVESU and Coordinator of COMBIMED, CESGRANRIO Foundation, Rio de Janeiro, 6 July 1973.

Lorenzato, Sergio. Assistant to the Director, Department of University Affairs, Ministry of Education and Culture, Brasília, 19 June 1973.

BIBLIOGRAPHY

Marques de Morais, Ceres. Special Assistant to the Rector, Federal Fluminense University, Niterói, 11 June 1973.

Mascaro, Carlos Corrêa. Special Assistant to the Secretary of Education, State of São Paulo, São Paulo, 27 April 1973.

Moniz de Aragao, Raimundo. Former Minister of Education, Rio de Janeiro, 3 July 1973.

Niny, Manoel Eduardo Cardeira. Director, Department of Administration, CESGRANRIO Foundation, Rio de Janeiro, 4 June 1973.

Nótrica, Victor Maurício. Director, Curso Miguel Couto, Rio de Janeiro, 16 June 1973.

Passarinho, Jarbas Gonçalves. Minister of Education, Brasília, 19 June 1973.

Pinto Cordeiro, Lourival. Superintendent of Instruction, United Association of Higher Education and Culture (SUESC), Rio de Janeiro, 25 June 1973.

Pontes de Medeiros Filho, Affonso. Professor of Chemistry, Catholic University of Petrópolis, Rio de Janeiro, 5 June 1973.

Potsch, Carlos. Dean, College of Philosophy, Santa Úrsula University Association, Rio de Janeiro, 7 June 1973.

Ribeiro Netto, Adolpho. President, Carlos Chagas Foundation and Member of CONVESU, Sao Paulo, 30 April 1973; Rio de Janeiro, 13 July 1973.

Rodrigues, Aroldo. Director, Department of Research, CESGRANRIO Foundation, Rio de Janeiro, 6 July 1973.

Sanches, Joel. Dean of Instruction, Bennett Integrated Colleges, Rio de Janeiro, 25 June 1973.

Serpa de Oliveira, Carlos Alberto. President of CONVESU and CESGRANRIO Foundation, Rio de Janeiro, 23 July 1973.

Soares de Meirelles, Alberto. President, Federation of Federal Isolated Colleges of the State of Guanabara, Rio de Janeiro, 24 May 1973.

Sucupira, Newton Lins Buarque. Former Director, Department of
University Affairs, Ministry of Education and Culture, Brasília,
18 June 1973.

Urbano da Silveira, Tito. Dean, School of Engineering, Souza Marque
Technical Educational Foundation, Rio de Janeiro, 5 June 1973.

ABOUT THE AUTHOR

JERRY HAAR is a Special Assistant in the Office of the Secretary of the U.S. Department of Health, Education, and Welfare. Previously he was a Research Associate in the Institute of Higher Education at Teachers College, Columbia University. He received his B.A. cum laude from the School of International Service, American University, in 1969 and the following year earned his Ed.M. from Johns Hopkins University. In 1974 he was awarded the Ph.D. degree from Columbia University. During the 1972-73 academic year, Dr. Haar was a Fulbright Scholar at the Getúlio Vargas Foundation in Rio de Janeiro, Brazil, where he conducted research on public administration and educational policy making. Dr. Haar has held research appointments in Columbia University's Institute of Latin American Studies and in the Department of Higher and Adult Education at Teachers College. His broad background includes work experience as a community college administrator in the United States and a technical research assistant with an urban planning company in Latin America. Dr. Haar has been a consultant to public and private organizations in the United States and abroad, and he has published research in the areas of public policy making, administration, educational planning, and technology.

RELATED TITLES
Published by
Praeger Special Studies

COMPARATIVE HIGHER EDUCATION ABROAD:
Bibliography and Analysis
                    edited by Philip G. Altbach

HIGHER EDUCATION IN DEVELOPING NATIONS:
A Selected Bibliography, 1969-74
                    Philip G. Altbach and
                    David H. Kelly

EDUCATION AND DEVELOPMENT RECONSIDERED:
The Bellagio Conference Papers
Ford Foundation/Rockefeller Foundation Report
                    edited by F. Champion Ward

BRAZILIAN ECONOMIC POLICY: An Optimal
Control Theory Analysis
                    Gian Singh Sahota

THE MAOIST EDUCATIONAL REVOLUTION
                    Theodore Hsi-en Chen

EDUCATIONAL PLANNING AND EXPENDITURE
DECISIONS IN DEVELOPING COUNTRIES: With a
Malaysian Case Study
                    Robert W. McMeekin, Jr.

POLITICS AND DEVELOPMENT IN RURAL MEXICO:
A Study of Socio-Economic Modernization
                    Manuel L. Carlos